A SLENDER MUSE

DOUG STEWART

An Even Money Book
Los Angeles

Even Money Press
Los Angeles
evenmoney.press
First edition. March 2018.
ISBN 978-0-9962204-8-4

Front cover: Fresco, Herculaneum, ca. 50 BCE. "A late Roman-Republican banquet scene. The woman wears a transparent silk gown while the man raises a rhyton drinking vessel." Naples National Archaeological Museum. Source: Wikimedia Commons.

Back cover: Tondo from an Attic red-figured kylix, ca. 490-480 BCE (Vulci, Italy). Brygos Painter. Symposium: a hetaira dances; a reclining youth holds an aulos. Kalos inscription: "PILIPOS KALLISTO" ("Philip is the most beautiful"). British Museum. Source: Wikimedia Commons.

For, when for the very first time, I placed my tablet
on my knees, Lycian Apollo said to me:
"[. . .] singer, [raise] your sacrificial victim
to be as fat as possible,
but your Muse, my friend, to be slender."
-Callimachus

CONTENTS

PREFACE

During the course of her 2009 interview of Philip Roth for *The Daily Beast* Tina Brown asked Roth about a remark he'd made about the future of novels.

> Tina Brown: You said in an interview that you don't think novels are going to be read 25 years from now. Were you being provocative or do you believe that to be true?
>
> Philip Roth: I was being optimistic about 25 years really. No, I think it's going to be cultic. I think always people will be reading them, but it'll be a small group of people—maybe more people than now read Latin poetry, but somewhere in that range.

Well, perhaps so, about reading novels, I mean, but Latin poetry? Cultic? It's certainly true that I've read far more Latin poetry than Philip Roth novels, and that's as of this year, not some 25 years into the literary future. Actually, looking *back* over the last 25 (and more), I'm not so sure I've read any: one less cult for me. But it's true these poets are not widely read, also that those who do read them are pretty passionate about it—a small but avid following. Doubly so for the Latin love poets, the amatory or erotic elegists of the late Roman Republic and Augustan era. And look at me, even I wouldn't be here if not for stumbling across a reference to a poem by Ovid (*Amores* 3.2) about a man trying to pick up a woman at the racetrack. And even that was just by chance, having set for myself a summer project to learn a little more about classical literature. Not that how I got here is of any importance, but still, from that one intriguing reference to this book—so unexpected.

What follows is a selection of their poems (Catullus, Propertius, and Ovid); the theme: the amatory poet's subjugation to a single mistress (*domina*), plus a look at their predecessors, in particular the Alexandrian, Callimachus, and the Greek tradition of erotic epigrams. There is also a sideways glance at a contemporary, the Greek Epicurean philosopher and poet, Philodemos.

The plan is fairly straightforward: present the poems with as little commentary and context as possible, moving most of that sort of thing over to Part Two. Commentary, notes, other texts, historical references, that's where you'll find them. You'll also find that I'm always present in this work, especially so towards the end of Part One where I do my best to update this tradition, although update is probably not quite the right word for what I've done, not unless *inspired by* counts as a continuation of one thing by another.

Los Angeles
January 2018

INTRODUCTION

As for *slender*, well, Part One is, Part Two, not so much, but certainly the poems and epigrams are—as this notion was interpreted by these poets (if not just as Callimachus intended). As for mine, my epigrammatic poetry, it's very much in a slender mode: small little sketches, nothing ponderous, few if any tedious cultural signifiers; no, it's just me, forever too slender to be concerned with any of that.

So the overall intent is to offer a slender presentation of the poems followed by a supplement—one truly fat enough for sacrifice—of historical context, notes, and commentary. In this I've tried to pick what I found most informative and least tiresome (though some is, still, unavoidably tiresome), but once you get started on something like this it's impossible not to become entranced by the endless minutiae of critical scholarship and commentary. I mean, just what did Callimachus mean by "slender?" At first it seemed fairly self-evident, but once I'd read what the scholars had to say I found myself getting lost in a critical haze of ever more fine and subtle distinctions; nothing slender about that (*see below), as for myself I shall always prefer to be "light on my feet."

The focus is, of course, on the three Latin elegists, Catullus, Propertius, and Ovid, even though I get way off course talking so much about Philodemos and Callimachus, but no matter, in the end it's all connected. So I let the poets, or the poems, speak for themselves, then in Part Two more or less bury you in commentary. But you certainly don't need to go there to appreciate these poets and their poems, though there are many subtleties and hidden connotations, not to mention literary, cultural, and historical lacunae, you might find worth knowing. The truth is: it's interesting to discover the contemporary nature of this material, but even more so to see it's really not.

A racetrack, a woman, what could be more familiar? Well, yes, but then no.

I should add that during the writing of this book I found myself increasingly taken with the notion of *exile* (Ovidian exile). It's a powerful current in what follows (as is: *the transformation of exilic suffering into art*), but mostly in Part Two. As a theme—both literary and personal—it's surprisingly compatible with my interest in these amatory poets and I've made no attempt to keep them separate (in the case of Ovid such an attempt would be pointless). Another surprise was my growing fascination with *person-poet/personae* and the slippage from one to the other. Like exile, it too became a persistent theme throughout this book.

*At first: brevity, not length; short and subtle works; avoiding the grand themes of mythological and historical epic (the fat, "noisy," bombast). And later: it's style, not genre; a concern for poetic style and quality in general; yes, small-scale, subtle, and original (and therefore "sweet") poetry, but *techné* is the more important criterion than length; hence the error of the Latin poets' *recusatio* to write specific genres (mostly full-length, heroic epic). But in either case a fine and delicate poetry, refined and original; not common but select (we take the untrodden path, though such a path may be narrow); the poet, too, subtle and refined, singing like the cicada.

Dates to bear in mind:
Roman Republic (133-31 BC).
The Augustan Age (27 BC-14 AD).
Catullus (Gaius Valerius Catullus; c. 84-54 BC).
Propertius (Sextus Propertius; c. 50/45-15 BC).
Ovid (Publius Ovidius Naso; 43 BC-AD 17/18).
Callimachus (c. 310/05-240 BC).
Philodemos (c. 110-40/35 BC).

A SLENDER MUSE

PART ONE

I hate and love. You wonder, perhaps, why I do that?
I have no idea. I just feel it. I am crucified.
-Catullus

AT THE TRACK

As I said, there's this business about trying to pick up a woman at the track (Ovid's *Amores* 3.2), and even though I've written about a similar occurrence in *The Bet*, this is something I've never actually experienced, not in *real* life, anyway, but then I've usually had a companion. Although *Amores* 3.2 has been translated any number of times, this is the version (Lee 1968) I prefer.

It's not the horses that bring me here
though I hope your favourite wins.

To sit with you and talk with you is why I've come—
I've come to tell you I'm in love.

If I watch you and you watch the races
we'll both enjoy watching a winner.

How I envy your charioteer!
He's a lucky man to be picked by you.

I wish it was me. I'd get my team
off to a flying start,

crack the whip, give them their heads
and shave the post with the nearside wheel.

But if I caught sight of *you* in the race
I'd drop the reins and lose ground.

Poor Pelops was nearly killed at Pisa
gazing in Hippodamia's eyes,

but being her favourite of course he won
as I hope your driver and I will.—

It's no good edging away. The line brings us together—
that's the advantage of the seating here.

You on the right, sir—please be careful.
Your elbow's hurting the lady.

And you in the row behind—sit up, sir!
Your knees are digging into her back.

My dear, your dress is trailing on the ground.
Lift it up—or there you are, I've done it for you.

What mean material to hide those legs!
Yes, the more one looks the meaner it seems.

Legs like Atalanta,
Milanion's dream of bliss.

A painter's model for Diana
running wilder than the beasts.

My blood was on fire before. What happens now?
You're fuelling a furnace, flooding the Red Sea.

I'm sure that lightweight dress is hiding
still more delightful revelations.

But what about a breath of air while we wait?
This programme will do as a fan.

Is it really as hot as I feel? Or merely my imagination
fired by your sultry presence?

Just then a speck of dust fell on your white dress.
Forgive me—out, damned spot!

But here's the procession. Everybody hush.
Give them a hand. The golden procession's here.

First comes Victory, wings outstretched.
Goddess, grant me victory in love!

Neptune next. Salute him, sailors.
Not for me the ocean—I'm a landlover.

Soldiers, salute Mars. I'm a disarmer,
all for peace and amorous plenty.

There's Phoebus for the soothsayers, Phoebe for the hunters,
Minerva for the master craftsmen.

Farmers can greet Bacchus and Ceres,
boxers pray to Pollux and knights to Castor.

But I salute the queen of love and the boy with the bow.
Venus, smile on my latest venture.

Make my new mistress willing—or weak-willed.
A lucky sign—the goddess nodded

giving her promise. And now I'm asking for yours.
With Venus' permission I'll worship *you*.

By all these witnesses, divine and human.
I swear I want you to be mine for ever.

But the seat's a bit too high for you.
Why not rest your feet on the railing in front?

Now, they've cleared the course. The Praetor's starting the first
      race.
Four-horse chariots. Look—they're off.

There's your driver. Anyone *you* back is bound to win.
Even the horses seem to know what you want.

My God, he's taking the corner too wide.
What are you doing? The man behind is drawing level.

What are you doing, wretch? Breaking a poor girl's heart.
For pity's sake pull on your left rein!

We've backed a loser. Come on everyone, all together,
flap you togas and signal a fresh start.

Look, their calling them back. Lean your head against me
so the waving togas don't disarrange your hair.

Now, they're off again—plunging out of the stalls,
rushing down the course in a clash of colours.

Now's your chance to take the lead. Go all our for that gap.
Give my girl and me what we want.

Hurrah, he's done it! You've got what you wanted, sweetheart.
That only leaves me—do I win too?

She's smiling. There's a promise in those bright eyes.
Let's leave now. You can pay my bet in private.
[*Amores* 3.2] (Lee 1968: 123-29)

So we've got Ovid plopping this fellow down next to an
attractive woman at the Circus Maximus (they're both there to
watch the chariot races), and he's relentless in his attempts to
gain her attention and favor. One does have to wonder if this
sort of thing really worked, though there's no doubt that's
implied (*there's a promise in those bright eyes*), a point he
reiterates in *Ars amatoria* ("The Art of Love")—his tongue-in-
cheek programmatic guide to meeting and seducing the
opposite sex—where he again mentions the track as an
excellent venue for meeting women (in a section he's entitled
"Where to Find Her").

Nor let the contest of noble steeds escape you; the spacious

Circus holds many opportunities. No need is there of fingers for secret speech, nor need you receive a signal by means of nods. Sit next to your lady, none will prevent you; sit side by side as close as you can; and it is good that the rows compel closeness, like it or not, and that by the conditions of space your girl must be touched. Here seek an opening for friendly talk, and begin with words that all may hear. Mind you are zealous in asking whose horses are entering, and quick! whomsoever she favours be sure to favour too. But when the long procession of ivory statues of the gods passes by applaud Queen Venus with favouring hand. And if perchance, as will happen, a speck of dust falls on your lady's lap, flick it off with your fingers; even if none fall, then flick off—none; let any pretext serve to show your attentiveness. If her cloak hangs low and trails upon the ground, gather it up and lift it carefully from the defiling earth; straightway, a reward for your service, with the girl's permission your eyes will catch a glimpse of her ankles. Then again look round to see that whoever is sitting behind you is not pressing his knee against her tender back. Frivolous minds are won by trifles: many have found useful the deft arranging of a cushion. It has helped too to stir the air with a light fan, or to set a stool beneath a dainty foot.

Such openings will the Circus afford to a new courtship, and the melancholy sand scattered on the busy Forum. Often has Venus' Boy fought upon that sand, and he who watched the wounds has himself been wounded. While he is speaking and touching her hand and asking for the book, and inquiring which is winning as he lays his stake, he feels the winged barb and groans with the wound, and is himself part of the show which he is watching. [*The Art of Love* Book 1.135-170] (Mozley 1979: 23-25)

Like I said, unlike winning bets, meeting women has never been my problem, which pretty much excludes me from membership in Ovid's unhappy amatory elegist's club.

2

....

AMATORY LATIN ELEGISTS

But this did make for an interesting, if brief, era (a few decades), these Latin love poets and their *inamorata*: autobiographical narratives; intense, ill-starred infatuations; *domina* or *puella* (mistress or girlfriend); women, real or imagined; learned courtesans and freedwomen, upper-class wives, widows, divorcées; obsessive, erotic desire, most often thwarted; the common arc—"erotic play, amatory rapture, and disillusioned rupture" (Keith 2012: 287); confessional verse; agonized internal dialogue; the tropes: *praeceptor amoris, servitium amoris, militia amoris* (the teacher of love, the slavery of love, the soldiering of love); the complete subjugation to a single mistress (our theme here): Catullus' Lesbia, Propertius' Cynthia, Ovid's Corinna.

But of these women, just who were they? Lesbia (Clodia Metelli) was a consul's wife, a woman who, if Cicero is to believed, was notorious for her misconduct. Cynthia may have been from an old Roman family, Propertius at one point remarking that he was pleased to hear that Augustus had rescinded one of his new marital laws threatening their affair (*for ever my mistress and for ever my wife*). And Ovid's Corinna, of whom he swears by all the gods *he will never seek another mistress*? No idea, most likely fictitious; but then weren't they all: these poets' amatory personae, their fanciful women, this sort of *love*?

Catullus

Catullus' famous *Lesbia cycle*, though here we track its mostly downward trajectory through mistrust and despair to bitter resignation. The autobiographical narrative, the agonized internal dialogue, the complete subjugation to a single mistress, the unique interiorized voice—all common features of Latin love elegies—make their first appearance here in Catullus' poetry.

Note that I've rearranged the commonly accepted order of these poems to better match my view of the rise and fall of this troubled affair. There's certainly no reason not to, since this traditional numeric order rests on groupings by poetic type (polymetrics: 1-60; the longer poems: 61-68; and the epigrams: 69-116), with little or no regard for thematic content or implied chronology (see Skinner 2007; esp. "authorial arrangement"). Actually, now that I think about it, this may be just the place for Tom Stoppard's remarks on the troubled (to say the least) history of these poems; remarks that hold true for many of the classical texts that somehow have managed to survive down to the present (see, for example, Butrica 2007, 2012). From his play *The Invention of Love;* Benjamin Jowett, the famous Oxford classicist, is speaking with (they're in Hades) A. E. Houseman:

Houseman: But isn't it of use to establish what the ancient authors really wrote?

Jowett: It would be on the whole desirable rather than undesirable and the job was pretty well done, where it could be done, by good scholars dead these hundred years and more. For the rest, certainty could only come from recovering the autograph. This morning I had cause to have typewritten an autograph letter I wrote to the father of a certain undergraduate. The copy as I received it asserted that the Master of Balliol had a solemn duty to stamp out unnatural mice. In other words, anyone with a secretary knows that what Catullus really wrote was already corrupt by the time it was copied twice, which was about the time of the first Roman invasion of Britain, and the earliest copy that has come down to *us* was written about 1,500 years after that. Think of all those secretaries!—corruption breeding corruption from papyrus to papyrus, and from the last disintegrating scrolls to the first new-fangled parchment books, with a thousand years of copying-out still to come, running the gauntlet of changing forms of script and spelling, and absence of punctuation—not to mention mildew and rats and fire and flood and Christian disapproval to the brink of extinction as what Catullus really wrote passed from scribe to scribe, this one drunk, that one sleepy, another without scruple, and of those sober, wide-awake and scrupulous, some ignorant of Latin and some, even worse, fancying themselves better Latinists than Catullus—until!—finally and at long last—mangled and tattered like a dog that has fought its way home, there falls across the threshold of the Italian Renaissance the sole surviving witness to thirty generations of carelessness and stupidity: the *Verona Codex* of Catullus; which was almost immediately lost again, but not before being copied with one last opportunity for error. And there you have the foundation of the poems of Catullus as they went to the printer for the first time, in Venice 400 years ago. (Stoppard 1997: 24-25)

No, nothing but extraordinary luck.

51
In my eyes he seems like a god's co-equal,
he, if I dare say so, eclipses godhead,
who now face to face, uninterrupted,
   watches and hears you

sweetly laughing—*that* sunders unhappy me from
all my senses: the instant I catch sight of
you now, Lesbia, dumbness gripes my <voice, it
   dies on my vocal

chords>, my tongue goes torpid, and through my body
thin fire lances down, my ears are ringing
with their own thunder, while night curtains both my
    eyes into darkness.

Leisure, Catullus, is dangerous to you: leisure
urges you into extravagant behavior:
leisure in time gone by has ruined kings and
    prosperous cities.
(Green 2005: 99)

5
Let's live, Lesbia mine, and love—and as for
scandal, all the gossip, old men's strictures,
value the lot at no more than a farthing!
Suns can rise and set ad infinitum—
for us, though, once our brief life's quenched, there's only
one unending night that's left to sleep through.
Give me a thousand kisses, then a hundred,
then a thousand more, a second hundred,
then yet another thousand then a hundred—
then when we've notched up all these many thousands,
shuffle the figures, lose count of the total,
so no maleficent enemy can hex us
knowing the final sum of all our kisses.
(Green 2005: 49)

7
You'd like to know how many of your kisses
would be enough and over, Lesbia, for me?
Match them to every grain of Libyan sand in
silphium-rich Cyrene, from the shrine of
torrid oracular Jupiter to the sacred
sepulcher of old Battus; reckon their total
equal to all those stars that in the silent
night look down on the stolen loves of mortals.
That's the number of times I need to kiss you,
That's what would satisfy your mad Catullus—

far too many for the curious to figure,
or for an evil tongue to work you mischief!
(Green 2005: 51)

68B [67-72, 134-37, 143-48]
He opened up enclosed land with a spacious driveway;
    provided a house for my mistress and me
where we could sink ourselves in our mutual passion.
    Hither my refulgent goddess with light step
came, setting her foot on the worn threshold
    with a tiny squeak of her sandal.
    . . .
    Yet
although the lady's not satisfied with one Catullus only
    she's modest enough, I can stand the occasional lapse—
being a stupid, jealous bore will get me nowhere.
    . . .
And anyway she never came to me on her father's
    arm, to a house fragrant with Assyrian scent,
but for one miraculous night brought me stolen presents
    filched from her, yes, her husband's, yes, ah, lap.
So it's enough if for me alone is reserved that
    day she designates with a *whiter* stone.
(Green 2005: 173-79)

86
Many find Quintia beautiful. For me she's fair-complexioned,
    tall, of good carriage. These few points I concede.
But overall beauty—no. There's no genuine attraction
    in that whole long body, not one grain of salt.
It's Lesbia who's beautiful, and being wholly lovely,
    has stolen from all the others their every charm.
(Green 2005: 193)

83
Lesbia keeps insulting me in her husband's presence:
    this fills the fatuous idiot with delight.
Mule, you've no insight. If she shut up and ignored me
    that'd show healthy indifference; all these insults mean

is, she not only remembers me, but—words of sharper import—
   feels angry. That is the lady burns—and talks.
(Green 2005: 191)

104
Do you really believe I could have cursed my darling,
   whom I cherish more than both my eyes? No way:
I couldn't, nor, if I could, would my love be so desperate—
   but you and Tappo made shockers of everything.
(Green 2005: 203)

107
If anything ever came through for one who so longingly
   yearned for it, yet without hope—that's balm for the soul.
So, there's balm for us too, than gold more precious,
   Lesbia, in this: that you've brought yourself back to me
and my yearning for you: yes, back to my hopeless yearning,
   to me, by your own choice. O brighter than white
day! Who lives happier than I do? Who can argue
   that life holds any more desirable bliss?
(Green 2005: 205)

109
You're suggesting, my life, that this mutual love between us
   can be a delight—and in perpetuity?
Great gods, only let her promise be in earnest,
   let her be speaking truly, and from the heart,
so that we can maintain, for the rest of our life together,
   our hallowed friendship through this eternal pact!
(Green 2005: 207)

87
No woman can say she's truly been loved as much as
   my Lesbia has been loved by me: there's no
guarantee so strong ever figured in any contract
   as that found, on my part, in my love for you.
(Green 2005: 193)

70

My woman declares there's no one she'd sooner marry
    than me, not even were Jove himself to propose.
She declares—but a woman's words to her eager lover
    should be written on running water, on the wind.
(Green 2005: 181)

72

You told me once, Lesbia, that Catullus alone understood you,
    That you wouldn't choose to clasp Jupiter rather than me.
I loved you then, not just as the common herd their women,
    but as a father loves his sons and sons-in-law.
Now, though, I *know* you. So yes, though I burn more fiercely,
    yet for me you're far cheaper, lighter. "How,"
you ask, "can that be?" It's because such injury forces
    a lover to love more, but to cherish less.
(Green 2005: 181-82)

75

My mind has been brought so low by your conduct, Lesbia,
    and so undone itself through its own goodwill
that now if you were perfect it couldn't like you,
    nor cease to love you now, whatever you did.
(Green 2005: 183)

92

Lesbia's always bad-mouthing me, never stops talking of me.
    That means Lesbia loves me, or I'll be damned.
What proves it? I'm just the same still—praying nonstop
    to lose her, But *I* love *her* still. Or I'll be damned.
(Green 2005: 197)

8

Wretched Catullus, stop this stupid tomfool stuff
and what you see has perished treat as lost for good.
Time was, every day for you the sun shone bright,
when you scurried off wherever *she* led *you*—
that girl you loved as no one shall again be loved.
There, when so many charming pleasures went on,

things that *you* wanted, things *she* didn't quite turn down,
then for you truly every day the sun shone bright.
Now she's said *No*, so you too, feeble wretch, say *No*.
Don't chase reluctance, don't embrace a sad-sack life—
make up your mind, be stubborn, obdurate, hang tough!
So goodbye, sweetheart. Now Catullus *will* hang tough,
won't ask, "Where is she?" won't, since you've said *No*, beg,
    plead.
You'll soon be sorry, when you get these pleas no more—
bitch, wicked bitch, poor wretch, what life awaits *you* now?
Who'll now pursue you, still admire you for your looks?
Whom will you love now? Who will ever call you theirs?
Who'll get your kisses? Whose lips will you bite in play?
You, though, Catullus, keep your mind made up, *hang tough!*
(Green 2005: 53)

76 [13-26]
It's hard to abruptly shrug off love long established:
    hard, but this, somehow, you must do.
Here lies your only hope, you must win this struggle:
    this, possible or not, must be your goal.
O gods, if its in you to pity, or if you've ever rendered
    help at the last to those on the verge of death,
look down on my misery, and if I've lived cleanly,
    pluck out of me this destruction, this plague,
which, creeping torpor-like into my inmost being
    has emptied my heart of joy.
I no longer ask that she should return my love, or—
    an impossibility—agree to be chaste.
What I long for is health, to cast off this unclean sickness.
    O gods, if I have kept faith, please grant me this!
(Green 2005: 185)

11 [15-24]
just find my girl, deliver her this short and
    blunt little message:

Long may she live and flourish with her gallants,
embracing all three hundred in one session,

loving none truly, yet cracking each one's loins
    over and over.
Let her no more, as once, look for my passion,
which through her fault lies fallen like some flower
at the field's edge, after the passing ploughshare's
    cut a path through it.
(Green 2005: 57)

58A
Caelius, Lesbia—*our* dear Lesbia, *that* one,
    that Lesbia whom alone Catullus worshipped
more than himself, far more than all his kinfolk—
    now on backstreet corners and down alleys
jacks off Remus' generous descendants.
(Green 2005: 105)

85
I hate and love. You wonder, perhaps, why I do that?
    I have no idea. I just feel it. I am crucified.
(Green 2005: 191)

But perhaps there's an alternative ending to this affair (and
ordering of these poems)? It's been suggested that the last "five
remaining Lesbia poems tell a simple story [i.e., 87, 92, 104,
107, 109], one perhaps best summarized in the trite but
timeless formula, 'They lived happily ever after'." (Dyson
Hejduk 2007: 272). Well, that's not how I see it, not at all,
but see the notes in Part Two.

Propertius

As with Catullus, I've reordered these poems to better depict that gradual, and apparently inevitable, shift from infatuation to bitter invective. This is, after all, the poetic genre where nothing ever seems to end well.

Cynthia's famous introduction in Book One (*Monobiblos*).

1.1.1-8
Cynthia was the first. She caught me with her eyes, a fool
who had never before been touched by desires.
Love cast down my look of constant pride,
and he pressed on my head with his feet,
until he taught me to despise chaste girls,
perversely, and to live without plan.
Already, it's been a whole year that the frenzy hasn't stopped,
when, for all that, the gods are against me.
(Katz 2004: 3)

1.3
She lay, Theseus' ship sailing away,
languid on lonely shores, the Knossian girl;
and Cepheus' daughter collapsed in first sleep
just free from the hard stone, Andromeda;
no less than Edonian bacchante, worn from dances,
when she fell by the grassy Apidanus:
so seemed she, breathing gentle quiet,
Cynthia, supporting her head on relaxed hands,
when I was dragging my feet drunk with much Bacchus,
and the boys shook the torch late in the night.

Not having yet completely lost sensation,
I try to approach softly, pressing on the couch,
and although a pair commanded me, gripped with lust—
Love on one side, Liber the other, each a hard god—
to test her lightly, lifting up her arm,
and to take kisses, my weapon in hand,

yet I didn't disturb my mistress' quiet,
fearing the outbursts of her well-known cruelty.

But I remained fixed, my eyes intent,
like Argus with the strange horns of Inachus' daughter.
And now I take the garland from my forehead
and place it on your temples, Cynthia.
Now I delight to redo your fallen hair.
Now I give furtive fruits to empty hands.
I lavish all these gifts on ungrateful sleep,
gifts that roll repeatedly from dangling breasts.
And each time you take breath with a sudden motion,
I am stupefied, believing in an empty sign,
that some vision has brought you unaccustomed fears,
or someone is forcing you unwillingly to be his,
until the moon, running across different windows,
the moon, busy with lingering moonbeams,
opens your composed eyes with its light rays.

So she speaks, fixing her elbow on the soft couch,
"Have another's insults finally brought you
back, expelled from her doors, to our bed?
Where *did* you consume the long hours of my night,
still languid, my god, with the stars disappearing?
If only you could experience the nights you always
force me to endure, you asshole!
At first I evaded sleep with the purple thread,
and again, exhausted, with the song of the Orphic lyre.
Now and then, I complained lightly to myself
the frequent long delays when your lover is about:
until sleep pushed me, slipping, with his delicious wings.
He at last cured my crying."
(Katz 2004: 11-13)

1.8B
She's staying! She swore she'll remain! My enemies be damned!
We won: she did not submit to unrelenting prayers.
Desirous envy can drop its false joys:
Cynthia's mine: she's abandoned going new ways.

She loves me, and through me, my beloved Rome.
Without me, she'll see no exotic kingdoms.
On the contrary, she prefers relaxing with me
on a narrow couch, mine on any terms,
to visiting the ancient kingdom of wealthy Hippodamia
and the riches Elis once procured from its horses.

Though *he* gave her much and promised more,
still she doesn't desert my embrace for greed.
I was able to sway her not with gold, nor with Indian
conches, but with the blandishments of alluring poetry.

So there *are* Muses, Apollo does not desert the lover.
Trusting them, I love. Rare Cynthia is mine!
Now I touch the highest stars with the soles of my feet.
Whether day or night, she is mine!
My rival cannot abduct a love so strongly founded.
That glory will know my old age.
(Katz 2004: 31)

2 .1.1-16
You ask how I can write so many love poems,
how such an effeminate book can come to my lips.
Neither Calliope nor Apollo sings this to me.
The girl alone erects my genius.

If I've seen her walk, radiant in Coan silk,
then this entire volume shall be made of silk.
If I've seen her hair falling loose across her face,
she goes contented, arrogant in my praise.
If she has struck a song on the lyre with ivory fingers,
I marvel at the art her agile hand commands.
When she lowers her demanding eyes to sleep,
I find a thousand new inducements to poetry.
When, nude, her dress ripped away, she wrestles with me,
then truly we compose lengthy Illiads.
Whatever she does, whatever she says,
the greatest story is born from nothing.
(Katz 2004: 81)

2.15.1-30, 37-40, 50-55
Lucky me! radiant night! and you
couch made fertile by my pleasures.

As many words as we shared while the lamps were on—
once light was removed, that many bouts ensued!
First she wrestles me with naked breasts,
then her concealing tunic brings delay.
She pushes open my lids, as they slip into sleep,
and says, with her expression, "So, you lie there spent?"
With such varied embrace we exchange positions!
So many of my kisses linger on your lips!

Venus does not enjoy corrupting in the dark:
if you don't know, eyes are the instigators in sex.
They say Paris himself was undone by the nude Laconian girl
as he stood up from Menelaus' bed:
and nude Endymion is said to have snared Apollo's
sister, to have gone to bed with the naked goddess.
But if you intend to go to bed and keep your clothes on,
you'll feel my hands ripping your clothing:
in fact, if excessive rage provokes me,
you'll be showing your mom your battered arms.

Drooping boobs don't yet preclude your play:
let her worry who knows the shame of having given birth.
When the Fates permit us, let us sate our eyes on sex:
a long night is coming for you, daylight never to return.
If only you'd agree that we are bound like this in mid-embrace
by a chain that no day would ever loosen!
Let joined doves be an example to you of love,
the male and female in complete union.
He is mistaken, who seeks a limit on love's madness:
true lust is incapable of moderation.
. . .
If she is willing to grant me such nights
with her, it will be a huge year in my life;
and if she'll give me many nights, I'll become immortal in them:
in a single night, she makes anybody feel like a god.

. . .
But you, while there's light, don't neglect the fruit of life!
If you give all your kisses, you give few.
And just as leaves fall from dried-up garlands,
and you see them floating, strewn over the wine bowls,
it's the same for us, lovers who now breathe vigorously:
perhaps tomorrow shuts in our fate.
(Katz 2004: 135-39)

3.8A
We had a great blow-up at yesterday's lamps,
so many curses from your insane voice,
when, drunk on wine, you push the table over and
cast full tumblers at me with insane hand!
Go ahead! Rip my hair
and scratch my face with your beautiful nails!
Threaten to set fire and burn my eyes!
Rip off my tunic, expose my bare breast!

No doubt signs of true heat are given me:
for no woman suffers, except from heavy love.
The invective a woman hurls with rabid tongue
is also uttered beneath lofty Venus' feet—

or she crowds him with flocks of chaperons when he goes out,
or she herself, like a besotted Maenad, scours the highways,
of ceaseless demented nightmares terrify the shy girl,
or the girl stirs her poor girlfriend with painted images:
I am a true prophet in torments of the soul.
I've often studied these signs of true lust.
It's not real passion that you don't turn to reproaches:
let a dull girl be my enemies' prize.
May my contemporaries see the wounds on my bitten neck:
let jealousy teach me to have had my girl with me.

I wish either to suffer from love or to hear suffering,
to witness either my tears or yours,
when you send words concealed in frowns,
or when you signal with your fingers your secret messages.

I hate the sleep that sighs never disturb:
I would be always pale to my angry one.

The fire was sweeter for Paris when, through a lively defense,
he could bear ecstasy to his Tyndarid:
while the Danaans conquered, while savage Hector lasted,
he waged the greatest war in Helen's pussy!

Either with you or for you against rivals, I'll always
be at war: with you, no peace will ever please me.
(Katz 2004: 259-61)

1.18
This is certainly the place, for one in pain—deserted, silent—
and Zephyr's air sits on the vacant grove.
Here one can release hidden grief freely,
if only the rocks can keep a secret.
Where can I first locate your contempt, my Cynthia?
What beginning of crying, Cynthia, do you give me?
Once I was numbered among the happy lovers,
now I am disgraced in your love.

What did I do? Which poem of mine changed you?
You think I've got a new girlfriend?
If so, come back, dove, as not one other girl
has placed her lovely feet upon my threshold.
My grief owes much of its bitterness to you,
but my rage won't come so rashly that I become
a constant and understandable source of anger to you, your eyes
deformed with crying so many tears.

Is it because my color shows no change,
and devotion doesn't scream in my expression?
You'll be witness, since a tree has loves,
beech and pine dear to the Arcadian god,
how often my words resound under your delicate shade and is
written in your bark the name, Cynthia!

Because your cruelty made me a nervous wreck?

These things are better kept behind locked doors.
Timid, I preferred to endure my proud one's
every command and not complain in shrill distress.
In exchange, I get sacred springs, cold
rock, and annoying quiet on this overgrown path.
Whatever my complaints can narrate
I am constrained, alone, to tell the shrill birds.

But however you are, let the woods echo my "Cynthia"
and let the rocks be full of your name.
(Katz 2004: 65-67)

2.5
Is it true that all Rome speaks of you, Cynthia,
that you betray me openly?
Do I deserve this? You'll pay the price, bitch!
The wind will blow me somewhere, Cynthia.
I'll find one girl yet out of all the cheats
who will enjoy becoming famous through my poetry.
She won't insult me with her imperiousness, and she'll
tear you to pieces! Then finally you who were loved too long will
    cry.

Now the anger is fresh, now's the time to separate.
Once the pain goes away, believe me, love will return.
Carpathian waves don't vary with the Aquilonian,
nor is a black cloud moved by uncertain Notus
as easily as fighting lovers change with a word:
while there's time, remove your neck from the unjust yoke.
You will not regret anything, except on the first night.
Everything painful in love, if you endure it, becomes light.

But please, by the happy laws of Queen Juno,
don't harm yourself, love, by your arrogance.
It's not just the bull who wounds his enemy with curving horns.
Even the injured sheep fights back his attacker.
I swear I won't tear the clothes from you body,
nor let my anger shatter locked gates.
Though enraged, I wouldn't dare to snatch your braided locks

or jab you with my hard thumbs.
Let some rustic look for these nasty scraps,
one whose head no ivies gird.
Let me write, then, what you aging may never erase:
"Cynthia, potent form; light word, Cynthia!
Believe me, although you deride the murmurs of reputation,
this verse, Cynthia, will be your pallor.
(Katz 2004: 97-99)

2.9A.1-2, 19-28, 41-48
That man there—that was me: but perhaps in time, when this
one's cast out, another will be even dearer.
…

But *you* couldn't be alone for one night,
you whore, couldn't stay one day by yourself!
You even led the drinking with raucous laughter:
and probably there was a lot of shit said about me.
You even looked up the guy who dumped you:
gods will it that you delight in that man and be stuck with him!
Were these my prayers for your health
when the Stygian waters were already around you head,
and we, your friends, stood circling your bed, crying?
This man, by god, where was he then, you faithless bitch?
…

The stars are witnesses and morning frost
and the gate opened secretly to despicable me,
that nothing in life ever pleased me as much as you:
now, although you are inimical, still there will be nothing.
No other woman will leave traces in my bed:
I'll be alone, since I can't be yours.
And I hope, if by chance I've lived a pious life,
that man may turn to stone while he is doing you!
(Katz 2004: 111-13)

2.17
To lie about a date, to deceive a lover with promises:
you might as well have hands stained with blood!
I am the poet laureate of this, so often I've spent bitter nights,
abandoned, shattered on both sides of the bed.

You may be moved by Tantalus' fate at the water,
how the liquid deceives his thirst, just beyond his parched mouth;
you may marvel at the Sisyphian toils,
how, with difficulty, he rolls the burden up the entire mountain.
Nothing on earth is harder than the fate of the lover,
nothing, if you only knew, that you'd want less to be.

Once, with admiring envy, they called me happy;
now I too am scarcely admitted every tenth day.
I'm not allowed to sleep on the street under a dry moon,
or to send messages through cracks in a gate.
Now I will lie, you slut, on a hard rock,
and take strong poison in my hands.

But even though it may be so, I'll avoid exchanging my mistress:
then she'll cry, when she has felt my fidelity.
(Katz 2004: 147)

1.10
What a great calm, when I was present at your
first love, a witness and partner in your tears.
It's such a pleasure to recall that night,
(I do it all the time with my prayers),
when I saw you, Gallus, swooning, wrapped
in her arms, drawing out each word in a long moan!

Although sleep was pressing my closing eyes
and the Moon with her horses reddened midway across the sky,
still I couldn't pull away from your sport:
so great was the ardor in your alternating voices!
But since you are not afraid to submit to me,
accept the rewards of our shared pleasure:
not only have I learned to keep quiet your pains,
there is an even greater promise, friend, in me.
I can rejoin separated lovers,
I know how to open a mistress' slow doors.
I can cure any recent pain,
not light is the medicine in my words.
Cynthia always taught me which things to pursue

and which to avoid: love has a certain effect.

Beware of fighting and making her unhappy,
don't boast too much nor be too long silent.
If she has asked for something, don't make a face.
Never let generous words fall to you unanswered.
She gets irritated when disrespected,
makes unjust threats in her rage.
The more you are humble, love's subject,
the more you will reap a good harvest.
He will remain happy with one girl
who will never be free, never thoughtless.
(Katz 2004: 37-39)

Only towards the end did I come to appreciate this poem. Initially, it seemed too farcical, but that was before I realized this marks Cynthia's last appearance ("in all her glory"). For that reason alone it needs to be here; here in this mythical chronology of this mythical affair. *At one point this too took place …*

4.8
Learn what scared the aquatic Esquiline last night
    When all who live near the New Fields came running,
When a sordid brawl was heard in an obscure *taverna*,
    If without me, not without stain on my good name.

An aged snake has long been guardian of the Lanuvium;
    An hour's delay is specially well spent there
Where the sacred descent vanishes into a dark cavern,
    Where enters (virgins, beware of all such journeys!)
The hungry serpent's due when he demands his yearly
    Food, with coiling hisses from earth's depths.
The girls sent down upon this sacred errand blench
    At blindly trusting their hands to the snakes mouth.
He snatches up the morsels offered by the virgin;
    Even the basket in the virgin's hand trembles.
If you've been chaste they return to their parents' embrace

And farmers shout "The year will be fruitful!'

It was here my Cynthia drove her close-clipped ponies,
 Juno the excuse, the real reason Venus.
 Appian Way, pray tell what a Triumphal ride you witnessed
 As her wheels raced along over your stones,
Herself a fine sight, seated, leaning over the yoke-pole,
 Daring to shake out the reins over rough places.
I'll not describe her smooth-faced toy-boy's silk-lined chaise
 And the dogs with fancy collars on their Molossian necks.
Later he'll have to sell his soul for filthy stodge
 When a shaming beard overcomes those hairless checks.

Because our bed was being wronged so often
 I meant to strike camp and change couch.
Next door to Aventine Diana there lives a Phyllis—
 When sober, rather dull; when drinking, quite delightful.
Another girl, named Teia, lives in Tarpeia's Grove—
 Pretty, but when drunk too much for one man.
By inviting these I planned to pass an easier night,
 Sampling once more stolen joys of unknown Venus.

There was one small couch for three on a secluded lawn.
 You ask how we lay? I was between the two,
With Lygdamus to mix the wine, and the summer glassware
 And the Greek bouquet of Methymnéan.
Nile, yours the piper, yours the castanet-girl, Baetis,
 Neat without art, prepared to be pelted with roses,
And Magnus too, the dwarf with misshapen limbs,
 Waved stumpy hands in time to the hollow boxwood.

But though the lamps were filled their flames kept flickering
 And the table collapsed on its hinged legs.
Besides at dice when I tried for the lucky Venus throw
 Always the losing Dog jumped out.
I didn't hear the singing, I was blind to naked breasts,
 I was on my own alas at Lanuvium's gates;
When suddenly the front-door grated on its hinges
 And muffled noises came from the entrance-hall.

Next moment Cynthia flung the folding doors wide open,
  Her hair a mess, but lovely in her fury.
My fingers lost their grip and dropped the glass,
  And loosened by the wine my lips turned pale.
Her eyes flashed and she raged as only a woman can;
  The sight was as frightful as a city's sack.
She dug her angry talons into Phyllis' face;
  Terrified Teia shouted "Neighbors, fire!"
Uplifted lights disturbed the sleeping citizens
  And every alley rang with midnight madness.
The two girls, dresses torn and hair disheveled, fled
  To the nearest tavern where the street was dark.

Pleased with her trophies Cynthia rushed back victorious
  And slashed my face with a back-handed slap
And stamped her mark on my neck, biting till it bled,
  And struck at my eyes, the chief offenders.
Then, when at last her arms were tired of hitting me,
  Lygdamus cowering behind the couch's head on the left
Was discovered and dragged out, begging my protection.
  Lygdamus, I couldn't help—like you, her prisoner.

But in the end with suppliant palms I sued for peace
  While she would hardly let me touch her feet
And said "If you would have me pardon your offence
  You must accept the list of my conditions.
You shall not strut about dressed up in Pompey's Porch
  Or when they strew sand in the ribald Forum.
Take care you don't turn round and stare at the upper Theatre
  Or let an open litter sweat while you delay it.
Lygdamus most of all, the whole cause of my grievance—
  Sell him, double-fettering his feet."

Such were her terms. I answered "I accept the terms."
  She laughed, exulting in the power I gave her.
Then, fumigating every place those girl intruders
  Had touched, she scoured the threshold with pure water
And ordered me to change my clothes again completely.
  And touched my head three times with fire of suphur.

Eventually when all the bed-clothes had been changed
   I answered and we laid down arms over the couch.
(Lee 1994: 121-24)

Ovid

Here, *Amores* 1.5, this era's most famous erotic poem, and
Corinna's first named appearance.

Siesta time in sultry summer.
I lay relaxed on the divan.

One shutter closed, the other ajar,
made sylvan semi-darkness,

a glimmering dusk, as after sunset,
or between night's end and day's beginning—

the half light shy girls need
to hide their hesitation.

At last—Corinna. On the loose in a short dress,
long hair parted and tumbling past the pale neck—

lovely as Lais of the many lovers,
Queen Semiramis gliding in.

I grabbed the dress; it didn't hide much,
but she fought to keep it,

only half-heartedly though.
Victory was easy, a self-betrayal.

There she stood, faultless beauty
in front of me, naked.

Shoulders and arms challenging eyes and fingers.
Nipples firmly demanding attention.

Breasts in high relief about the smooth belly.
Long and slender waist. Thighs of a girl.

Why list perfection?
I hugged her tight.

The rest can be imagined—we fell asleep.
Such afternoons are rare.
(Lee 1968: 15-17)

Yes, *ecce, Corinna venit*!

And this sly pair—perhaps a truer account.

Amores 2.7
So that's my role—the professional defendant?
I'm sick of standing trial—though I always win.

At the theatre I've only to glance at the back rows
and your jealous eye pin-points a rival.

A pretty girl need only look at me
and you're sure the look is a signal.

I compliment another woman—you grab my hair.
I criticize her—and you think I've something to hide.

If I'm looking well I don't love you.
If pale, I'm pining for someone else.

I wish to God I had been unfaithful—
the guilty can take your punishment.

As it is, you accuse me blindly, believing anything.
It's your own fault your anger cuts no ice.

Remember the donkey, putting his long ears back—
the more he's beaten the slower he goes.

So that's the latest count against me—
I'm carrying on with your maid Cypassis?

Good God, if I wanted variety
is it likely I'd pick on a drudge like her?

What man of breeding would sleep with a slave
or embrace a body scarred by the lash?

Besides, she's your coiffeuse—her skill
makes her a favorite of yours.

I'd be mad to ask a maid so devoted to you.
She'd only turn me down and tell.

By Venus and Cupid's bow
I'm innocent—I swear it!
(Lee 1968: 79-81)

Amores 2.8
Cypassis, incomparable coiffeuse
who should start a *salon* on Olympus,

no country lass, as I know from our encounters,
but Corinna's treasure and my treasure hunt—

who was it told her about *us*?
How did she know we slept together?

I didn't blush though, did I? Said nothing by mistake
to betray our secret?

I may have argued no one in his right mind
would have an affair with a maid,

but Achilles adored his maid Briseis
and Agamemnon fell for his slave Cassandra.

I can't claim to be greater than those two.
What goes for royalty is good enough for me.

Corinna looked daggers at *you* though.
And how you blushed! I saw you.

But I saved the day, you must admit,
by swearing my Venus oath.

—Dear goddess, bid the warm south winds
blow that white lie over the ocean!—

So in return, my black beauty,
reward me today with your sweet self.

Why shake your head? The danger's over.
Don't be ungrateful. Remember your duty to *me*.

If you're stupid enough to refuse I'll have to confess
and betray myself for betraying her.

I'll tell your mistress where and when we met, Cypassis,
and what we did and how many times and how we did it.
(Lee 1968: 81-83)

Another pair: a lover's jealousy, anger, and a plea.

Amores 3.11
To hell with love! I've been a martyr long enough.
You're quite impossible.

I've slipped my shackles. Yes, I'm now a free man—
I can blush to remember how I forgot myself.

Victory at last. I've planted my foot on Cupid's neck.
I didn't know I had it in me.

'Stick to it' I tell myself, 'don't weaken.
It's painful, but think of the pain as medicine.'

Did I really lie down like a tramp on the pavement
all those nights you locked me out?

Did I really stand guard at your door like a slave
while you were hugging another man?

I well remember seeing your lover leave the house
and stagger home—invalided out.

The worst of it was that he saw me—
I could wish my enemies nothing worse.

Was there a single day when I didn't report for duty
as your personal escort, your friend, your lover?

My company made everybody love you.
My passion for you started a male fashion.

I can't forget the lies you fed me,
the promises you fooled me with,

the nods to lover-boys at parties,
the sly remarks in obvious code.

Once, I heard you were ill, rushed to your home in a panic
and found you in bed—yes, in the arms of my rival.

These and other unspeakable insults have made me hard.
Find someone else to play the martyr.

My ship's in harbour, garlands hanging from the stern,
deaf to the roar of the rising storm.

Don't waste sweet words and bygone witchery on me.
I've learnt some common sense at last.
(Lee 1968: 165-67)

Amores 3.11.B
Love and hate, here in my heart, at tug of war—
and love I suppose will find a way to win.

I'd sooner hate. If I can't, I'll be the reluctant lover—
the dumb ox bearing the yoke he loathes.

Your behavior drives me away, your beauty draws me back.
I adore your face and abhor your failings.

With or without you, life's impossible
and I can't decide what I want.

Why can't you be less lovely or more true?
Why must your faults and your figure clash?

I love what you are and hate what you do—
but your self, alas, outweighs your selfishness.

By the bed we shared, by all the gods
who let you take their names in vain,

by your face my holy icon, by your eyes that ravished mine,
take pity on me.

Be what you will, you'll still be mine—but you must choose—
do you want me to want to love you or be forced to?

Make life plain sailing for me please
by helping me love what I can't help loving.
(Lee 1968: 167)

Augustus' Rome; the sorry plight of the poet: a remarkably revealing poem about class, wealth, status, and resentment.

Amores 3.8
Does anyone these days respect the artist
or value elegiac verse?

Time was when imagination meant more than money
but today *poor* and *boor* mean the same thing.

'I adore your poetry' she says,
and allows it where I can't follow.

After the compliments the door curtly closes
and I, her poet, moon about humiliated,

displaced by a new-rich upstart, a bloody soldier
who butchered his way to wealth and a knighthood.

Him in your lovely arms! You in his clutches!
Light of my life, how could you?

That head wore a helmet, remember—
that obliging flank a sword.

His left hand, flashing the new equestrian ring,
once griped a shield. His right has killed.

How can you hold hands with a killer?
Have you no sensibility?

Look at his scars, marks of a brutal trade—
that body earned him all he has.

I expect he even brags about his killings.
How can you touch him after that, gold-digger,

and allow me, the priest of Phoebus and the Muses,
to serenade your locked door in vain?

No man of taste should waste his time on art—
he'd better enlist and rough it under canvas.

Don't turn out couplets, turn out on parade.
Homer, join up if you want a date!

Jove Almighty realized gold's omnipotence
when he cashed himself to seduce a girl.

Before the transaction father looked grim, daughter prudish,
her turret steely, the doorposts coppered.

But when the crafty lecher arrived in cash
she opened her lap and gave as golden as she got.

Long ago, when Saturn ruled in the kingdom of heaven,
Earth sank all her capital in darkness—

stowed bronze and silver, gold and heavy iron in hell.
Ingots were not yet known:

she had better things to offer—crops without cultivation,
fruit on the bough, honey in the hollow oak.

No one tore the ground with ploughshares
or parceled out the land

or swept the sea with dipping oars—
the shore was the world's end.

Clever human nature, victim of your inventions,
disastrously creative,

why cordon cities with towered walls?
Why arm for war?

Why take to the sea—as if happiness were far away?
Why not annex the sky too?

We have, in a modest way—by defying Bacchus
and Hercules and Romulus and now Caesar.

We dig for gold instead of food.
Our soldiers earn blood-money.

The Senate's barred to the poor. Capital is king,
creates the solemn judge and the censorious knight.

Let them own the world—knights controlling Campus and
        Forum,
Senate dictating peace and war,

but hands off love! Sweethearts shouldn't be up for auction.
Leave the poor man his little corner.

As it is, if my girl were chaste as a Sabine prude
she'd crawl for anyone with money.

So I am locked out. When I'm around she's scared of her
    husband.
He'd vanish quick enough if I could pay.

O for a god in heaven to right a lover's wrongs
and turn fat pickings to a pile of dust!
(Lee 1968: 151-55)

But as I've said, it was short, this era of amatory Latin poets: Augustus' new adultery laws, Ovid's relegation to the Black Sea town of Tomis (for both, see Part Two) . . . well, the time had come to write about something else.

3

....

ALEXANDRIANS

It needs to be noted just how indebted these Latin poets (these *new* Latin poets, Cicero's *Neoterics*) were to the Greeks, Callimachus in particular: those clever Alexandrians, scholar-poets, light on their feet, sophisticated epigrams, restrained, amused, learned allusiveness, the calculated quip, the apt phrase, brevity, originality—a *slender* poetics. Like Catullus' *urbanitas* and *uenustas*: a learned sophistication free of pedantry, a seductive elegance "under the sign of Venus." "It was from them that the *Neoterics* acquired . . . their distaste for long, sprawling, pompous and cliché-ridden poetry (epic in particular) [and] . . . their personal rather than public preoccupation." (Green 2005:10) Callimachus explains this, his *slender* Muse, as follows, in the opening lines of his most important poem, the *Aetia*. First, a faithful translation of the fragment (for fragments are all we have):

> Often the Telchines croak at my song, fools, who are not friends of the Muse, because I did not complete one continuous poem either on kings? [. . . or . . .] heroes in many thousands of lines, but I [told] my tale bit by bit like a child, though the decades of my years are not few. [. . .] to the Telchines I [say] this: "tribe [. . .] that knows how to waste your liver [. . .] was of few lines. But bountiful Demeter drags down by far the long [lady?], and of the two the [. . .] taught that Mimnermus is sweet, not the large lady . . . [. . .] may the crane rejoicing in the blood of Pygmies [fly . . .] to Thrace from Egypt, and man the Massagetae shoot at their man, [the Mede], from afar. Thus are [nightingales] sweeter. Begone, baneful race of Envy. And in turn [judge] poetry by its *technê*, not by the Persian rope. Do

not ask me to produce a loud-sounding song: to thunder is not mine, but Zeus's." For, when for the very first time, I placed my tablet on my knees, Lycian Apollo said to me: "[. . .] singer, [raise] your sacrificial victim to be as fat as possible, but your Muse, my friend, to be slender. [And I bid you] this also: go there where wagons do not trundle; [drive your chariot] not along the same tracks as others; nor along the broad path, but the [unworn] ways, even though you will drive along a narrower course." [I obeyed him.] For we sing among those who love the clear sound of the cicada, not the din of asses. Let another bray just like the long-eared [beast]; may I be the small, the winged one, ah truly, that I may sing feeding upon the moisture, the morning dew from the divine air, and that in turn I may shed old age, which is a weight upon me as great as the tricorn island upon destructive Enceladus. [. . .] as many as the Muses look upon with favorable eye when they are children, these friends they do not lay aside when they are gray. [. . .] no longer to move its wing [. . .] then the most vigorous . . . . [Fragment 1.1–40 Pf (Pfeiffer), with additions] (Acosta-Hughes 2012: 32)

And then this more polished version.

The Telchines, who know nothing
of poetry and hate the Muses, often
snipe at me, because its not a monotonous
uninterrupted poem featuring kings
and heroes in thousands of verses
that I've produced, driving my song instead
for little stretches, like a child, though the tale of my years
is not brief.
   Well, here's what I say
to the Telchines:
    "Born eaters
of your own hearts, [the Coan poet]
was not, admittedly, a man of few verses
but all the same his bountiful Demeter far
outweighs the woman he celebrated

at length.
             And of the two books
Mimnermus wrote, not the one that tells
of the big woman, but the one composed
with a delicate touch, displays
the poet at his sweetest.
                      Let the crane
who revels in the blood of Pygmies fly
far from Egypt, and the Massagetai
shoot at the Mede long range: nightingales
are sweeter like this.
                  To hell with you, then,
spiteful brood of Jealousy: from now on
we'll judge poetry by the art,
not by the mile. And don't expect a song
to rush from my lips with a roar:
it's Zeus' job, not mine to thunder."
  The very first time I sat down and put
a writing table on my lap, my own
Lykian Apollo said to me:
                    "Make your sacrifice
as fat as you can, poet, but keep
your Muse on slender rations. And see that you go
where no hackneys plod: avoid the ruts
carved in the boulevard, even if it means
driving along a narrower path."
                And so I sing for those
who love the shrill cicada's cry, and hate
the clamour of asses. Let someone else,
loud as any long-eared brute, bray
for their amusement. As for me,
I would be small and winged—yes,
even so, to sing
with dew upon my lips, the food
of morning culled from air divine, shedding
the years that weigh on me
like Sicily on Enkelados.
                The Muses

won't repulse in grey old age
the man on whom they smiled in his youth.
. . . no longer stir its wing
. . . [sings] most effectively, then.
[*Aetia* Prologue] (Nisetich 2001: 63-64)

Callimachus makes a similar point in his *Hymn to Apollo*.

Envy whispered into Apollo's ear:
"I don't like a poet who doesn't sing
like the sea." Apollo kicked
Envy aside and said: "The Assyrian river
rolls a massive stream, but it's mainly
silt and garbage that it sweeps along. The bees
bring water to Deo not from every source
but where it bubbles up pure and undefiled
from a holy spring, its very essence."
Farewell, Lord! Let Criticism go where Envy's gone!
[*Hymn to Apollo* 126-35] (Nisetich 2001: 27)

Let me just say that I too find this new aesthetic personally
appealing: not being swept along by a massive stream; taking
the less worn, narrower path; the endless braying of asses in my
ears; as for feeding on the morning dew or singing like the
cicada ... perhaps not.

Callimachus' Erotic Epigrams

31 Pf
Up and down the hillsides, on the track
    of every rabbit, every deer—that's your hunter,
Epikydes, braving frost and snow. But if someone says.
    "There it is, wounded!", he leaves it alone.
My passion is like his: expert at chasing
    what runs away, it passes by what doesn't.
(Nisetich 2001: 173)

28 Pf
I hate recycled poetry, and get no pleasure
    from a road crowded with travellers this way and that.
I can't stand a boy who sleeps around, don't drink
    at public fountains, and loathe everything vulgar.
Now you, Lysaniës, sure are handsome ... But before I've
        repeated
    "handsome", Echo's "and some ... one else's" cuts me off.
(Nisetich 2001: 173)

46 Pf
How fine a lover's charm, Polyphemos hit on!
    By god, that Cyclops knew his stuff.
Poetry, Philip, shrinks a lover's swelling,
    poetry's a drug for every ill.
Only hunger—good for nothing else—is as good
    at rooting out the craze for boys.
When Eros comes on strong, I let him have it:
    "You might as well clip your wings, sonny!
I'm not afraid of you. I have at home
    both charms against your cruel wounds."
(Nisetich 2001: 173)

41 Pf
Half my soul's living still, half's in Love's or Death's
    clutches—I don't know which, only that it's gone.
Is it chasing one of the boys again? Over and over
    I've warned them, "Have nothing to do
with that runaway." Steered by lust, worthy of stoning,
    she's off, I know, on her usual rounds.
(Nisetich 2001: 174)

29 Pf
Fill the cup: time for another toast "To Diokles"
    and leave the water out! His looks (handsome,
all too handsome) demand it neat. If anyone disagrees,
    I'm the only connoisseur of beauty here!
(Nisetich 2001: 174)

52 Pf

Hate him four times over, if he hates me, love him
   if he loves me—Theokritos, I mean, the dark beauty
just now ripening on his chin. Hear me, Zeus: by
    Ganymede,
   you too were a lover once. Need I say more?
(Nisetich 2001: 174)

32 Pf

I *know* my pockets are empty. By the Graces, Menippos,
   don't tell me my own dream! It hurts and hurts
hearing you, my friend, remind me of it. Of all
   that comes from you, this is least like a lover.
(Nisetich 2001: 174)

42 Pf

If, Archinos, I sang at your door on purpose,
   never forgive me; but if I couldn't help it,
let it go. Wine at full strength and love are to blame,
   the one for dragging, the other for keeping me there.
Nor did I shout, "It's so-and-so son of so-and-so", but
    kissed
   the doorpost: if that's a crime, I'm guilty.
(Nisetich 2001: 174)

44 Pf

There's something hidden here, yes, by Pan,
   by Dionysos, there's fire under this ash.
Careful, now: don't get too close! Often a river
   eats away at a wall, bit by bit, invisibly.
Even so, Menexenos, I fear you'll slip
   under my skin and topple me into love.
(Nisetich 2001: 174-75)

45 Pf

"You will be mine, Menekrates! Meanwhile, play hard to
    get",
I said on the twentieth of June, and on the tenth (or so)
of July the bird came willingly to hand. He's mine,

Hermes, all mine: the twenty days are OK.
(Nisetich 2001: 175)

25 Pf
Kallignotos swore to Ionis he would never love
    anyone, male or female, more than her.
He swore, but it's true, what they say: the vows
    of lovers never reach the ears of the gods.
Now he burns for a boy, and the poor girl
    (as they also say) is out in the cold.
(Nisetich 2001: 175)

30 Pf
Is it you, Kleonikos of Thessaly? By the sun's rays,
    I couldn't tell. Where in the world have you been?
Nothing but hair and bones! Has the god I worship
    got you in his clutches? Is that what's happened?
I knew it: Euxitheos was the one. You saw him too
    and had no eyes for anything else.
(Nisetich 2001: 175)

43 Pf
The guest kept his wound hidden. How painful
    the breath he drew (did you notice?)
at the third toast, and the petals drooping
    from the man's garlands littered the floor.
He's done to a turn. By god, that's plain as day:
    I've been there myself, I know the way.
(Nisetich 2001: 175)

Others of Note

From what I put on my head at the time—
expensive auburn ointments, fragrant garlands—
faded on the spot, and the food
that went between my teeth
and into my ingrate belly, of that too
nothing remained in the morning:
                        what I put

in my ears alone stays with me still
[*Aetia* 2.49-54 (i.e., fragment 43.12-17)]
(Nisetich 2001: 88)

And this, a personal favorite: Heraclitus, whose nightingales (poems) still live (two versions).

2 PF
Someone, Heraclitus, mentioned your fate, and brought me to tears, remembering how many times the two of us had sunk the sun in conversation. But you, my friend in Halicarnassus, lie somewhere, gone long long ago to dust. But your nightingales live: Hades, who seizes everything, will not lay his hand on them.
(Tueller 2014: xiii)

Your death, a casual remark, moved me to tears,
    for I recalled, Herakleitos, how often you and I
put the sun to bed with our talking. But all that's left
    of you is ashes now, my friend in Halikarnesos.
Your *Nightingales* are alive, though: Hades who rips
    all things away will never lay a hand on them.
(Nisetich 2001: 180)

Elegant Callimachus, quintessential scholar-poet, court poet of the Ptolemies.

4

....

EROTIC EPIGRAMS FROM BOOK 5
OF *THE GREEK ANTHOLOGY*

Push this sort of thing back far enough and you arrive at the origins of the Greek epigrammatic tradition. Here are my picks for best erotic or amatory epigrams from Book 5 of the *Greek Anthology* (Tueller 2014). Yes, but do I have a favorite? I do. It's by Posidippus (note: for information on the recently discovered papyrus bookroll of heretofore unknown epigrams by Posidippus, see Part Two, Chapter Four).

213
Posidippus
If Pythias has someone with her, I'll go, but if she sleeps here alone, by Zeus, I'd like her to invite me in for a little while. Tell her this token: that drunk, and through thieves, I came with daring Love as my guide. [*Pythias* was prostitute's name in antiquity.] (Tueller 2014: 357)

Led by Love, drunk, and through thieves ... who hasn't?

18
Rufinus
We, who take no pleasure in costly intrigues, choose slaves over proud ladies. The latter's skin smells of perfume; they snigger with pride, and intercourse with them ripens to danger. But the beauty of the others' skin is their own, and their beds are amenable to gifts, without regard for their cost. I am like Pyrrhus, Achilles' son, who preferred his servant Andromache to his wife Hermione. (Tueller 2014: 213)

19
Rufinus
No longer mad for boys, as before, I am now called mad for women; now my discus is a rattle [The discus was a boy's toy, the rattle a girl's, but an obscene allusion is concealed.]. Instead of the unadulterated complexion of boys, I am now fond of chalked skin, accented with the blush of rouge. Dolphins will feed on tree-crowned Erymanthus, and swift deer in the foaming wave of the sea! (Tueller 2014: 215)

23
Callimachus
May you, Conopium, sleep in the same way that you make me bed down on this chilly porch. May you sleep, you fiend, like you put your lover to bed: you have not met even a dream of compassion! Your neighbors take pity on me, but you—not even in a dream! Presently your gray hair will remind you of all this.
(Tueller 2014: 217)

51
Anonymous
I desired her, I kissed her, I got her, I did her—I am loved. Who am I? And she? And how? Only the goddess [Aphrodite] knows. (Tueller 2014: 237)

60
Rufinus
A silver-footed maiden was bathing, letting the water fall on the golden apples of her breasts, with flesh like curdled milk. Her rounded buttocks, their flesh more fluid than water, gyrated back and forth. Her outspread hand covered the swelling Eurotas—not all of it, but as much as it could.
(Tueller 2014: 243)

66
Rufinus
Luckily, I saw Prodice sitting alone; I pleaded with her, clasping her ambrosial knees, and said, "Save a man who is

nearly lost, and grant me my waning breath of life." When I said this, she cried, but wiped away a tear and, with her tender hands, showed me out. (Tueller 2014: 247)

70
Rufinus
You have the beauty of Cypris [Aphrodite], the mouth of Persuasion, the body and freshness of the spring Seasons, the voice of Calliope, the intelligence and prudence of Themis, and the hands of Athena; with you, dear, the Graces are four. (Tueller 2014: 249)

72
Palladas of Alexandria
This is life, this is it: life is luxury; away with cares! Brief are the years of men. Now we have the Deliverer, [i.e., Dionysus; wine delivers one from cares.] now dances and flowery garlands, now women! Let me experience every good thing today—tomorrow is revealed to no one. (Tueller 2014: 251)

75
Rufinus
A girl Amymone (an Aphrodite!) was my neighbor, and set my heart on fire not a little. She would tease me, and whenever I had the chance, I made an attempt. She would blush—but what was the use? She felt the pang. After much effort, I succeeded. Now I hear that she is giving birth. So what do I do? Do I stay or do I go? (Tueller 2014: 253)

77
Rufinus
If a woman had as much charm after sex, a man would not weary of keeping company with his wife. For all women are displeasing after sex. (Tueller 2014: 253)

83

Anonymous

If only I were the wind and you would walk in the sunlight, bare your breasts, and take me to you as I blow. (Tueller 2014: 257)

93

Rufinus

I am armed against Love with the breastplate of reason; he will not defeat me, one on one; mortal versus immortal, I will withstand him. But if he has help from Bacchus, what can I do, one against two? (Tueller 2014: 263)

98

Anonymous or Archias

Take up your bow and arrows, Cypris, and go in peace after another target; I have no more room for a wound. (Tueller 2014: 265)

104

Marcus Argentarius

Lift this bed netting, procrastinator; stop moving and twisting your hips on purpose. The folds of your thin dress cling well to you; all of you is seen, and unseen, naked. If you think this is amusing, I will take this, which sticks straight out, and wrap it in gauze. (Tueller 2014: 269)

111

Antiphilus (of Byzantium)

I said even earlier, when Tereine's charms were still in their infancy, "She will burn us all up when she grows up." They laughed at my prophecy; but see, the time I once foretold is here, and I have long acknowledged my wound. (Tueller 2014: 273)

127

Marcus Argentarius

I was deeply in love with the virgin Alcippe, and once, having succeeded in persuading her, I had her secretly in her bed.

Both our chests were pounding at the thought that anyone would happen upon us—that anyone would witness the secrets of our overflowing desire. But her mother overheard the chattering of the bed and, looking in suddenly, said, "Daughter, Hermes shares." [The saying is proverbial; Hermes grants luck in finding things but then requires the finder to share his good fortune with others. But Argentarius also intends a more literal interpretation: Hermes is the ithyphallic god, and the mother wishes to share the lover's erect penis with her daughter.] (Tueller 2014: 285)

158
Asclepiades
Once I was fooling around with seductive Hermione, and she wore, Paphian goddess [Aphrodite], a colorfully embroidered girdle with golden letters. There was written, "Love me to the end, and don't be distressed if someone else has me." (Tueller 2014: 307)

162
Asclepiades
Insatiable Philaenium wounded me; though the wound does not show, nevertheless the pain reaches to my fingertips. I am gone, Loves, I am a dead man, I am done for, for half asleep I stepped on the prostitute, and when I touched her, she bit. (Tueller 2014: 309)

164
Asclepiades
Night, I call you, and no one else, to witness how Nico's Pythias insults me, habitual deceiver that she is. I have come by invitation, not uninvited! I hope that she has this experience later, and complains to you while she stands at my porch. (Tueller 2014: 311)

183
Posidippus
Four are drinking at the party, and a girl is coming for each. That makes eight; one jar of Chian wine is not enough. Go,

boy, to Aristius and tell him the first he sent was half full: it is two gallons short certainly, I think more. Go quickly: we are all gathering at the fifth hour. [i.e., about 11 a.m.] (Tueller 2014: 327)

184
Meleager
I knew it! You didn't fool me; why call on the gods? Oh no, you haven't fooled me; I knew. Don't go on swearing you didn't; I know everything. This is what happened? This, oath breaker? That you have long slept alone—alone?! Oh, her brazen impudence! Still she continues to say "alone"! That looker Cleon didn't . . . ? I say, if you won't . . . But why make threats? Get out, you evil beast of the bed—get out quickly! No, I will do just what will please you best: I know you want to see him, so stay where you are my prisoner. (Tueller 2014: 329)

186
Posidippus
Don't imagine that you are deceiving me with your persuasive tears, Philaenis. I know: you love absolutely no one more than me—as long as you're lying beside me! But if someone else were holding you, you would say that you love him more than me. (Tueller 2014: 331)

189
Asclepiades
The night is long and it is winter weather, and it sets to the midst of the Pleiad—and I am pacing by her porch in the rain, wounded by desire for that treacherous woman. It was not love that Cypris hit me with, but a painful bolt made of fire. (Tueller 2014: 333)

203
Asclepiades
Lysidice dedicated to you, Cypris, her horse-riding spur, the golden goad of her shapely leg, with which she trained many a supine horse, while her own thighs were never reddened, so

lightly did she bounce. She completed the course without the goad, and therefore hung up the golden implement between your gates. (Tueller 2014: 341)

209
Posidippus or Asclepiades
By your shore, Paphian Cytherea, Cleander saw Nico swimming in the blue waves, and burning with love he took to his heart dry coals from the wet girl. Though he was on the land, his ship was sinking; she, stroking the sea, was received by the gentle beach. But now both are equally in love, for the prayers were not in vain that he prayed on that shore. (Tueller 2014: 347)

222
Agathias
Whenever the girl took the plectrum and struck her harp, her music was the echo of Terpsichore's strings; whenever her voice broke forth into a tragic strain, she reproduced the hum of Melpomene herself. And if there were a contest for beauty, Cypris herself would more likely lose to her, and Paris would overturn his decision. But hush! Let us keep it to ourselves, lest Dionysus overhear and long for this Ariadne's bed too. [The wife of Dionysus also had the name Ariadne.] (Tueller 2014: 359)

241
Paulus Silentiarius
"Farewell" is on my tongue, but I winch back the sound and stay near you again. For I shudder at this horrid parting as at the bitter night of Acheron. Your glow is like daylight; but while that is mute, you also bring to me that talk, sweeter than the Sirens', upon which all my soul's hopes depend. (Tueller 2014: 375)

5

....

PHILODEMOS' EPICUREAN GARDEN

Like our Latin elegists, Philodemos' narrator often finds himself in a bit of difficulty, even more so since he's an Epicurean presumably committed to *ataraxia* (that is: peace of mind; tranquility; the absence of mental disturbance, fear, and anxiety; a life of continuing, undisturbed mental activity). One could, I suppose, rearrange the order of these epigrams to better reflect that struggle (which is just what I've done). Making it clear how following the teachings of Epicurus was no easy matter; so many potential stumbling blocks along the way—a beautiful woman, adultery—but apparently (thankfully!) hard-fought equanimity comes with age, perhaps even with a proper marriage to a proper (Epicurean) woman (like Xanthippe/Xanthos), living a quiet life in the Garden.

11
Demo is killing me, and so is Thermion, the one being a hetaera, Demo
    not yet knowing Aphrodite.
And one I touch, the other I may not. I swear by you, Kypris; I do not know
    which I should say is the more desirable.
I will say it is Demarion the virgin; for I do not want that which is at hand,
    but I have a passion for all that is under guard.
(Sider 1997: 101)

12
O foot, O leg, O (I'm done for) those thighs,
O buttocks, O bush, O flanks, O shoulders, O breasts,
O delicate neck, O hands, O (madness!) those eyes,

O wickedly skillful walk, O fabulous kisses,
O (slay me!) her speech.
And if she *is* an Oscan—a mere Flora
who does not sing Sappho's verses—
  Perseus too fell in love with Indian Andromeda.
(Sider 1997: 104)

13

My soul, knowing my earlier tears and desires, tells me in advance
to flee
  passion for Heliodora.
It speaks, but I have not the strength to flee; for shamefully
indeed the
  same (soul) both foretells and, while foretelling, desires.
(Sider 1997: 110)

15

All the times I dare whether by day or evening to come to rest on
Kydilla's
  bosom,
I know that I cut a narrow path along a precipice, I know that
each time I
  risk my head on the throw of the dice.
But what's the use? For she is bold, Eros, each time when she
drags me
  and altogether knows not even the dream of fear.
(Sider 1997: 116)

25

You cry, you ask for pity, you look me up and down, you are
jealous, you
  keep touching me and kissing my hand.
These are the deeds of a lover, but whenever I tell you I am ready
and you
  hold back, you have absolutely nothing of the lover in you.
(Sider 1997: 147)

26

I came having stolen away from my husband in the middle of the night,
    and having gotten wet into the bargain in a driving rain.
Was it for his that we (now) sit doing nothing, and talking we do not go
    to bed as lovers should?
(Sider 1997: 150)

Yes, but revels must come to an end, and then … what? Marriage?

4

Seven years are coming up on thirty; papyrus columns of my life now being
    torn off ;
now too, Xanthippe, white hairs besprinkle me, announcing the age of
    intelligence;
but the harp's voice and revels are still a concern to me, and a fire smolders
    in my insatiable heart.
Inscribe her immediately as the koronis, Mistress Muses, of this my madness.
(Sider 1997: 73)

5

I fell in love. Who hasn't? I reveled. Who is not an initiate of revels? But
    whose fault is it I went mad? A god's, isn't it?
Let it go, for already grey hair rushes in to take the place of black—grey
    hair the proclaimer of the age of wisdom.
And when it was right to play we played; and since it is right no longer, we
    shall lay hold of loftier thoughts.
(Sider 1997: 78)

6

To have white-violet wreaths yet again, harp songs and Chian wine again,
    and Syrian myrrh yet again;
to revel again, and to enjoy a drunken whore—this is what I do
not want.
    I hate these things that lead to madness.
But bind my brow with narcissus and give me a taste of cross-flutes and
    anoint my limbs with saffron myrrh
and wet my lungs with wine of Mytilene and wed me to a stay-at-home girl.
(Sider 1997: 81)

7

Philainis, soak with oily dew the lamp, the silent confidant of acts which
    are not to be spoken of,
and then leave. For Love alone does not desire living witness.
And shut
    the door tight, Philainis.
And you, dear Xantho, (to) me—but now, O lover-loving wife, learn what
    Aphrodite has left for us.
(Sider 1997: 85-86)

And now that we've attained a more proper Epicurean state, let's turn to something Epicureans made much of, the Epicurean dinner, here presented first in the form of a dinner invitation to Philodemos' patron, Piso (Lucius Calpurnius Piso Caesoninus, whose daughter, Calpurnia, was Caesar's third wife), owner of what is now referred to as Herculaneum's Villa dei Papiri (see Sider 2005). So named because it was here among the ruins of this magnificent villa (buried by Vesuvius, AD 79) that some 1800 charred papyrus scrolls were discovered (mid-1700s), most of which were works of Piso's mentor, Philodemos. Was this Philodemos' personal library, left with his patron's family after his death? We really don't know, but it's clearly an Epicurean's library of some sort.

27
Tomorrow, friend Piso, your musical comrade drags you to his modest
    digs at three in the afternoon,
feeding you at your annual visit to the Twentieth. If you will miss udders
    and Bromian wine *mis en bouteilles* in Chios,
yet you will see faithful comrades, yet you will hear things far sweeter than
    the land of the Phaeacians.
And if you ever turn an eye to us too, Piso, instead of a modest
    feast [Twentieth] we shall lead a richer one.
(Sider 1997: 152)

And this, which suggests a modest meal, one appropriate for Epicureans (though with a touch of elegance); a likely gathering of friends or students, the guests responsible for the bulk of the food; *symposiastic*: dining and teaching. All well known aspects of the Epicurean lifestyle: the communal dining, the dinner invitations, the lectures. Virgil was one such friend and student, probably present at such affairs in Herculaneum or nearby Naples.

28
Artemidoros has given us cabbage, Aristarchos *baccalà*, Athenagoras spring
    onions,
Philodemos a small liver, and Apollophanes two pounds of pork (three
    are left from yesterday).
Slave, give us Chian wine, wreaths, sandals, and myrrh: I want to have them
    in at 4 P. M. sharp.
(Sider 1997: 161)

Somber in tone, this epigram appears to have been written at Piso's villa (where Philodemos' school may have been located; it was certainly nearby). Two of their friends have died. Suddenly, it seems. A modest meal, reflections on "an all powerful death," a mood of "quiet realism." (Gigante 1995: 59)

29
Philodemus: Already the rose and chickpea and first-cut cabbage-stalks

   are at their peak, Sosylus,
and there are sautéed sprats and fresh cheese curds and tender curly

   lettuce leaves.
But we neither go on the shore nor are we on the promontory, Sosylos,

   as we always used to.
Sosylus: Indeed, Antigenes and Bacchius were playing yesterday, but

   today we carry them out for burial.
(Sider 1997: 164)

Life in the Garden.

6

....

EXILE [in L.A.]

I can hardly claim it's the same as Augustus' relegation of Ovid, but a form of exile nonetheless. As for *Tristia* or *Epistulae ex Ponto*—the *Sad Things* of exile or *Letters from Pontus*—my L.A., my Black Sea, well, perhaps just a bit.

But why exile? It's mostly self-imposed, of my—or our—own doing. If not a straightforward choice then no one but Accident sent us here.

There was certainly no august decree, no *duo crimina, carmen et error* (two crimes: a poem and a mistake) to regret. Repenting nothing, regretting nothing, yet no less shocked and displaced. But exile implies—demands—a homeland (*ex-silium;* out of the soil; a literal separation from the land). Exiled here from there where I'd rather be, from where I feel most at ease, though I really can't say where that is; there seems to be no such *place*.

But perhaps it's an inner place, this homeland, in which case I've been exiled to an inappropriate externality. I find myself there when I wish to be here; here in this hidden homeland.

And the temporal: displaced now from then? Perhaps that's the more profound exile. Caught up in ceaseless change, this poor, doomed creature, captive (always) to a finite moment.

7

....

MY OTHER DAYS AT THE RACES

At the races, and with a woman; more often than not that's been the case.

1
Fate's hands are clean. No reason, just random, or no reason we could ever fathom; indifferent, aloof, uncaring. But that it happened to you, here, now, for this reason and none other, or maybe again just as before, is—ironic. There's your nemesis. Oh? You'd bet against it?

2
Winning isn't luck, just losing. Losing isn't luck, just winning. Blink your eyes, it's all different.

3
The Pick Six *down at old Del Mar*: Vigorously Juan, Angel Allie, Veronica Bay, Hold That Smile, Touching Rainbows, and R Sunday Surprise paid $190,443.80 for a single winning ticket bought in Las Vegas—no way your favorite color or birthday; not even your lucky number.

4
Once, she leaned down, laughing, to tell us it was the name of a childhood friend. We—those of us sitting in my box—just looked at one another, pondering the vicious irony. But then she whiffed on a trifecta. Took a mournful misstep with not enough cash and too many possible combinations; when an anticipated but un-bet longshot tagged third to ruin her day.

5

She's never happy when we leave like that, like losers. That evening—that night—she's miserable and I'm increasingly desperate. I find my mind wandering … Epicurean Gardens … *ataraxia* … but I usually just wander.

6

Every day at the track starts anew, but no day ever ends older. That's how it is with her, too.

7

First, I met the older one—nice lady—not nearly as crazy as her little sister. And she, well … she *was* the wild one. Later, I drove her out to Van Nuys to No Way Out Bail Bonds. Had to settle up. She'd slapped her boyfriend around. It happens. Why I found it hard to cut her loose is hard to explain. You may know such a woman, who, when she drinks is just *out there*. Sometimes it's even worth the risk being out there with her. I'm not necessarily recommending it, of course, but …

For sure—and this may seem odd, but then you have to understand her demimonde—I was the first guy she'd ever slept with lacking tattoos. But I won't even wear a watch; limiting my textuality to the page; not one to visibly display my look-at-me narcissism. Not an issue for her, if she even noticed.

How'd it end? Not my fault. I'm steady—so steady—one always knows just where I stand, but she'd wanted something unexpected, which is just what *I'd* expected. Really, there's just no dodging that implicit predictability. In that, she was just wasting her time.

8

She was a crazy bettor, too. Such excitement, such anticipation and certitude—like that would ever make any difference to Chance. Chance that we met, almost chance why she bet, but nothing else was particularly random.

9

Another time she bet Gary Stevens, then he won on a longshot. Since he won so often to continue seemed like the smart play; that was her thinking. Well, [amazingly] he's still at it. And her? Loser? Winner? I really have no idea, but at some point all streaks do end.

10

We'd driven up to Vegas on our way to New York for her internship at Columbia. We got checked in at the Mirage, then rushed downstairs to place a few bets in the sports book. Caught the last two races at Del Mar. She bet her favorite jockeys and won [of course]; cashed some big tickets. She *is* lucky. It never deserts her.

11

We were at this huge handicappers' banquet. They had a raffle. The big prize was a hundred dollar bill. She won. I wasn't surprised and neither was she. She has so much luck she just takes it for granted. She's never spent it.

12

Frosty called to tell me he saw her over at Carmine's in Beverly Hills. He said he was outside waiting for his car to be brought around when she pulled in with some guy driving one of those lame looking Maseratis. Did she see him? She did, but he said she acted like she didn't know who he was. Understandable, I suppose. So when she walked past him he said, oh so softly, "Who do you like?" Then he winked. No, I don't think we do want to know any more than that; that ticket was cashed a long time ago.

13

These guys all wintered in a trailer park down in Boca Raton. Otherwise, they were over at Suffolk Downs. I told them, "Bet Stevens." They were reluctant, California horse, California rider, California trainer too, but they did. I was their hero from then on. "Who do you like" all the time.

14

Told this Asian gentleman the same thing in a betting parlor
in downtown Chicago. His English was just passable. Kept
referring to the jockeys as *the drivers*. But it only paid
$2.10—the least a winning two dollar bet can pay. Some tip.

15

Desperate day chasing winners we never caught. Reduced to a
state of blunt idiocy we decided to buy one. Full field—bet
everyone. Paid $4.60: winners at last!

16

Sunday's was a killer: a Pick Six payout of $568,696—Doc
Curlin ($7.00); Muny Spunt ($38.60); Beautiful Shot
($16.40); Bird is the Word ($5.60); Sir Sampson ($6.20), and
Action Hero ($25.40)—favorites, longshots, a DQ, and there
you have it. All on just one winning ticket from United Tote
in Brooklyn. But then everybody knew about the bird.

17

I believe they'd been down at the Grey Goose cart near the
main stretch in front of the grandstand. Believe, because I
can't claim to know for sure, but they'd surely been
somewhere. Coming back, she'd made her bets—we all sat
and waited. Screaming and yelling: Chilled Martini.
Something like that—I'll never get over.

18

For a long time she only bet Argentine horses, then there were
the Misses: Misbehave, Misunderstand, Misadventure,
Mistake—no misnomer; cascade effect.

19

The surest thing, bet against me. She smiled. "You try so
hard to understand everything. All I need to understand is
that you never will." It was never the same with her after that.

20

Hot, muggy day at Saratoga, wandering the shaded paddock, gliding through the close air to the grandstand where she finally sees a horse she likes. I'm torn, but I give her a hundred bucks. I say, "Whatever you do, do twice for me." It's a chump's bet, but I can see she's got the luck, her golden hunch, the gods always on her side [they're never on mine—I know that; I know she's their darling]. After the race I wait while she cashes our tickets. She hands me $3,711. I've nothing to say. Even now.

21

Every loss there's a litany of excuses. She's told me, "I should never listen to you." Anger, and all day, that night, the next day, days and nights when I'm not welcome in my own bed. Or if I've somehow managed to get there I'm getting no further. I did once hear a guy, a drunk young man, actually, walking down my street, who stopped to sit on the wall across from my house: "Nobody loves a fuckin' loser." Over and over that same singsong refrain before he got up to stumble on down the hill. I told her about it. "It's true," she said.

22

I was thinking about her that last day at Hollywood Park. They'd sold it, now it was going to be a football palace. All those minorities, those poor people of color who spent their days there, who lived nearby, were fated to disappear. But we'd made a special point to attend the wake. I wondered if I'd see her there—she'd loved Hollywood Park—but if so our paths never crossed. That seemed impossible.

23

I often tell this story because nothing better illustrates the odd quotidian *otherness* of life at the track. It's this ancient little man with ten thousand dollars in his pockets. Two big fat rolls of one hundred dollar bills, fifty per roll. I silently count along as he double-checks his stake, his winnings, his whatever they represent. Then I see that no one but me has noticed. It's so outlandish, so outré: just me, just him, just those one hundred hundred dollar bills. The last I see of him he's at the large transaction window. So, a large bet, but all, or just some? My fear: forsaking sane [if there is such a thing] probability, he's sucked into a wormhole of randomness popping up again somewhere else lost to us in the infinite reaches of space and time, there at a racetrack in an alternate universe where he's the most pitiful loser anywhere everywhere. No, I can't imagine how this has a happy ending.

24

"I like to think of it as the interpretation of chance."
"No, you're just a loser."
"There's nothing wrong with losing that winning won't fix."
"You've been saying that for years."
"So?"
"When's the fix?"

25

I've left blinded as much by cheap margaritas as losing bets, but then my sight's restored by a winner; nightcap to the rescue; healed by that last chance best effort. It's never the luck. I always say that.

26

Los Borrachos won yesterday's first leg of the pick six.
And after five more: *la noche* de los borrachos.
Losers most, I suppose.

27

My first *signer* was at Santa Anita—an improbable pick four—a visitor from random happenstance with the wrong address.
"I told you!" I told her.
"You always tell me," she said.

28

She was incredulous. "What are you talking about? I've seen you upset."
"But not because I lost, it's the irony."

"There wouldn't be any irony if you stopped second-guessing yourself."
"But—"
"You see!"

8
....

THE SLIPPAGE FROM PERSON TO PERSONAE

Did Aristotle really say thirty-seven was the proper age at which to marry? If so, then I've been both too early and too late: driven by a love too new and a love that grew. But now I seem to have reached a proper age, stumbling upon an Epicurean Garden at four o'clock in the afternoon, the twentieth day of the month—finally, a bit of tranquility. I *should* turn to more weighty matters. Isn't that so? When what burns—as the Latin poets once noted—has burned, leaving cooling embers, dreams and memories recalled with a groan, a sigh, a shrug—but life never truly satisfies.

1
At some point it no longer matters who or what; the real
becomes imaginary; the impetus merely creative; the truth [of
no] [no longer of any] importance.

2
I had a very disturbing dream last night: panic-stricken, I
suddenly realized I'd somehow managed to forget a woman
I loved. How strange, even in my dream I wondered how
that was possible. Making it worse, for some reason I was
unable to remember her name or even what she looked like.
Nevertheless, the memory that there was such a woman
awoke in me a profound longing. In my dream it was all
but unbearable.

I haven't had this dream in some time. Then, I usually awoke
in a panic, quickly rolling over to look at the woman who
slept beside me. No, thankfully I hadn't forgotten *her*. But
then any dream can become a memory, and somewhere in my

dream last night I did recall having dreamt this before, or at least I dreamt that I had.

Well, there's always a woman in your life you wish you still knew even if you're happy to see the woman who's in your bed. And it's true that there was a time when I might have erred, when I might have rolled over and found the wrong woman. I certainly remember my panic over that, dream or no dream. But none of that happened, even though there was this one moment when I might have lost her.

3

An exhausting all-day drive in from Nevada. Our first night together: a hooker's motel on Ventura. North Hollywood, Studio City—today, I have no idea where it was.

When she went in to get the room the guy said, "For the whole night?" "Uh," she said, smiling, "For this guy—yeah, that's what it will take." But mostly we slept; in the morning I was leery of using the shower. I can't remember where we had breakfast, but it wasn't Du-par's.

The next night we spent at the Woolamaloo in West Hollywood—a gay B&B run by Aussies. For dinner we drove over to Pink's on La Brea and I walked across the street to buy tall boys [Colt 45]. The Woolamaloo seemed deserted even at breakfast: English muffins with orange marmalade.

Tired of noir and bohemia we tried the new downtown Sheraton. Just opened. A plumber had to come up to fix the faucets in our room. We overlooked the 110. For lunch: the Pantry. It's still there.

The next day, I drove a carload of women out to The Wine House on Cotner [it's also still there]. There was a cheap popular Sonoma red: Glen Ellen. I used the corkscrew I kept in my car and we passed the bottle round on the drive down Wilshire.

Women love Bacchus (still!): the most dangerous of the surviving gods. The mindless frenzy: torn limb from limb. To me, it tasted mostly of merlot.

4

Then there are those dreams that seem like variations on a common theme. It's a woman I want to impress or make a connection with, some emotional, sexual, or psychological connection that always seems to elude me. We're going to have sex but we don't. We're talking or just hanging out but I fail to capture her interest or hold her attention and she drifts away.

One of the defining characteristics of these dreams is the happiness I feel at being with her, and sometimes this happiness is quite profound, but then it always fades away as she once again eludes me.

It's not that she's unattainable, she's not, it's just that I never quite get there. It's frustrating. It's also an existential statement of sorts, a comment on a deeper level about a particular mode of being, but then it's also about a woman I once knew of which all this was true.

What I now wonder is why this still matters to me and how her story became entangled in this larger existential issue.

5

For years I've borne her scar on my thumb. It's where she gouged me; a garbled sign of both her resistance and her desire. *Do* pursue me, but *never* catch me. The truth was: you never will catch me—I won't be caught. So my thumb reminds me: not caught by me.

6

We'd first made love the year before in the midst of a monsoonal downpour. Sultry evening, dark clouds, the crack of thunder, her windows wide open, ozone, the humid air filling the room with the tang of rain in the desert. "Yes, I'm a real blond," she'd said to mask her embarrassment. Later, she jiggled her feet as we talked. With her there was always a sense of anticipation.

7

Led by passion, our acts [are we really surprised by this?] can't escape unanticipated meaning, unforeseen consequence; it's our nature. Where things will go from there—just try to predict.

8

Because she did come to see me one evening while I was alone. I knew. She was lonely: the end of another disappointment. We were very young, but then you'd turn to a friend, even the boyfriend of your best friend. "We shouldn't," she said, one last bit of face saving self-deception as she wrapped her legs around me. "No, but we will." And with that she took me in hand.

9

I was in graduate school—this was in Boulder—and one summer morning I took a friend out for breakfast at the old dining hall up at Chautauqua. Tired—we'd been up most of the night—we hardly spoke. Later, back in my car, at her request we just sat. She was pensive, moody, staring out the window at the Flatirons. Finally, I just asked, "What is it?" Turning to look at me, moist eyes, maybe a quiver in her upper lip, she spoke: "It's Duke." "Ah, so you *are* out of here." "In December." And that was how it began to end; a finality that fed her passion. Years later we both agreed: it might have been the best six months we'd ever had … anywhere … with anyone.

10

I drove her to the airport when she left for Los Angeles. As we sat in the terminal waiting for her plane she said, "Come with me. I'll take care of everything." I'm sure she would have, and she did write a few letters before it all faded into nothingness.

11

She bore an amazing resemblance to a woman I knew eight or nine years later who wrote her last letter to me from Africa. The resemblance truly was uncanny, which was part of the attraction. She once invited me over to her apartment and we got as far as her telling me she couldn't, but with a little encouragement she changed her mind.

12

Late one summer night—or very early one summer morning—I heard her at my window whispering my name. It must have been August: night-scented dry grasses and stubble, dew in the air, a soft sigh and lapping breeze. At times like that we're prone ... driven ... to do things ... [magical things] ... that look like nothing in daylight. And she knew my bed as I knew hers. But I wondered why she'd come like that. When unexpected, what someone does is sure to portend something unanticipated ... she'd come to say goodbye.

13

A small cottage behind a restaurant on a busy street ... fenced ... lush foliage ... high heat ... swamp cooler ... cinder block and bare concrete floor ... late lunch but returned ... now aloof ... uninterested ... a perfunctory hug ... I said goodbye. I never bothered to find out why nor pursued her after that ... one last chance ... not something I had any interest in.

14

She wrote me a letter. A letter! I'd been at her apartment but she'd been awkward, unsure, more than hesitant but never just *no*. But it was the no I remembered—it was never answered.

15

She insisted, so I let her drive my car. No, I'm not a good passenger, but she's a worse driver. Even worse, any road rage—and sooner or later it was going to find us—would be focused on me. "Don't do that," I'd pled. But she'd laughed,

cut them off, finger when they honked. Woman as the
aggressor; scares the hell out of me.

16
"Here's the deal. In my old hometown newspaper you're
going to find articles that mention me performing solos, being
at summer band camp, that European concert tour ..."
"Not me."
"I know."
"Although I still might be in there somewhere."
"In the police log?"
"We *were* just kids."
I got that look. And she was right: that did still typify us;
nothing had changed. Not really.

17
She finally just said it, that she found me too complicated,
that she preferred a man less so, one less burdened by
reflection and wonder, one more focused on just her. "But
isn't that saying you think I think about you too much?
Because I do think about you." She smiled. She patted my
hand. "I'm leaving now," she said.

18
Just today I found out what became of her. Good things, I'm
pleased [surprised] to say, which now looks foolish, that worry
I no longer have. So that clears up one mystery, but I'd still
like to know more about her friend—my close friend. Just
what are we supposed to do with all these things we'll never
know?

19
Once, and this was some time ago, we'd all tried to live
together, but she'd blown it all apart with her bottomless
desire. Now here she was teasing me. *Again.* I found it hard
to believe she still had such effect on me, but there I was
with one hand down her pants, the other on her breast, while
she, laughing, smiled, knowing she'd always have that with
me no matter what I said.

20

I'd been drinking. Down on the mall with friends until
closing. Now, and this was what, like 2:30 in the morning,
and I'm sitting in my car shocked to see her waiting for me in
one of those big lawn chairs on my front porch. "Oh. She's
back." At that point anything was possible.

21

It was that long yellow t-shirt she wore when she spent the
night at my place. Up over her hips, lying back on the table;
awkward, not that comfortable. Quick, hard, the first time;
the second, longer, rhythmic; there were beads of perspiration
on her upper lip; a lost look in her eyes.

22

Late at night: deep, endless snowfall, soft light through her
thin curtains; she was cold, her nipples like hard little pebbles
in my mouth. She took my hand—I'd never felt a woman
more aroused. Later, a moment of infinite peace and
certitude as I lay bathed in the beautiful light pouring in
through her bedroom windows. I felt safe and warm in her
bed, knowing outside the snow was relentlessly piling up. At
the quietest time of night on the quietest possible night I
heard nothing but the gentle sound of her breathing. *Nothing*
that happened later added to or changed in any way what I
knew in that moment.

23

If you're not going to stay – it's been a long time – she had on
that orange jacket she bought when I was with her – I saw her
all the way across the quad,

and she was glad to see me. Red nose – cold afternoon – but
we got all warm and tangled under the covers up in her room.

She'd been unschooled, ready to find out all about it – eager
to. She'd said, "I have no idea what I'm supposed to do."
"Just do this," I'd told her.

"Baby, I'm yours" – or she said something silly like that in one of those impossible post-coital moments, but we never really mean it, do we?

24

October; a time to reflect; maybe it's the light; a dry sun.

A cool evening, deep black sky; jackets, maybe a sweater, but temperate, sitting in my car, my hand up her skirt, and when I found her she leaned back. She laughed then, told me tomorrow her roommate would be away.

I undressed her. It's what she wanted. "Let's not rush." She always said that, like it would take her some time, but it never did.

I hadn't called. I just showed up. She liked that. The surprise. My need. She held me in her arms a long time. This was afterwards. "This man, I know him." That was her thought.

So she was like that, intensely intimate, repeatedly, then talk. Now I'd swear it was the oxytocin.

25

I heard her friend—a roommate—on the phone, something about some guys they'd met. But not just overheard, I was meant to hear.

I didn't say anything as we left, not even in the car, but she was upset, embarrassed, caught in what would have been a lie if I'd asked; if she'd replied.

The roommates: I have no idea how that played out, or if it did. At this point it doesn't really matter. As for why it didn't then ... I'm not really sure.

26

She tells me she's ready for me any time. "I'm next?" That's what I said, because I know she's just nearing the end of her string of friends. So I said, "You know, I'd rather not, I prefer being unique." "Can I still use your car," was her response.

27

"Who you got in there?"
    Banging on the front door.
"I know you got someone in there!"
    Across the alley from Archie's
of Hollywood; my little walk-up
    apartment.
Ventura Boulevard.
    Still a crummy looking block:
rundown, cheap, tawdry.
    She was one of the ladies who
worked a few doors down at
    Thai Massage.
We're friends,
    but not like my new friend,
the psychiatrist, and I are.

I'll call her Lauren;
    Lauren who laughed when she
sat up in bed
    (yes, she's really a psychiatrist—
I like dating doctors),
    asking: "Well?"
Big moments so often go unspoken,
    or often so when no speaking
is necessary;
    a relief, since anything I might
have said would have sounded lame
    or been a lie.
So I pulled on my pants,
    then standing on my side of
the still unopened door,
    said:

"I'm not home.   Come back later."

Actually, that's not what happened,
    it was Lauren—
impatient, listening to the banging,
    wondering who this woman was,
interested
    (professionally, would be my guess)
in my reaction, embarrassment,
    hesitation (I was just signifying
all sorts of shit; but clueless)
    —who got my bathrobe
and went to the door.

Lauren loves to dance. We met at
    this Mexican restaurant in
Northridge that hosts a weekly
    Tuesday morning Big Band show.
Johnny Vana and the Big Band Alumni.
    Veteran L.A. studio musicians
who've still got their chops.
    Big Band old-timers who live
scattered from West Hollywood
    to Calabasas.
Lauren lives out there too.
    Tarzana; one of those Fifties tract
homes with a pool.
    And she?
Attractive; several times married and
    divorced;
kids grown;
    a sensual, middle-aged lady
who'll stay in bed all day under
    the right circumstances.

So this is sort of embarrassing
    because after they'd talked—
I hid under the covers—
    Lauren came back and said this

when she threw my bathrobe
   on the bed:
"Your Thai gal will be back later."
   Then very still, staring at me
a moment (a professional's gaze)
   before smiling:
"It's up to you to make this right."
   "You don't think I can?"
She laughed as she dressed;
   there were parting words when
she reached the bedroom door:
   "Three can't be happy.
Two, maybe.
   One, never."

Delphic.
   Oracular.
But did that mean the sacrifice
   would be mine?
I really have no idea.

9

....

EXILE

Isolated, estranged, displaced, and alienated. Exiled, enforced or chosen, here or there, now or then, inner or outer. I suppose at some point it no longer really matters—something's been lost. Irretrievably? So it seems.

1
My bedroom was downstairs
almost in the basement.

I sat on my bed . . . an empty, hollow
feeling . . . that was my future.

So alone in that, though we all felt it.
Something I now see.

Just out of synch.
Knowing I didn't belong.

But someone must have.
Nothing came to an end.

Everything came to an end.
Something I now see.

The present, a wrenching, twisting, tearing, discontinuity;
the future, all shredded with jagged, torn edges.

How many bright dawns will it take, how many
quiet evenings, for there to be *that* moment?

There was a time when I sought such moments,
but they've become too rare.

Now is almost always a mundane space.
What was once memorable becomes forgettable;

just another member of that class of all classes
of moments just like any other.

It's a space, a familiar space that's never felt like home;
a cheap room downtown in a men's-only flophouse.

A prison-house of delimited spaces.
Delimitation. De-limits all around.

It's a time, or the passage of a time so slow yet so brief;
when each day of endless duration is summed so quickly.

Everywhere limits; the ends, the starts, the in-betweens;
the sums equaling naught.

A handful of zeros; it's always just zeros.
There *is* no summing up.

2
Down at the end of that patchy asphalt road there's this big
river, but there's nothing special over there on the other side.

First, up and across those shiny rails,
then find your way down through the green thicket.

You step out into the open; the bright sun.
You stand alone on the bank.

It's rolling [roiling] muddy waters:
a swift expanse of bobbing swirls and snags.

Yes, a muddy brown bank, bright sun,
and there's that smell of a world so alive.

Oddly, I've never been there.
Not since conception.

3

There was something troubling about that first day back in town, and not just how it oscillated between never left and never been. And then she told me she wasn't that surprised to see me again. This was standing in the parking lot up at Star Market.

Well ... what I wanted to say was I could have been killed, but I knew she would have just laughed: "You?" That's how she thought in those days, that we were all escapees from finitude. Like: "Really? That still bothers you?" So I let it pass.

We rendezvoused that evening at Carmine's. I hadn't been in four years; or had it been even longer? And people remembered me, or pretended to; too embarrassed not to. Baked ziti pasta—what I'll always get at Carmine's. That was something [else] I saw: that I could tell—now—what I'd always do. But knowing that, was that a good thing, or not?

I broached the subject with her over dessert [sorbet]: "Listen, if you knew what you'd do—I mean beforehand—and this was always going to be the case . . . " and then I ran out of words.

Holding her spoon in mid-air, sort of staring into space, or at least over my head, and of course I knew just what she was about to say, if she'd spoken, that is, which, of course, she did not: "But I do." What she did say was "Umm" as she licked her spoon [cantaloupe], and of course I knew what that meant as well.

4

Learn to say no: I think not. There's very little that isn't a choice; unacknowledged, of course. And you're left with nothing—an excellent place to begin.

5

Few beliefs. Fewer assumptions. No certitudes.

6

Back and forth [interweave] the thoughts, but there's no thread. No place to pause. Really, there's nothing even to see—or what you see is nothing.

7

Ellipsis ... omission ... struck through ... the barest notion ... no notion at all.

A SLENDER MUSE

PART TWO

I'm in the last outback,
at the world's end.
-Ovid

INTRODUCTION

In "Whose Reading of What Propertius" Tara Welch seeks to draw a distinction between what she calls immersive reading and discursive, or critical, reading: "The immersive reader (engaged in 'ludic' reading) desires to get lost in a text and experience the emotions it generates. The discursive reader remains aware that a text is a discourse defined and housed in a set of discourses such as prior literary works, history, memory, etc. Of course, the immersive reader can never fully abandon discourses, nor can the discursive reader avoid an initial reaction. But these two terms are important in understanding Propertius', or any other poetry." (Welch 2012: 7-8) Well ... but if I were forced to choose I suppose I'd opt for immersive, after all, I've already said this book is not a work of scholarship. Yes, but on the other hand I'm really troubled by this notion of *getting lost in the text* or *experiencing the emotions it generates.* Does anyone really read like that? I certainly don't. So, on second thought, now I'm tempted to say that what I've done is a bit of both, but that here in Part Two we're shifting more towards the discursive. As for *discourses,* let's just say that what *I'm* doing is providing a bit of commentary and context.

But what of: *whose reading of what Propertius?* Welch answers:

> Which Propertius are we reading? The question goes deeper than an allegiance to an editor, text, or a set of critical principles. To a large degree, try though we might to recover an authentic text, we must all admit that we are reading our own Propertius. The reader does much to constitute the text, approaching it with a set of expectations or at the least with a set of experiences in reading poetry, Latin love poetry, Augustan literature, Greek epigram, Ezra Pound, or snippets of prose in a Latin primer to name a few, or having visited

> Assisi, or being in love with a woman named Cynthia, or being in any fiery and difficult romance. (Welch 2012: 7)

The same, of course, goes for any of the poets in this book, though I'm troubled by this notion that we *constitute the text*. And what is *authentic* even supposed to mean in this context? We know, for example, that we don't have the texts as written by Propertius or Catullus, just as we know that what we do have is the product of scribal error, editorial selection, scholarly correction, and guesswork.

> It is clear that all existing manuscripts of the works of Propertius descend from a single *exemplar* which can for the most part be reconstructed with relatively little difficulty. Where editors differ is on how far we should trust the text of the archetype thus reconstructed. (Butrica 2012: 46-7)

Not only was the ordering of these poems arbitrary—the numeration—so were the choices made as to where to divide the text into separate poems.

> In analyzing the structure of an ancient book we must rely on basic principles thoughtfully applied, and not simply follow the numeration of our editions as if that were a thing of authority and not historical accident. (Heyworth 2012: 231)

> The division of each book [of any of these poets] into separate poems depends on the suggestions made by readers in the Middle Ages and the centuries since. In no case does the conventional numeration have particular authority. (Heyworth 2012: 221)

Nor do we really know just how these poems were meant to be read, or were read; not with any certainty. But *constitute*? Like we're adrift in a textual multiverse? Where each text is the work of one of us? Why not just say we each *interpret* the text in light of who we are and what we've read, experienced, and understood? Such interpretive acts don't create new texts, just different takes on *a* text. And Welch says as much (my italics): "The irony is that critical readings help *recuperate* for the modern reader some of the *circumstances* that might have *conditioned* an ancient *reading*, offering us a pathway toward an *immersion* into the text that is no longer possible. To those of us who learned Latin as adults, all Latin texts are somewhat exotic. What must Propertius' poetry have sounded like to a native speaker? What *frames of reference* were available to ancient audiences?" (Welch 2012: 8-9) So, yes, let's not quarrel over *reified text* or *objecthood*, recuperate, circumstances, conditioned, reading, immersion, frames of reference, will do just fine.

And as long as we're being more discursive, perhaps this is the time to talk about elegiac metre.

Latin love elegy gets its name from its metre, the elegiac couplet. Metres in the ancient world tended to have associations with particular kinds of subject matter. The hexameter is the metre of epic, iambics are associated with invective and insult, and elegy is the metre of lament. In English, the word 'elegiac' conjures up a muted, possibly nostalgic sadness, and lament was the basic association of elegiac metre in the ancient world. Love elegy was the genre of the lover's lament and complaint. . . .

Ovid's claim that Cupid stole a foot from his epic hexameters [see below: *Amores* 1.1] provides a neat description of the elegiac couplet, which is made up of two lines, one of six metrical feet (the hexameter) and the other of five (the pentameter). Ovid reminds us, outrageously, that when you shorten every other line of the epic metre by a foot it becomes elegiac. The elegiac couplet shares the same basic metrical foot with the hexameter, namely the dactyl, which consists of a long syllable followed by two shorts (- u u, or, phonetically, 'dum da da'). So the simplest schema for an elegiac couplet looks like this:

-uu-uu- // uu-uu-uu-u
-uu-uu- // -uu-uu-

The slanting lines mark the point where there is usually a break (called a caesura) between one word and the next, dividing the line into two parts. In the pentameter, a more conclusive feel is given to the line by making the fifth foot a spondee (two longs) and dividing it between the end of the first half of the line and the end of the second half. Putting it phonetically (with commas marking off the feet):

Hexameter:
Dum da-da, dum da-da, dum // da-da, dum da-da, dum da-da, dum da.

Pentameter:
Dum da-da, dum da-da, *dum* // dum da-da, dum da-da, *dum* (the italicized 'dums' between them produce the fifth foot).

Latin metre is quantitative, based on the length of syllables, whereas English metre is based on stress. Whether one can write quantitative verse effectively in English or not is debated; there have been many attempts to do so, more or less successful. But we can get a sense of the rhythm of an elegiac couplet form Coleridge's English version of it, which is also a description:

In the hexameter rises the fountain's silvery column;
In the pentameter aye falling in melody back.

In order for the first line to work as a Latin hexameter you need to put a stress on the first word, 'In', and on the second syllable of the word 'hexameter' (hex*am*eter). But not all of this line can be read as dactylic. The word 'fountains', for instance, consists of two long syllables, a foot called a spondee (- -). Since Latin metre is quantitative, marked by the time it takes to pronounce a syllable, a long syllable is regarded as equivalent to two shorts, and in the elegiac couplet spondees can be substituted for dactyls in all but the penultimate foot. This allows necessary variation in the lines, which would be monotonous if they were always made up entirely of dactyls. (Fitzgerald 2013: 56-59)

But if you prefer a more *literary* explanation . . .

This coupling of hexameter and pentameter has seemed to critics to possess an intrinsic character of a formal kind arising from the encounter between two dactylic lengths which are different yet closely related. Georg Luck's paragraph-long attempt to capture this inherent tension in elegiac meter is particularly suggestive:

> The charm of the elegiac couplet – a charm easily felt but hard to describe – may be explained in a number of ways. There is an element of surprise in the pentameter: it seems to begin like the hexameter which has preceded it, but instead of rolling along majestically, it suddenly stops and reverses, becoming its own echo. Moreover, there is an intensely "personal" element in the pentameter: instead of reaching out to embrace the world, it hesitates, it reconsiders and ends on an abrupt final note – whose abruptness is softened immediately by the renewal of the rolling beat in the following hexameter. The break in the middle of the pentameter and the echo-like effect of its second half are highly characteristic. (Luck 1969, 28)

[O]ne aspect of the movement of the elegiac couplet that has exercised the metaphorical talents of other critics besides Luck is its "hesitant" quality, the way the confidence and ambition of the hexameter seem to be stymied in the pentameter. Ovid likes to represent it as a metrical limp . . . whilst Barchiesi borrows Heinze's metaphor of breathlessness . . . What all these responses to elegiac metrical form have in common is a recognition that the metrical scheme stages a dynamic encounter. The power of the pentameter largely resides in its role as an answering voice to the hexameter it does and yet also does not resemble. Another shared insight . . . is what we might call the "infolding" quality of the couplet, the very strong tendency of couplets to be syntactically independent of each other. In Heinze's words, "The elegiac distich, metrically a self-contained unit, strives constantly after syntactic unity as well," in contrast to the expansive, unconstrained quality of continuous hexameters [as in epics] . . . and this is an implication also of Luck's remark on the pentameter's "abrupt final note". (Morgan 2012: 206-07)

And then there's epigram [viz., Martial's short, witty poem with a sting in its tail: quick-witted, clever; the hexameter making a paradoxical statement the pentameter explains with a witty point (Fitzgerald 2013: 81-82)], also written in elegiac couplets though of much shorter length, two to ten lines being typical versus, say, Propertius' elegies that can run to thirty-five, or Ovid's to fifty. There are other significant differences, of course, but for those you'll need to turn to Part Two, Chapter Five.

Ovid's Battle with Cupid (*Amores* 1.1)

My epic was under construction—wars and armed violence
in the grand manner, with metre matching theme.

I had written the second hexameter when Cupid grinned
and calmly removed one of its feet.

"You young savage" I protested "poetry's none of your business.
We poets are committed to the Muses.

Imagine Venus grabbing Minerva's armour
and Minerva brandishing love's torch!

Imagine Ceres queen of the mountain forests
and Diana the huntress running a farm!

Or longhaired Phoebus doing pike drill
and Mars strumming the seven-stringed lyre!

You've a large empire, my boy—too much power already.
Why so eager for extra work?

Or is the whole world yours—the glens of Helicon included?
Can't Phoebus call his lyre his own these days?

Page one line one of my epic rises to noble heights
but line two lowers the tone
and I haven't the right subject for light verse—
a pretty boy or a girl with swept-up hair."

In reply the god undid his quiver and pulled out
an arrow with my name on it.

"Poet' he said, flexing the bow against his knee,
"I'll give you something to sing about—take that!"

Alas his arrows never miss. My blood's on fire.
Love has moved in as master of my heart.

I choose the couplet—rising six feet, falling five.
Farewell, hexameters and iron wars.

Garland your golden hair with myrtle from the seaside,
hendecametric Muse, my Elegia. (Lee 1968: 3-5)

1

....

AT THE TRACK

Commentary on *Amores* 3.2

This might be more commentary than you care to see (and there's even more in Appendix One), but it's such an interesting poem—the setting, the insights into Roman daily life, the poet's obnoxious persona, the ominous foreshadowing of his own sad fate—it's worth it.

Although there are many ways to approach this poem the one I'm pursuing asks two questions: who is this woman, and who's "Ovid" speaking to (or is he speaking at all)?

All critics are agreed that this is a delightful and vivid poem, almost unique in ancient literature (perhaps the nearest approach to it, for intimate social realism, is Theocritus' Fifteenth Idyll, the *Adoniazusae*), a monologue addressed to a girl at the races, which not only displays great psychological acumen but offers us an all-too-rare glimpse of Romans enjoying their leisure in a credible and recognizable manner. The scene is as clearly etched as Frith's *Derby Day*. What would seem to have struck nobody, however (and this remains true whether we treat the poem as fiction or as reportage), is the curious ambiguity of the relationship between Ovid and the object of his advances; the girl utters not one word from start to finish. Why not? And how have they come to be where they are in the first place?

It makes a crucial difference how we read the scene. There are the girl and Ovid next to one another in the front row, against the railings (63–4). She has (it would appear from Ovid's complaints) one strange man to her right, and another behind her (20–24), leaving Ovid himself on her left.

Thus she must, inevitably it would seem, be either alone, or else Ovid's acknowledged guest. Which is it? If she had come alone–unlikely in any circumstances–she would have, almost by definition, to be a *meretrix*, a prostitute. Who else would haunt the Circus, of all places, unescorted? But if she was a prostitute, the poem, would be meaningless, since Ovid employs considerable sympathy and subtlety to make an impression on her, and in the penultimate line (83) merely *thinks* he sees the promise of capitulation in her eye. Whatever this monologue may be, then, it is *not* Ovid's account of how he propositioned a tart.

Such being the case, a natural inference would be that Ovid and his latest girl-of-the-moment are attending the races together–a pleasant excursion with decidedly modern associations. Too modern, indeed, by a long chalk, as we at once realize on reflection. Social difficulties beset this idyllic scene. Under what circumstances, we ask ourselves, could or would a young man legitimately appear in public accompanied by an unchaperoned lady who was not his wife? Again the answer forces itself upon us: only with a *meretrix* or (the next best thing) a *libertina*, a name with unfortunate but hardly accidental associations. But Ovid's companion is clearly neither whore nor freedwoman. He treats her with delicate social respect, as an equal: no easy touch there. An unmarried girl of good family, then? Unthinkable. A married lady? Equally unthinkable: discreet private adultery was one thing in Rome, but (except in very special circumstances) flouting public conventions for the whole world to see was quite another. At this point the exasperated reader may well object that if Ovid could not have brought this girl with him, and is not picking her up either, then what in heaven's name is supposed to be going on?

Let us compare this poem, for possible illumination, with a related sequence in the *Ars. AA* 1.135–64 takes the basic material of *Am.* 3.2, but transposes it into didactic advice for others. What Ovid there says, quite clearly, is that the Circus provides admirable conditions for *approaches...to a new courtship* (*aditus... novo... amori*). The lady is referred to as *domina* (139), but whether this implies prior acquaintance, or merely hope for the future, is uncertain. What a day at the races can provide, Ovid seems to suggest, is that intimate *physical proximity* essential for the preliminaries of seduction. Now in both these passages (*AA* 1.139–42; *Am.* 3.2.19–20) what rates specific emphasis is *the convenience of the seating-arrangements*. Spectators were packed in close, side by side, irrespective of sex, and a hopeful lover could, by careful manoeuvring, get himself near, or even next to, the lady of his choice. The great advantage, clearly, of such contact lay in its apparent fortuitousness: the occasion both gave it social acceptability and robbed it of any overtly scandalous implications.

This suggests a rather different scene from those hitherto proposed. Ovid has fallen in love with a respectable, and almost certainly married lady. He has not yet made love to her (27–36), and does not even know for certain whether she returns his feelings of passion (83). One possible solution is to seat himself next to her at the races. The poem describes this occasion–but what it discreetly omits (partly on grounds of literary economy, but also as a private social joke, and a hint at Ovid's own obsessional state of mind) is all direct mention of the *other people* who must have been participants in the scene: the lady's husband, probably her maid, perhaps even Ovid's own wife. The scene, in its public aspects, now becomes socially innocuous.

On the other hand, Ovid's monologue most certainly does not. No *vir* in the world, however complaisant, is going to sit by while a young poet and gadabout not only flirts outrageously with his wife, but tells him, the husband, to sit a little less close to her (21–2). It is those lines that first give us an inkling of what Ovid is up to. 'Hey, you on the right there, *whoever you are* (*quicumque es*)', he says: the joke is shared between poet and percipient reader, who will (knowing Roman social rules) have instantly deduced the husband's unseen and unspoken presence, and chuckle at this cheekily oblique reference to him. But, finally, why does the husband keep so obligingly quiet during this elegantly seductive monologue, which subjects his wife to a species of lingering verbal rape? For the same simple reason, I would argue, that the girl herself says never a word either: *because they do not hear what Ovid is saying.* The entire monologue (and not line 83 alone) is conceived as an elaborate fantasy going on in the poet's head, perhaps encouraged by one casual flirtatious glance. Not a word of it–except perhaps Ovid's exhortations to the charioteer, which are legitimate on such an occasion–is to be thought of as being spoken aloud. Of course, if the scene portrays Corinna, and Corinna was in fact here based on Ovid's first wife, then the social proprieties are at once restored, and the joke will lie in Ovid's use of a respectable marital outing to hint at elegant seduction. (Green 1982: 310-313)

The fact that inverted commas did not exist in the ancient world is surely relevant to a responsive reading of this poem. Save for J. C. McKeown in his 1987 text, modern editors enclose lines 1-82 in them and most do the same with the final line. However, it may well be that this gives today's texts too clear-cut an appearance: direct speech as straitjacket. The Loeb translator comments that the poet is here relating "what he said to a fair one at the races". Yet even the most literal-minded reader will have to acknowledge that he also addresses *(inter alios)* her neighbors, the goddess Venus, and the charioteer. The inverted commas demand an answer to the question of who it is that the poet is talking to, but without them the poem becomes far more open-ended. In this brief essay, I shall be suggesting that we are in fact listening in on the poet's silent stream of consciousness.

What is the situation that the poet has set up? We can all, I hope, agree that he leads us to believe that he has seen a woman who attracts him and has contrived to sit next to her at the races. Whether in actual fact or simply in his mind, he's on the pull. It seems that he does not know her in any meaningful way. He reacts to her entirely as a physical entity. Appropriately enough for a poem set at the *spectacula* (65), he looks at her, feeding his eyes on her (5-6): he is blind to any qualities of personality, indeed apparently quite uninterested in them. While he employs the language of poetic love, it would surely be an accurate assessment of his feelings to say simply that he really fancies her. There may well be an element of absurdity, of self-mockery in his wish at 61-2 that this potential pick-up should be his mistress for ever.

A further point is that the poet asserts at the outset that his motive for being at the races is not a passion for thoroughbred horses. Yet the poem makes clear, through its detailed evocations of the seating arrangements and the description of the race and its prelude, that he knows all about the racing scene. He has been here many times before. (He may in fact be something of a racing bore, the type who buttonholes his neighbour with unwanted descriptive chatter.) In his *Ars Amatoria* 1.99-100, Ovid comments on women's motives for going to the theatre:

> *spectatum ueniunt. ueniunt spectentur ut ipsae;*
> *ille locus casti damna pudoris habet.*

(Dryden's memorable translation runs:

> To see, and to be seen, in Heaps they run;
> Some to undo, and some to be undone.)

If the poet's main motivation for attending the races is not dissimilar, it would certainly be in line with this poem's amoral, hedonistic stance.

Which takes us back to the inverted commas. Are we seriously to believe that the poet addressed these words to the woman? In forcefully alliterative lines (23-4) he accuses the man behind her of lacking a sense of shame as he presses his legs against her back. But the poet himself is spectacularly deficient in this quality too. To take lines 25-36 as an especially egregious example, here he undresses her in his imagination (Peter Green refers to "a species of rape"). Up to the poem's final couplet, the reader will have been comically agog, wondering whether the poet actually had the brazen impudence to address the woman in such terms. Here we enter the speculative realm of female psychology, but, with the right woman, it may indeed prove an effective means of seduction for the would-be lover to overwhelm her with the power of his attention and his failure to restrain his amorous language. Ovid may be illustrating something of the kind in *Heroides* 20 and 21, where Acontius wins Cydippe with his unremitting barrage of emotional verbal artillery. And so our poem may be a literal address.

Speaking for myself, I cannot believe that this is the case. After all, the woman does not need to hear his account of the introductory procession (43-5) and the race itself with its aborted start (65-79). She can see them for herself. What the poet could be doing is tracing the contours of his own thoughts as he ponders his emotions, the excitement of the race, the involvement of a great crowd, and, above all, what he would like to say to the woman. All of this is communicated brilliantly to the reader, but does a single word of the poem have to be addressed to anyone else? Is it rather, to use John Henderson's expression, "a running conversation in one head"?

Whether or not we are listening in on the poet's silent stream of consciousness, what are we to make of the passage in which he distances himself from all divinities apart from Venus (47-57)? Of course, an appeal to Venus is of obvious relevance in a declaration of love. The rejection of the other gods is decidedly less so. Lines 49-50 are, in fact, a statement of a poetic programme, the espousal of *amor* and *pax* as opposed to *arma* (the first word, of course, of Virgil's *Aeneid*), the embrace of love elegy and the rejection of epic and its hexameters. This embrace of *amor/Venus* and concomitant denial of epic can be located in an important area of Augustan aesthetics, the *recusatio* ('refusal', usually to write an epic). For other examples, see Horace, *Satires*, 1.10.31-7; Virgil, *Eclogues*, 6.1-5; and Propertius 1.6, 3.1, and 3.9.

Apart from its status as a poetic manifesto, this passage with its rejection of sport (hunting [51], boxing and horsemanship [54]) among other things, throws into perspective the poet's imagining of himself as a charioteer (9-

14), as well as his self-identification with the real-life charioteer (9, 67-70) and with active characters from mythology (15-17, 29-30). Such vicarious indulgences are manifestly ludicrous. In his imagining, the love poet is hoping to win his race not through dynamic athletics but his elegiac gift of the gab. The bathos here shows him in self-mocking vein, very much aware of his self- delusion.

How does the poem end? The use of the third person and the perfect tense in the penultimate line (*risit et argutis quiddam promisit ocellis*) suggest objectivity. There is an expectation of closure. But this is undermined by the indefinite *quiddam*. All we know for a fact is that the woman has laughed or smiled. The poet, of course, reads a promise in her eloquent eyes, quite possibly the poem's final line: *hoc satis hie ; alio cetera redde loco* ('This is enough for here; give the rest somewhere else'). If so, it is surely the product of his mind, not of her tongue. It could also be the poet's own (absurdly complacent) comment - It's in the bag! - and this, too, would no doubt be unspoken. Either reading would seem to confirm that the poem up to the final couplet has been equally unvoiced, and to lead one to share Peter Green's feeling that the entire monologue is conceived as "an elaborate fantasy going on in the poet's head". It certainly leaves open the possibility that the poet is deceiving himself. After all, she could simply be smiling because the charioteer whom both she and the poet were supporting has won, or laughing at the man who has been looking at her so intently, or at something altogether different. "Ovid" has convinced himself that he will soon have won the palm, that is, achieved the conquest of the woman. But the Ovid who has created him and followed what I take to be his silent thoughts is very aware that they may be illusory wish-fulfillment.

Even if it is all in the imagination, as well as being shot through with the spirit of comedy, Ovid's poem remains deeply subversive of Augustan values. According to Suetonius, the emperor kept women separate from the men as spectators at games: "he did not allow women to watch even gladiatorial shows except from the higher rows, though it was previously the custom for them to be watched by mixed crowds" (*Vit. Aug.* 44.2). We do not know when he introduced these measures and they did not apply at the races, but the man who imposed them could be expected to find no common ground with the poet who regarded such places of mass entertainment as offering opportunities, whether or not they were fulfilled, for members of the opposite sexes to make contact, especially when he reworked the material of *Amores* 3.2 as a straight (if humorous) pick-up manual in a later poem (*Ars Amatoria* 1.135-62). There would be trouble ahead. (Morwood 2011: 14-18)

I find this insightful. Without context, and we aren't Romans and this isn't two thousand years ago, its easy to miss the sly humor, the knowing wink. This is all so much more sophisticated than it at first appears, and not necessarily in the way we might expect, but then this is Ovid, this is what he does.

Green's More Specific Notes on 3.2

11–12. The chariots ran anti-clockwise, past a central barrier known as the *spina*, which they kept on their left. At the turns, a skillful charioteer would edge as close to the end-posts (*metae*) as he could without actually touching them.

15–16. The myth of Pelops and Hippodameia is, to put it mildly, odd. Hippodameia was the daughter of Oenomaus, King of Elis, who nursed an incestuous passion for her, to which she did not respond. To add to his frustration, Oenomaus had been warned by an oracle that his future son-in-law would be responsible for his death. When suitors came seeking Hippodameia's hand, Oenomaus sent them off in their chariot, with his daughter, and himself pursued them. If they got to Corinth ahead of him, they could marry Hippodameia; if Oenomaus caught up with them (which he invariably did) he speared them to death. By the time Pelops came along, there were a dozen suitors' heads nailed to the king's gable. Hippodameia, however, fell in love with Pelops, and bribed Oenomaus' charioteer, Myrtilus, to weaken the linchpins in the wheels of the king's chariot, so that he crashed and was dragged to his death. Even so, Pelops had a narrow escape when he slackened rein at sight of Hippodameia, and just missed being skewered by her urgent father.

19–20. The seating-places in the rows were marked off from each other by a groove (*linea*) carved in the marble.

29–30. Atalanta, daughter of Iasus, was, like Artemis/ Diana, a virgin huntress, who took part in the famous hunt for the Calydonian Boar, and wrestled successfully against Peleus. When her father wanted her to marry, she made her suitors race against her, giving them a slight start, and herself running armed. Like Oenomaus in similar circumstances, if she caught the suitor, she killed him. However, if he kept his distance, he married her. Various suitors were neatly dispatched; Atalanta remained a virgin. Milanion, knowing the conditions, brought with him some golden apples he had obtained from Aphrodite. These he dropped at intervals during the race. Atalanta, being both greedy and curious, stopped to pick them up; thus Milanion won both the race and his desired bride.

43–4. The races were preceded by a procession (*pompa*) of ivory images of the gods, borne on wagons or floats, and escorted by officials. The *pompa*, setting out from the Capitol, made its way through the Forum and the Forum Boarium, and so to the Circus by way of the Via Sacra. Once there, it paraded the entire length of the racetrack, with the spectators applauding their patron deities.

54. Castor's reputation as a horseman, and Pollux's as a boxer, go back to Homer's time: see *Iliad* 3.237.

66. The praetor gave the signal for the race to begin by dropping a napkin.

73–4. Races could be stopped and restarted, by public demand among other reasons, in the manner here described. (Green 1982: 313-314)

2
....

AMATORY LATIN ELEGISTS

General Remarks

Roman erotic elegy is one of the most influential genres in the history of western poetry. It is not too much to say that our conception of romantic love as the passionate attachment of one person to another, to the exclusion of all other concerns—money, fame, social propriety—was first codified by the Roman elegists. It was from the elegists, and Ovid in particular, that the medieval poets of courtly love derived their most famous and influential conceits. Likewise, the love sonnets of the Renaissance poets from Petrarch to Shakespeare would be unimaginable without the elegiac predecessors from which they self-consciously drew. The sonnet tradition, in turn, established the conventions for romantic devotion and the life of love that have dominated western culture until at least the beginning of the twentieth century. In short, to study the elegiac poets is not just to study a genre of poetry practiced by a people long dead, in a tongue no longer spoken, and in a far away place. To study Latin elegy is to uncover the storehouse of themes and images from which our modern notions of love and commitment have been constructed." (Miller 2002: 1)

Even so, this is of little interest, not to me, not here, anyway, where the focus is these poets, their poems and personae, the putative extra-textual reality of these *dominae*, the unusual nature of these depicted relationships, poet and mistress, and the social, literary, and historical contexts.

But biographical speculation is tempting.

Writing towards the end of the first century CE, the epigrammatist Martial catalogues the canonical Roman writers of erotic verse and their mistresses:

> Cynthia made you a poet, sprightly Propertius; fair Lycoris was Gallus' genius; beauteous Nemesis is the fame of clear-voiced Tibullus; Lesbia, elegant Catullus, dictated your verse. My poetry neither the Paelignians nor Mantua will spurn, if I find a Corinna or an Alexis. [*Epigrams.* 8.73.5-10] (Martial 1993: 217)

Autobiographical in form, Latin erotic elegy records the speaker's love for a beautiful, usually unavailable, woman who is celebrated under a Greek pseudonym. The elegiac mistresses Martial names—Propertius' Cynthia, Gallus' Lycoris, Tibullus' Nemesis, Catullus' Lesbia, and (Ovid's) Corinna—occupy pride of place in their poets' amatory collections and are variously addressed in the poems as *domina* ("mistress"), *puella* ("girlfriend"), *uita* ("life") and *lux* ("light"). Speculation concerning the identity of the women behind the pseudonyms started in antiquity, apparently encouraged by the poets themselves.

C. Valerius Catullus (*c.* 84–54 BCE) sets the precedent for the naming practices of the Augustan elegists by concealing the identity of his beloved behind a pseudonym, Lesbia, which evokes the Greek poet Sappho. But he seems to invite his readers to identify her as a Roman aristocrat named Clodia in an epigram (*c.* 79) that names her brother, Lesbius, by his cognomen Pulcher ("pretty boy"):

> Lesbius is a Pulcher/pretty boy. Why not – since Lesbia prefers him to you and your whole family, Catullus. But nonetheless, this pretty boy would sell Catullus, along with his family, if he could find three friends' kisses.

Few readers have been able to resist the invitation of these lines to biographical speculation. Indeed, the challenge posed by Catullus was taken up already in antiquity, as a passage in the *Apology* of the second-century CE orator and philosopher Apuleius shows (*Apologia* 10):

> But in the same manner let my opponents accuse Gaius Catullus because he names Lesbia for Clodia; and Ticidas, similarly because he wrote Perilla when she was Metella; and Propertius, who says Cynthia to conceal Hostia; and Tibullus because he loved Plania in his heart, Delia in his verse.

(Keith 2012: 285-86)

Yes, but tempting or not there are important, complicating factors to consider. For instance, just how realistic, how autobiographical, are these poems? And what of these *dominae*? Are these real mistresses, or are they fictive and or meant to be metaphorical?

The emphasis of Roman love elegy is then the opposite of what might have been expected: the lover's primary concern is for himself and not for his beloved. This may be seen in other ways too. To approach elegy with the expectation of finding powerful character portraits of beautiful and tempestuous women is to invite disappointment. The focus is instead on how the woman affects the male lover. Relatively few authenticating details are revealed of the women of love elegy; rather, a highly conventional beauty and temperament are ascribed to them. Some details, for example, of Cynthia's looks are concentrated in the second and third poems of Book 2, enough at least to build a picture of a tall woman with blond hair, long thin hands, a snow-white complexion and striking eyes (2.2.5-6; 2.3.9ff.). But these are the generic looks proper to goddesses and heroines (such as Dido in the *Aeneid*), and elsewhere in his poetry Propertius, like the other elegiac poets, is mostly content with general and unspecific references to hair, eyes, clothes and looks (see further Wyke

2002: 19ff.). In addition, while elegy does offer the alluring appearance of a beginning-to-end narrative of the elegists' relationships with their women, a closer look reveals that it is impossible to construct a chronology for the affair of (e.g.) Propertius and Cynthia from the former's variously conflicting statements about its length and episodes (Allen 1962: 112-18); few recent scholars have even tried to do the same for the various affairs of Tibullus and Ovid. One ancient writer, Apuleius, some two centuries after the elegists, it is true, claims in his *Apologia* (10) to provide the names behind the pseudonyms of Cynthia and Delia (although not, interestingly, the Nemesis of Tibullus' second book, or the Corinna of Ovid). But suspicions that Cynthia and her ilk may be (mainly) a fiction must be raised further when it is observed that such characteristics as are given to the women of elegy are often said equally to be characteristics of the elegist's poetry. This may be seen most clearly in Ovid *Amores* 3.1.7-10, where Elegy herself is given a female form whose details replicate features attributed elsewhere to Cynthia and Corinna (see Wyke 2002: 122-4). *In other words, readers of elegy must live with the constant suspicion that when elegists talk of their mistresses they are talking also about their poetry* [my italics]. One other indication of the strong implicit connection between the women of love elegy and elegiac poetics is that each of Lycoris, Cynthia and Delia bear a name also known to be a cult title of Apollo, god of poetry, while Corinna's name recalls that of a famous Greek poetess (McKeown 1987: 19-24: Wyke 2002: 27-8). (Gibson 2004: 165-66)

In other words, it's poetry; a specific poetic genre with its own conventional nature. There's our context, within which, for Roman readers, the *domina's* poetic function was well understood.

The *puella*, then, is not a person. She is not even a fully formed literary character. Cynthia speaks rarely, Lesbia, Delia, Nemesis and Corinna never. Her physical features are described in passing and in the most general terms. Her social status is clear only in the case of Lesbia, who is a *matrona*, while the rest appear to be *meretrices*, though their portrayal is not always consistent. However, the *puella* is not simply a literary construct. While she may not refer, even in the case of Lesbia, to a single extra-textual reality (Clodia's lived experience was certainly not what Catullus or Cicero portrays), she is only intelligible to the poets' readers and able to function within their texts to the extent that she embodies certain sets of pre-existing erotic, social, moral, legal, political and poetic assumptions. What the *puella* does substitute for is the ability of these values to coincide: the impossible figure that reconciles amorous plenitude with social recognition, poetic perfection with political legitimacy, law with transgressive desire in first century Rome. (Miller 2013: 178)

More specifically, the details of this poetic genre's depiction of the relationship between poet and mistress—it's anti-conventional conventions—are, as follows (note the *nominally*):

Roman elegy is predicated on clearly defined roles for the elegist and his female mistress. The elegist, typically, portrays the male in the traditionally passive and subservient role of women and, at the same time, depicts the female beloved as masterful, active, and dominant. The elegists often refer to their mistresses as *dominae* (female rulers) who subject their lovers to the torments of abandonment and betrayal. The elegiac enterprise, in general, seems to subvert Roman conventions of masculinity by assigning to the male narrator traits typically associated with women: servitude (*servitium*), softness (*mollitia*), and triviality (*levitas*). The male lover thus presents himself as devoted, dependent, and passive, and in turn often depicts his mistress as *dura* (hard, strong)—an attribute associated chiefly with men. The elegist's apparent servitude to his mistress, at least *nominally* [my italics], accords his mistress complete domination and control over him. (Greene 2012: 257)

For now, that's enough context. More will follow at the end of this chapter, and there's much more in Appendix Two: Love elegy: social and literary contexts.

Notes and Commentary on Individual Poems

Catullus

But before we start: who was Lesbia/Clodia? And what function does she really have in Catullus' poems?

> Famous for her beauty (Cicero called her "ox-eyed," Homer's epithet for Hera), she [Clodia Metelli; born c. 94] was, despite scholarly doubts almost certainly the model for Catullus' Lesbia. She probably met him in 61, and their on-again, off-again relationship seems to have lasted almost until Catullus' death c. 54. Her other lovers included M. Caelius Rufus, whom Cicero defended in 56 against charges largely instigated by Clodia herself, making her a laughingstock in the process. Till then she had been constantly involved in political affairs; after the trial she vanishes from public life. Much, though by no means all, of the evidence against her was clearly hyped up by her enemies. It used to be the fashion to believe all of it; today conventional wisdom has gone to the other extreme and dismisses it wholesale as fiction. The truth, as always, lies somewhere in the middle. As a high and arrogant aristocrat she pleased herself, in sex as in other matters. (Green 2005: 283-84)

> But Lesbia, in the fictional world of Catullus' poetry, has always struck readers as a real person with specific Catullus traits, at least too much so to serve merely or principally as an allegory for things like poetic writing, the genre of elegy, or the book of poems itself, as Cynthia so often does in Propertius. (Wray 2012: 26-27)

> Lesbia, however, is exceptional in her role as an elegiac *puella* not only because she is the first so named, [but] because she is

the sole *puella* to have an established *extra-poetic identity* [my italics]. (Miller 2013: 169)

Lesbia . . . alone, no matter how stylized the portrait, seems to be indubitably based on a real person. Thus leading scholars of elegy as different as Veyne, who views the entire genre as an elaborate game (1988), and James, who views it as a window onto the complex commerce that governed relations between upper class men and the women who erotically served them (2003), agree that Lesbia constitutes an exception. But if this is the case, does that mean that Lesbia also constitutes an exception to the methodological strictures laid down at the beginning of this chapter? Do we, therefore, not seek her meaning through the pattern of substitutions that characterizes her position within the textual economy of the Catullan corpus but rather predicate it on a pre-existing knowledge of her reality that allows us to read the poetry? The fact is, however, that the textual construct Catullus has produced only functions within the symbolic world that constitutes Roman life: the dividing line between poetic construct and pre-poetic reality within that symbolic world is impossible to establish. (Miller 2013: 167-68)

As for Catullus and his "reality," Wray points out that with Catullus we get much more of what Veyne calls the "classical illusion," by which he means "the strong impression that the speaker of Catullus' poems is a man in the world, or at least a character in a realist drama, talking—maybe to someone else, maybe only to himself—but just talking, the way people talk in the world." It's this "impression of directness and authenticity" that makes Catullus unique. But is this really just an impression?

Extant Latin poetry offers no other reading experience that has felt to so many readers like the experience of getting close to another human being. No amount of talk on the part of us scholars about things like performativity and ironized self-presentation has yet succeeded in making Catullus walk that way for most of his readers, especially when coming to his poems for the first time. (Wray 2012: 27)

He seems very real.

The man Catullus' poems make us think we are getting to know is one who voices his feelings with the heraldic intensity of an aristocratic spirit that brooks no constraint because it has never been broken, never been taught to curb or dissemble its passionate nature across the whole range of human emotion, from love to hate, from joy to grief, from anger to fear and shame. (Wray 2012: 32)

And then Wray notes this striking contrast between Ovid and Catullus; one that may get us closer to the truth of the matter.

Ovid is implying, and expecting his readers to understand, that being a Roman love elegist had come to mean something comparable on some level to what it meant in this culture to be a philosopher. That is to say, the choice to be a Roman elegist could be held up as not just a choice to mold written language under the constraints of a certain literary form on a given day, or to have a particular kind of poetic career, but rather a once-for-all decision, forced on the poet more than taken by him, to be a certain kind of human being and live a certain kind of life. Catullus, whose poetry gives as strong a sense of poetic vocation and poetic ambition as any poet who ever wrote, never hints that he thought of being a love elegist in this way or had even heard of the possibility of doing so. (Wray 2012: 27)

Commentary

51

Wilkinson's idea that this free translation of three stanzas from a well-known Sappho poem was Catullus' first shot in his courting of Lesbia/Clodia has a lot going for it. Looked at in this way, it is a cautious enquiry, despite the naming of the addressee as "Lesbia." If the lady returned his feelings (or at least wanted to take things further) she would know what he meant: otherwise it was simply a poetic translation sent by one literary aficionado for the enjoyment of another, and nothing (of course) to do with present company. In the latter case "Lesbia" was simply the "girl of Lesbos" apostrophized by Sappho; but if Clodia wanted the cryptonym, it was there waiting for her. The speaker's envy of the (probably licit) freedom possessed by this addressee's companion to enjoy her company is at least consonant with the scenario in which Catullus is commemorating his first encounter with Clodia, probably in 61/0, and at home, in her husband's company.

The fourth and final stanza is a puzzle. It corresponds to nothing in Sappho's Greek . . . and it is, to say the least, startling to find a crypto-declaration of love, followed up, as Fordyce well puts it, by the reflection, "Your trouble Catullus, is not having anything to do." Of the two main current theories, one suggests that this stanza . . . ended up by scribal vagary, attached to a poem where it did not belong; the other, perhaps more psychologically plausible, argues that Catullus added this note of depressed self-recrimination much later, when the affair had gone very sour, or was already over. (Green 2005: 228)

5

The affair with "Lesbia mine" is now presented as an ongoing, open scandal, vulnerable to gossip and "old men's strictures." . . . [Here he wants] to frustrate jealous attempts at hexing . . . by means of the evil eye. Just as knowledge of a secret name or possession of a victim's nail pairings or hair clippings, could, on the principle of the part for the whole, be used against their owner, so Catullus affects to believe that an accurate tally of his and his lover's kisses may confer a similar power. (Green 2005: 214)

7

We can picture Lesbia—Clodia Metelli, if it was indeed she— reading or hearing 5, and asking amusedly, "All right, then, how many kisses *would* satisfy you?" Cf. Lynn . . . a sensitive and sympathetic analysis, pointing out in detail how "the ingredients of the poem (humor, urbanity, extravagance, warmth, and a touch of sentimentality), and the proportion and ordering of these ingredients, must allow valuable insight into the personalities of both Catullus and Lesbia and into how the two interact." This poem, together with 2, 2a, 3, and 5, clearly belongs to an early stage in her affair with Catullus. (Green 2005: 215)

68B

This poem is generally considered the first example of the elegiac genre. It offers the length and complexity typical of the form and anticipates later uses of mythological exempla. The poem is also important because it gives us a rare glimpse into the overall narrative of the Lesbia affair. Here Catullus clearly states that it is an adulterous affair, but that he nonetheless conceives of his relationship to Lesbia as a kind of marriage. Such a demand for fidelity in an adulterous liaison would have been highly unusual in the Roman world and highlights the eccentric nature of the affair portrayed by Catullus. It is this commitment to a woman to whom one would normally owe no such thing that signals the unique status of the elegiac romance in Roman life. This poem also foreshadows later developments in the genre by showing that Catullus' sense of commitment was not shared by his beloved. It is this presumed inequality of feeling that lies behind the common elegiac theme of *servitium amoris* or "the slavery of love." One feature of this theme is the casting of the beloved in the figure of the *domina*, the poet's literal mistress, an inversion of the normal Roman hierarchy of gender relations. This poem features the first use of the word *domina* in an erotic context. (Miller 2002: 109)

Poem 68, generally regarded as Catullus' elegiac masterpiece, locates the poet at his family home in Verona in the aftermath of his brother's death in the Troad (*c.* 68.1–40) and offers a poem of thanks to a friend for making available to him and his mistress a house in which to pass a night of love (*c.*

68.41–160). Lesbia (unnamed in the poem) enters the borrowed house, *domus*, as the poet-lover's mistress, *domina* (*c.* 68.67–74). Catullus' friend thereby endows Catullus' girlfriend with a household and thus invents, as far as we can tell, the amatory metaphor of *seruitium amoris*, the "slavery of love," for the Latin word *domina* denotes a woman in charge of the household slaves, a property owner. (Keith 2012: 287)

In Part B Catullus recalls Lesbia's arrival for an assignation: she put her gleaming foot on the worn threshold, and the sole of her sandal tapped on it. It is not only Lesbia who stands on a threshold but western literature itself, for two things begin here. What has fixed itself in the poet's mind is something oddly ordinary, a contrast of textures, shining shoe on stone, the moment marked by the sharp sound. Here is a new feeling for the particularity of small, ordinary experiences, realized through visible and audible detail; we shall meet it again in Virgil. Second, we have here a fragment of narrative: Catullus is beginning to tell a story. And this in turn is the beginning of what we shall come to recognize as Latin love elegy: the protoplasm seems to be evolving before our eyes. (Jenkyns 2016)

Catullus clearly is, or pictures himself as being, at that stage in his affair with Lesbia, where, thoughtfully conscious of her promiscuity, he is prepared to put up with the "occasional lapse" as a man of the world—and in the knowledge that complaint would be counterproductive. . . . The irony is poignant . . . the acknowledgement that Catullus and Lesbia are not married at all, but restricted to stolen and furtive pleasure. Indeed, a careful study of the sequence strongly suggests that this may have been the *only* complete night they ever spent together. Wiseman observes, "Only now, and only for a moment, do we catch a glimpse of 'Lesbia' as she may have been in life—the adulterous noblewoman cheating on her husband again for a night with an adoring lover. How much did it matter to her that he saw her in his fantasy as his bride? He should be glad she found time for him at all." Poignant irony again: Catullus will settle for being Lesbia's favorite, but not her only, lover. [T]he white stone is the equivalent of a "red letter day." (Green 2005: 254-55)

86

Here Catullus reveals more characteristics of what educated Romans regarded as an attractive woman: she should be, *inter alia*, fair (i.e., pale-skinned, protected from the sun, not a field-worker), tall, and hold herself erect. (We should not assume from this ideal, tempting though it is to do so, that most Roman girls were short, dark, and slouched.) She was also expected to be not only literate, but versed in literature: a salon queen, in fact [note: *salt* means wit].

Catullus' word for "beautiful," *formosa*, he uses here only, yet he would seem to have injected new subtlety into it. Before him it was used of anything well-shaped or well-formed of its kind, whether physical or abstract . . . But for Catullus it meant good looks plus subtle charm, and after him this usage became "one of the hard-worked words in the love-poet's vocabulary." Quintia was good-looking, but lacked that special magic. Lesbia for Catullus incorporates the Sapphic and Hellenistic ideal. Skinner suggests that "Quintia and Lesbia stand for contrasting approaches to the Latin elegiac distich, one traditional and the other innovative." (Green 2005: 261)

T. D. Papanghelis (1991) has demonstrated that this epigram encodes a powerful literary statement in its association of Lesbia with the critical terminology of neoteric poetics (*uenustas, sal*) and, by extension, with the elegiac poetics espoused by the Alexandrian poet Callimachus, whose *Aetia* Prologue delineates a contrast between rival poetic styles symbolized by women (*Aet.* fr. 1.9–12 M). For Catullus here uses the term *uenustas*, "charm," in the sense of "modesty of size and slenderness of form, which are central preoccupations of the Neoteric-Callimachean poetics" (Papanghelis 1991, 385). A preference for the charming and dainty Lesbia over the tall Quintia thus pointedly recalls Callimachus' expression of disdain for "the tall woman" (or long poem) in the *Aetia*

Prologue and his espousal of the sweetness of a more modestly sized woman/poem. Catullus thus also seems to be responsible for naturalizing in Latin elegy the Hellenistic delineation of a poetic project in the metaphor of female anatomy (Wyke 2002).

83

On the assumption that Lesbia is Clodia Metelli, this poem must be dated earlier than the sudden death of her husband Metellus Celer in March 59. Quinn wonders whether the affair has in fact begun: does Catullus hopefully interpret the abuse as proof of love, or is it a cover-up for an affair already in full swing? Almost certainly, I would argue, the latter: the cumulative evidence points back to 61 or early 60 as the likeliest date for the assignation arranged by Manlius. In either case, the psychological subtly is considerable: seeming dislike may hide love. And the husband may be a mule (nice insult, mules being sterile), but he is still, maddeningly, the one officially entitled to Clodia's favors. (Green 2005: 260)

104

This has to be a fairly early poem, since there exist quite a few late attacks (e.g., most particularly, 11 and 58) which would, in most people's opinion, qualify as "cursing" or "speaking ill of" Lesbia. Goodwin also stresses the alleged incompatibility of Catullus' attitude here with that in 92, where Lesbia's bad-mouthing of *him* is taken as proof of love. But perhaps Catullus would explain the lines as wrongly interpreted on just this basis? In any case, Whitman's apothegm applies: Catullus in love is quite ready to contradict himself. (Green 2005: 266)

107

The Latin stutters with emotional excitement: elisions pile up, line 3 (if the text is not corrupt) contains a nice asyndeton in *carius auro*, Catullus' incredulous delight at Lesbia's return after estrangement is beautifully conveyed. The white mark for a lucky day was a commonplace cliché. (Green 2005: 267)

109

Inevitably, in English translation this poem looks more optimistic than it does in Latin. The Latin terms for "pact" (*foedus*) and "friendship" (*amicitia*), especially when juxtaposed, as in the final line, normally mean a *political* alliance or treaty, though as we have seen [see note for 76] Catullus tries to adapt them to a new kind of emotional relationship. But as Godwin asks, and Catullus surely wondered apropos his own situation, "Did any *foedus* last for ever? Or any *amicitia*? And when did the gods ever show interest in promoting the fidelity of mortal lovers? Catullus' poem subverts its own desperate hopes, not least that of "quasi-spousal fidelity." (Green 2005: 267-68) [For a completely different interpretation of 87, 92, 104, 107, and 109, see Dyson Hejduk, below]

87

This belongs to the same disillusioned group as 72, 75, and 85. The mood in which Catullus' own single-minded loyalty is invoked is not one of self-righteousness but rather one of despair. Note the switch in the last line to direct apostrophe: emotion has got the better of third-person distancing. Catullus startles the reader here, brings Lesbia suddenly, and directly, into the reckoning. (Green 2005: 261)

70

It would not have been at all surprising had Catullus raised the possibility of marriage after her (Lesbia/Clodia) husband Metellus Celer's death in March 59—indeed, it would have been surprising had he not—and equally predictable that his *inamorata,* elusive as always, would waffle: "Yes, you're the person I'd like to be *married to,* but maybe not to *marry.*" This poem is an adaptation of an epigram by Callimachus (25 Pf.), but Catullus gives it his own characteristic twist, and the notion of writing on the wind seems without ancient parallel. The reference to Jupiter, though proverbial, hardly suggests stability: the god's brief and lustful infidelities were notorious, and Catullus' overall mood is one of cynical resignation, backed by a handful of stock literary allusions. (Green 2005: 256)

72

This poem takes up where 70 left off. It is remarkable on several counts. The contrast between the love the common man has for his *amica* and Catullus' feeling of respect and affection for Lesbia is made all the more striking by the poet's resort to comparing his feelings to those of a father for his sons. Traditional Latin vocabulary had no way of expressing affection between a man and a woman that was not fundamentally sexual in nature. Catullus is making an analytical distinction that is unprecedented, and he has no way to do so other than to express his feelings in terms used to describe relations between men or homosociality.

The contrast between Catullus and the common man is balanced by one between present and past. Catullus is now disillusioned, but his passion burns the more, even as Lesbia has fallen in his esteem. The opposition between present and past, in turn, refers back to poem 70. (Miller 2002: 116)

75

Thomson finds this "an intermediate stage in compression of thought" between 72 and 85. For Fordyce, Catullus' confusion between passion and affection is a "pathetic paradox." Quinn, on the other hand, sees these lines as "ruthlessly clear-sighted." Take your choice. But the emotional conflict is real and expressed with bitter vigor. (Green 2005: 257-58)

92

A summation of the thought expressed in 83, but clearly written at a later stage in the relationship: there is a sense of continuity now in Lesbia's bad-mouthing and Catullus' reactions: each keeps maintaining a position in what has become an established affair with a history. These are "the words of a man who is eagerly looking for confirmation of what he feels sure of." (Green 2005: 262)

8

[W]ritten at a much later stage, when the affair had reached a point of bitter recrimination. (Whatever the arrangement of the poems may have been, it was certainly not chronological.) . . . The triple-thud line endings of the choliambic metre, together with the absence of enjambment, are extraordinarily effective in conveying the notion of reiterated determination. (Green 2005: 215)

76

This is the sole poem by Catullus, other than 68, to have the length and range of emotional development to be able to lay claim to being a true elegy rather than an epigram. In many ways, it is a summary of the affair. Catullus claims that he has been *pius* (respectful of his obligations) and shown *fides* in his affair with Lesbia, but these good works have gone unrewarded. He therefore prays to the gods for justice. He does not seek to make Lesbia love him, but asks merely to be freed from the bonds of this affair, which is pictured as a disease that gnaws at the poet's entrails. This is a powerful poem and a fitting summary of the affair as portrayed in 70, 72, and 75. (Miller 2002: 117)

Catullus here sets in play the metaphor of love as an illness. . . . With striking irony, the poet makes his plea on the basis of an adulterous relationship (cf. *c.* 68). In so doing, he establishes a framework that subsequent Latin elegists will make conventional to the genre. (Keith 2012: 288)

This is a crucial poem, and Godwin's basic analysis is very much to the point, together with Lynn's analysis of Catullus' use of terms borrowed from formal diplomacy or even from interstate politics (*amicitia* ["friendship," "alliance"], *foedus* ["solemn treaty," "covenant"]) to hammer out a new vocabulary of the ideal *personal* relationship, the *foedus amicitiae*, a permanent "marriage pact of friendship" based on affection as well as passion. As lines 23-26 make clear, "after all the rhetoric, the use of medical language and the pious prayers, we are left with a man in love with a woman who does not love him and does not care." (Green 2005: 258)

11

Perhaps the bitterest of the late Lesbia poems: contrast with the violent delineation of Lesbia's *nostalgie de la boue* the sad image of Catullus' love as a crushed flower, with its echo of Sappho. Note that Catullus will not even address Lesbia personally, but sends a message. . . . It cannot be a coincidence that this final repudiation of his faithless lover by Catullus returns to the metre (the Sapphic stanza) in which what was clearly his first poem to her, 51, was written, and which he employs nowhere else. (Green 2005: 216)

The equally famous Poem 11, delivering its speaker's bitter message of dismissal to a lover proved false, closes on a literal cut inside an unforgettable figure. When he likens his love to a flower that falls after "it has been touched by the plow" (*tactus aratro est*, 11.24), the speaker has plowed his own utterance straight down its furrow to an untoppable and unanswerable closure, by hitting on a poem-final phrase that manages to nail, with overweening aptness, no fewer than three things at once: the steely brutality of the heartlessness he imputes to his beloved; the slashing intensity of his own retaliatory anger; and the wilting pathos of the self-pitying aggrievement that underlies that anger as the source and secret principle of it, and that a psychologically subtle poet lets us discern through and beneath the words of his poem's speaker. (Wray 2012: 30)

58A

Whether the accusation is literally true or not is impossible to determine; certainly it is not impossible, and history offers comparable cases. This, among the bitterest of Catullus' reflections on his former lover, must be dated to a period after his return from Bithynia, and also (if we grant that Lesbia is Clodia Metelli) after her break-up with her other lover, M. Caelius Rufus, that is, to 56 or 55. This would postdate the famous prosecution of Caelius (April 56) and his defense by

Cicero, itself in large part a calculated attack on Clodia. Caelius referred to her at that time as a "two-bit Clytemnestra," and her apparent disappearance from the social scene after that prosecution failed is consonant with the kind of public low-life behavior that Catullus etches so dramatically. His invocation of Caelius, indeed, is all too apposite: "*You've had her too*, the implication goes, *you know what I'm talking about.* (Green 2005: 231)

85
The greatest two line poem ever written, 85 sums up the whole dilemma of the Lesbia affair as outlined in 70, 72, 75, and 76, while its language enacts the wrenching conflict it describes. (Miller 2002: 119)

[C]onventional to the genre, though honed to minimalist perfection, is Catullus' expression of the lover's emotional torment in the grip of unrequited love. (Keith 2012: 288)

There can be few better-known Latin poems than this pungent and desperate distich. Thomson sees it as "the ultimate stage in a process of condensation of thought and expression" that began with 72 and 75. Logic (*nescio*) has failed; all that remains is feeling (*sentio*), painful to the point of torture (*excrucior*). The juxtaposition remains inexplicable, but a brute fact. (Green 2005: 261)

But perhaps I've got it wrong: Dyson Hejduk's alternative "happy" ending (her translations; her order).

As I hope to demonstrate in this chapter, however, the impressionistic portraits of Lesbia that emerge from the different sections of the collection are so utterly different from one another – whatever the reality that inspired them – that this very difference *must* [my italics] be essential to the meaning of the poems. With the exception of Homer, whose Penelope is a match for the cunning Odysseus in every way, Catullus is the first author to depict a romantic relationship between a man and a woman as true *amicitia*, "friendship," *a meeting of minds* [my italics] presupposing both social and intellectual equality. So radical was this move that it was followed, as far as I can tell, by no other author before Jane Austen. Yet if we accept the division of Catullus' poems into three sections – the polymetrics (1–60), the longer poems (61–8), and the epigrams (69–116) – it is only in the third that the idea of Lesbia as the poet's "friend" emerges. (Dyson Hejduk 2007: 255)

In poem 86, the poet concedes that Quintia is physically beautiful, but – here is the crucial difference – he denies that physical beauty constitutes true "attractiveness." What Quintia lacks is "salt," that is, "wit": Lesbia, by implication, possesses this essential quality. Although this is Catullus' only explicit reference to Lesbia's mind, it highlights the metamorphosis in his depiction of their relationship. The epigrammatic Lesbia has something more distinctive to offer than the perfume of sexual allure.

The five remaining Lesbia poems tell a simple story, one perhaps best summarized in the trite but timeless formula, "They lived happily ever after."

87
No woman is able to say that she's been
loved so truly
as my own Lesbia has been loved by me.
No faith so great was ever found in any
pact
as has been found, from my side, in your
love.

92
Lesbia's always cursing me, and never
keeps quiet
about me: damned if Lesbia doesn't love
me!
What proof? Because I'm exactly the same:
I rail against her
constantly – but damned if I don't love

her!

104

You think that I could hurl abuses at my
Life,
one who is dearer to me than both my
eyes?
I couldn't—nor, if I could, would I love so
desperately:
but you, with Tappo, do all monstrous
things.

107

If ever anything comes to a man who is
longing, wishing,
but hopeless—that is sweet to his spirit
indeed!
Therefore this is sweet to me, this is dearer
than gold:
you restore yourself, Lesbia, to me in my
longing,
you restore to a longing and hopeless man,
on your own you return
yourself to me. Oh day of more radiant
note!
What happier man lives than me only? Or
who will be able
to name a thing more to be wished in life
than this?

109

You declare to me, my Life, that this our
mutual love
will be pleasant and last for all eternity.
Great gods, see to it that she be able to
promise truly,
and that she say it sincerely and from the
heart,
so we may be allowed for our whole life to

continue
this everlasting pact of holy friendship.

Our final glimpse of the polymetric Lesbia is utter
degradation, shucking all comers in back alleys. Our final
glimpse of the epigrammatic Lesbia is in an "everlasting pact
of *holy friendship* [my italics]," *amicitia*, a word denoting not
only reconciliation but *true equality* [my italics]. The *puella*
has grown up. (Dyson Hejduk 2007: 272-73)

*Must ... holy friendship ... true equality ... a sentimental
meeting of the minds?* No, I just don't see it, which is why I've
ordered these poems differently; telling a story that seems far
more likely, if not also likely true. (See the commentary,
above, for 76, 11, and 85, in particular) But I leave it to you.

This is amusing. Originally, Catullus 2A and 3 were not
included in this (my) series. There were two reasons. First,
chronologically, they're not that important, and second, I find
them tedious. Well, they are, nevertheless, famous, and subject
to much scholarly debate. Fine. But then I ran across a poem
by Dorothy Parker that makes reference to them, and that
poem is good enough that it was necessary to throw them in
for context.

2A
Sparrow, precious darling of my sweetheart,
always her plaything, held fast in her bosom,
whom she loves to provoke with outstretched finger
tempting the little pecker to nip harder
when *my* incandescent longing fancies
just a smidgin of fun and games and comfort
for the pain she's feeling (I believe it!),
something to lighten that too-heavy ardor—
how I wish I could sport with you as she does,
bring some relief to the spirit's black depression!

3

Mourn, Cupids all, every Venus, and whatever
company still exists of caring people:
Sparrow lies dead, my own true sweetheart's sparrow,
Sparrow, the pet and darling of my sweetheart,
loved by her more than she valued her own eyesight.
Sweet as honey he was, and knew his mistress
no less closely than a child her mother;
nor from her warm lap's safety would he ever
venture far, but hopping this and that way
came back, cheeping, always to his lady.
Now he's travelling on that dark-shroud journey
whence, they tell us, none of the departed
ever returns. The hell with you, you evil
blackness of Hell, devouring all that's lovely—
such a beautiful sparrow you've torn from me!
Oh wicked deed! Oh wretched little sparrow!
It's your fault that now my sweetheart's eyelids
are sore and swollen red from all her weeping.

And here's Parker's response.

From A Letter From Lesbia

...So, praise the gods, at last he's away!
And let me tend you this advice, my dear:
Take any lover that you will, or may,
Except a poet. All of them are queer.

It's just the same – quarrel or a kiss
Is but a tune to play on his pipe.
He's always hymning that or wailing this;
Myself, I much prefer the business type.

That thing he wrote, the time the sparrow died –
(Oh, most unpleasant – gloomy, tedious words!)
I called it sweet, and made believe I cried;
The stupid fool! I've always hated birds...
(Parker 1944: 452)

121

Commentary

2A

Lesbia's sparrow is too firmly entrenched, both by Catullus and by its subsequent history, to dislodge, but was probably in fact a blue rock thrush, popular as an Italian pet, real sparrows being dowdy, mean, and virtually untamable. Nevertheless, evidence for the *passer* and other birds as pets goes back as far as the plays of Plautus in Rome (as well as featuring in the *Greek Anthology*), and the sparrow, as we know from Sappho, was sacred to Aphrodite (the poem, incidentally, parodies the formal structure of a hymn to a goddess). It also (as Chaucer was aware) enjoyed a reputation for lechery—one reason why, ever since the Renaissance, a running debate, still open, has gone on as to whether this poem contains an obscene double entendre, since *passer* and its modern Italian descendant *passero* are both found as a slang term for the penis. This being so, it is hard to believe that Catullus did not at least let the ambiguity cross his mind, with the thought that it might also cross that of his reader; Martial (7.14, 11.6.15-16) certainly took it that way. (Green 2005: 213)

3

If 2 takes off from a hymn, Catullus here neatly fuses the Greek concept of the dirge with that highly Hellenistic genre, the epitaph, and under both we find (Quinn) "a delicately ironical, graceful love poem, wary of any sentimentality." It is also unique. As Fordyce says, "the simple emotion which turns the lament for the dead pet into a love lyric, and makes commonplace and colloquial language into poetry, owes nothing to any predecessor." Nor was the effect repeatable: neither Ovid's elegy on Corinna's parrot (*Am.* 2.6) nor John Skelton's *Lament for Philip Sparrow* comes near Catullus' subtlety, charm—and wry humor. The last two lines reveal the true reason for Catullus' grief: the bird's demise has upset Lesbia. (Green 2005: 213-14)

Propertius

And Cynthia, who was she? The common view now seems
to be she wasn't, or at least not outside the confines of a book
of poems. And here, an extreme version, in which she's more
like a life coach, an erotic life coach who liberates, who
facilitates a Roman version of self-actualization.

> As an emblem of the erotic imperative, she stands for much
> more than the services that a highly skilled (and highly paid)
> sex-worker can provide for her customers. The gifts she
> bestows (or withholds) are very much carnal in nature, but
> they are not merely carnal. If she proffers her trick or long-
> time companion delights that he cannot expect to get at home
> from his wife or his slaves, she is no less lavish in her
> willingness to awaken in him emotional energies,
> psychological pleasures, and expanses of imagination that are
> as vivid as—and sometimes more vivid than—the bodily
> thrills that accompany them. She (or such women as she
> symbolizes) cannot fabricate for him a new identity, but she
> can help liberate him from the codes, the sign-systems, the
> ideologies, that he was born into and that have, until she got
> hold of him, prescribed for him not just who he thought he
> was and thought he out to be but also what he valued and
> chose and did. This freedom allows him and indeed
> encourages him to assume a new identity, one that requires
> him to fashion for himself a new set of ethical norms, ones
> that provide his existence, his daily life, his sense of himself
> and the world, with new directions, new meanings, new
> purposes. Whether as ideal or an illusion or a bit of both, she
> is the catalyst of a new style of self-fashioning. (Johnson
> 2009: 94)

Ideal type or an illusion isn't much of a choice, but this
notion that Cynthia has a function more than an identity is an
interesting one. We'll see it again.

Commentary

1.1

" . . . Cynthia, the beautiful, accomplished, and imperious woman whom the Propertius lover is obsessed." (Booth 2009: 66)

So begins Propertius' first book, immediately conveying interests that will be of key importance in what follows. In first place the name of his beloved Cynthia, its primacy stressed by the addition of *prima*. The poet is unhappy (*miserum*), disorganized, mad, and ill-fated: this will turn out to be normal—love for him is never easy. (Heyworth 2011: 1)

To pursue Cynthia the poet has abandoned the life indifferent to love, but because his suit has been rejected and he now seems to have exhausted the resources of strategy, he lives aimlessly from day to day. (Richardson 1977:147)

'Cynthia first . . .' – the opening phrase indicates that she dominates both his life and his verse. He calls his affair 'worthlessness'; he says that she has taught him to shun nice girls and to live a life without aim; and he describes himself as 'good for nothing', his situation as slavery. Propertius hopes, so he says, to 'give up his last breath to this worthlessness'. So does he enjoy his servitude, or does he hate himself for it? Does he regret the worthlessness, or is he a rebel against the conventional respectability that gives this name to a style of life that he enthusiastically embraces? Part of the fascination is that he seems not to know himself: we are shown the tossings and turnings of a restless and uncertain spirit. There is a touch of death wish, which, perhaps, he knows himself to be more than half a pose. Many, he adds, have perished in a long love gladly; in their number may the earth cover him too. And he imagines the young visiting his tomb and calling him the 'great poet of our own love'. He also gives us the lover as aesthete, presenting himself as a man whose sensibility is steeped in literature and visual art and who brings his care for such things to his experience of Cynthia. (Jenkyns 2016)

1.3

The aesthete is to the fore at the beginning of one of his masterpieces, the third poem of Book 1. He begins with a series of pictures: like Ariadne as Theseus' ship left her abandoned, like Andromeda in slumber after being rescued from the rocks, like an exhausted Bacchant collapsed on the grass – such did Cynthia seem to him asleep. But then the poet smashes the lovely serenity that he has created, as he lurches into the scene, drunk and randy. He thinks of possessing her as she lies unconscious, but then thinks again, remembering her fierce tongue, and instead turns sentimental, laying his garland on her, rearranging her hair and putting apples in her hands – the aesthetic impulse again – until a moonbeam wakens her. She angrily reproaches him for unfaithfulness, and there the poem ends. The beauty of this lies in its openness. Did they make up their quarrel, or did they not? Did the night end in lovemaking, or in bitterness? We do not know. We are simply offered the fragment of a story, a small lighted space, with darkness before and beyond it. Some of Propertius' motifs are likely to have derived from Greek epigram: the moonlight through the shutters, the narrator having his wicked way with a sleeping girl. But these elements are now incorporated into a more complex and unfolding narrative. And the woman now counts: her fierceness checks his sexual urge. Like Tibullus, he has an idea of how he would like her to look and be, but the real living woman will not remain the passive picture that he has sought to make of her. (Jenkyns 2016)

1.8B

[1.8 A] is addressed to his mistress, a long, fervent entreaty in which the poet tries to dissuade her from setting out on a voyage, [and 1.8B] is addressed to the reader, an account of her reaction to the inner poem [of 1.8A], her decision not to go after all, and his jubilance. . . . [In 1.8B] Propertius drops the pretense that the first part is a spontaneous outpouring of argument and prayer and admits it is a carefully composed and controlled literary composition. This makes us look at the second part with a fresh eye and ask to what extent it, too, is artificial. (Richardson 1977: 166)

2.1

In this poem, which ranges easily from the subject, touching on many but exploring none, Propertius puts before us a program of subject matter we may expect to find exploited in the poems that follow and an apology that his scope is not more ambitious and varied. The first sixteen lines are addressed to his readers in general, who may find his poems curiously slight and of a single focus; to these he replies that his life shows the same restrictions, that he is entirely taken up with his mistress. The remainder of the poem is addressed to Maecenas [Augustus' friend and advisor; patron of many poets] and falls into three sections: a *recusatio*, in which he apologizes for not celebrating the victories of Augustus, a feverish essay at accounting for the hold his mistress has on his life and imagination, and a final oblique prayer that Maecenas will forgive him his shortcomings after his death. (Richardson 1977: 211)

The passion and immediacy of the Cynthia elegies have long provoked interest amongst Propertius' readers in the autobiographical origins of his elegiac poetry, and he himself plays on public curiosity about the intimate details of a real love affair at the outset of his second book (2.1.1-4). Few readers have been able to resist the invitation of these lines to biographical speculation about Cynthia, her looks and her morals.

Propertius here apparently denies poetic inspiration altogether, insisting on the primacy of his mistress' toilette and activities to spur his literary imagination. Nonetheless it is possible to trace clear debts to both Catullus and Gallus in Propertius' onomastic practice, which contradicts this disavowal of literary inspiration. . . . Significant too is Propertius' debt to the example of Gallus, for the name Cynthia, like Lycoris, is a feminized form of a cult title of the god Apollo Cynthius, divine patron of poetry. Propertius thus endows his girlfriend with a name that bears an intensely literary resonance.

Social historians and literary critics alike, moreover, have called into question whether the identification of a supposed historical girlfriend concealed behind Propertius' pseudonymous Cynthia can provide meaningful access to the historical woman and the circumstances of her life, let alone explain her literary significance in Propertius' poetry. . . . Even if we accept the biographical speculations of historical and philological scholarship . . . it is incumbent upon us to explore Cynthia's symbolic import in Propertian elegy by considering carefully the literary valence of the themes and images with which our elegist associates her throughout his verse. (Keith 2012: 291)

2.15
[T]he play is on the theme of what is eternal and what is transient, the night of love being the merest moment of time and yet granting immortality, and simply the climax of a love that cannot be limited in any way. (Richardson 1977: 255)

In perhaps the best of all his poems . . . triumph is mingled with darkness and defiance. He exults in the 'shining night' that he has enjoyed, the teasing, the nakedness, the shared delight, and he meditates future possibilities – bruises and ripped clothing. The eyes, he insists, are the guides of love: he does not care to do what he cannot see. But then his thought moves to another night – that long night which day will not follow. He ends by passionately urging his beloved not to lose the fruit of life: if she gives him all her kisses, they will not be enough. 'As the leaves drop from withering garlands, which you see strewn about, swimming in the cups, so for us, lovers who now breathe big, tomorrow's day may perhaps close our destinies.' Leaves suggest the brevity of our existence, as they have since Mimnermus, but they now float on the vivifying surface of the wine – a detail that is both visually acute and emotionally expressive. It is late in the party, but the party has been very good. For these final lines are a paean of praise to the goodness of life, and although death casts its shadow, the very last word is 'day'. There is a strength in this that we might not have expected from the wilting amorist presented in his earliest works. Sometimes he is more straightforwardly outrageous. (Jenkyns 2016)

3.8A

1-10: I enjoyed last night's absurd quarrel with you. Do continue your aggressive behavior towards me; when you throw a table or a goblet, it is a sign of your deep love for me. 11-18: The woman who hurls mad abuse is a subject of Venus: crowds of guards, Maenad-like behavior, terrifying dreams, jealousy of a picture—any of these is evidence of love. 19-28: Fidelity may be turned to a row: let my enemies have an unemotional girl. Let my friends see love-bites on my neck. I want to feel pain or witness the pain of another. I do not like sleep without sighs, and wish to always love an angry girl. 29-32: The violence of the Trojan War made the love of Paris for Helen sweeter; the greatest battles were in her lap. 33-40: I shall always have fights with you or for you. A curse on my rival: if you are given the chance to steal a night, it will only be because she is angry with me . . . the oddity of a poem that celebrates a physical assault by a lover. (Heyworth 2011: 174-75)

In one poem, looking back on another night of rough lovemaking – bites and scratches again – he declares that sex ought to have the spice of violence, and he scorns those whose love life goes smoothly. Paris enjoyed his passion all the more, he adds, when he came to it straight from the battlefield of Troy; while the Greeks are winning, while that barbarian Hector remains on the field to fight for his country's survival, he fights the biggest battle of all on Helen's breast. This is deliberately provocative and, for that matter, deliberately unserious: no one can seriously put Paris's inconstancy above his brother's gallantry. (Jenkyns 2016)

1.18

Propertius plays with the idea of separation from Cynthia . . . Here the escape is to the forest to soothe his anguish with a complaint he dares not utter in her presence . . . He comes to the forest to ask mournfully why Cynthia now scorns him and to try to find an answer among various possibilities: first that she is jealous and suspects he has been courting another love, then that he has given too little proof of his affection, last that he had been morose and resentful in his behavior. Each he claims is groundless, but the last he cannot entirely deny. So he is left to cry her name through the wilderness.

It is a touching and attractive poem, full of tenderness, with a sensitive development of the landscape by seemingly casual touches. The lover's despair, his gentleness and patience come through with remarkable clarity for so short a poem. . . . We recognize the poet of the other elegies of the first book only hazily, and the contrast with Cynthia, a ruthless, capricious, and self-assured vixen, is the stronger. (Richardson 1977: 196-97)

2.05

This poem, the first in this book [Book Two] to mention Cynthia by name, is also the first rebuke to his mistress and a powerful revelation to the reader of the degeneration of a love affair. The poet is no longer the romantic worshiper, spellbound, suffering only from the anxiety that he may lose Cynthia and his failure to understand and please her every moment; instead he sees her as heartless, an incorrigible liar, frivolous and unworthy of his devotion. Yet he cannot quite bring himself to accept what he sees and knows is the truth, so he is reduced to toying insincerely with the idea of abandoning her, to pleading with her and making vague threats. This new attitude of ambivalence in the poet and a tension between love as he had imagined it and insisted on it in the first warm raptures and the grim realities of his liaison that he now perceives are what give the second book of elegies its greatest strength and are responsible for much of its difficulty for the reader. The poet can, as he says and shows us in this poem, change at a word and go from anger to pleading, from high seriousness to wry irony, from romantic rhapsody to laughter at his own fatuity. On such sudden changes of pace and attitude, incongruous juxtapositions, shifts and leaps of a cultivated intelligence caught in an emotional tangle alien to it many of the succeeding poems depend. (Richardson 1977: 224)

2.09A
[Here, the] poet's mistress has been stolen from him by a rival, and he explores his emotions and contemplates his revenge. . . . written in a highly controlled, cold fury. . . . he knows exactly what he wants to do, to turn the tables, showing her up as a vicious, self-centered cheat, pitting one man against another for her amusement. . . . Before the poem is over it becomes a thinly disguised plea for reinstatement. (Richardson 1997: 235-36)

2.17
[T]he outraged cry of a man cheated out of a rendezvous with his mistress. This begins overly abruptly, even for Propertius, and ends with an almost equally abrupt relapse into patient resignation. (Richardson 1977: 263)

1.10
In it appear those familiar strands of Propertian elegy, the poet as *praeceptor amoris* [the teacher of love] and the *seruitium amoris* [the slavery of love], but it is quite unlike any other poem. The incident from which it springs is surprising, and the movement of the poem from ebullience to melancholy and foreboding, though characteristic of Propertious, is apt to seem enigmatic

The poem opens on a note of high excitement. The poet has been witness to an intimate scene between Gallus and a girl he has just fallen in love with and cannot restrain himself from telling of the pleasures he derived from it and promises his assistance in the affair. The joy of the first moments that he experiences vicariously turns gradually to a bittersweetness as he thinks of developments to follow, and finally almost sour at the end, as the poem turns its focus from Gallus and his mistress to Cynthia and Propertius. (Richardson 1977: 173)

4.8
Johnson's (overly) "immersive" commentary, with additional comments by Miller (in brackets), adding just a hint of discursive scholarship.

[The poem is notable for the way in which Cynthia is presented in a clearly masculine role, while Propertius occupies the feminine position. It is Cynthia who journeys out into the world while Propertius stays home. Both lovers are equally faithless to each other, but only Propertius is chastised. It is Cynthia who uses violence and physical force to seek retribution for her betrayal, exercising a masculine prerogative. Lastly, although Propertius seeks to console himself with two high-priced professional women, he is unable to perform because of his preoccupation with Cynthia. He is thus *mollis* (soft), and emasculated.] After a brief, opaque statement in which he alludes to a squabble in a low dive, one which somehow involved him, even though he did not participate in it, he drops the story of the mysterious altercation and launches into what promises to be a properly Callimachean investigation into the nature and meaning of a venerable Latin religious ritual. . . . No matter. We quickly learn that mention of Lanuvium was . . . an introduction to a lengthy anecdote about Cynthia and the part she ended up playing in the tavern brawl with which the poem opens and which turns out to be almost the culmination of the story that is the real subject of 4.8. . . . [She's] on her way to Lanuvium . . . . furiously whipping the horse that draws her carriage, racing hell for leather along the Appian Way, while her companion (it is doubtless *his* carriage and it is he who should be grasping the reins) lolls back on his silken seat, fondling his pedigree dogs, a rich kid, smooth and gleaming from a recent wax job. [Depilated . . . hence both an effeminate and wealthy youth.] [Cynthia is presented as transgressing all boundaries of propriety . . . driving through areas of low repute, whose boundaries a respectable *matrona* would not cross . . . violating the laws of gender by driving when she has a male escort.] Cynthia's pretext for this journey (the excuse she offers Propertius for her absence) was her need to worship at Juno's shrine on this holy day . . . [Why] the young gentleman is accompanying her on this pilgrimage to Lanuvium is left in doubt. One gathers he is her newest boy toy, and more to the point, he is her new (surprisingly youthful) sugar daddy. Propertius jealously opines that, at the rate he is squandering his fortune, he'll end up eating filthy food at a school for gladiators as soon as he gets his full beard and needs to shave. So, Cynthia's motive for her visit to Lanuvium is probably not so much piety as business or lust or lust combined with business. Perhaps she wants to get Boy Toy in the sack as quickly as she can (before he changes his mind?). . . . Whatever her reasons, she has lied to the poet—worse, she has apparently jilted him (if only temporarily, but it has happened before, and doubtless will again).

The poet refuses to take this treachery lying down—or rather, he will take it lying down, in his own fashion. . . . He gets out the Roman equivalent of his little black book (which he has retained, for all his protestations of fidelity to Cynthia). There's a Phyllis, of course, whose stomping grounds are near Diana's temple on the Aventine [Note . . . the juxtaposition of presumed virginity (Diana) and promiscuous sexuality (Phyllis).] Sober, she's kind of a bore, but with a few drinks in her, a barrel of fun. And then there's Teia, who hangs out in the Tarpeian Groves [Tarpeia also combines ritual purity and promiscuous sexuality.]; very lovely, and in her cups, more than one guy can handle. . . . When the girls arrive and the poet is comfortably sandwiched between them, the party begins in earnest. Few passages in Latin poetry can match, in verve and charming details, its representation of pagan fun. Lygdamus . . . is mixing the excellent wine and decanting it into elegant wine cups [Using glassware, a luxury reserved for summer.]; an Egyptian piper and an Egyptian girl on the castanets provide the music; there are plentiful roses ready to have their petals strewn about the happy scene; and there is a dwarf, Magnus, dancing energetically to the Egyptian music.

In the midst of this infectious merriment occur three bad omens. The lamps, just lit and full of oil, begin to gutter, then the table collapses, and, as Propertius is trying his luck at dice (a lucky "Venus" throw would presage him a good time with his ladies), he tosses instead the dreaded "Dog-throw." [The best throw was Venus, with all four dice showing different numbers. The worst was the dog, with all four dice showing ones. There is a clear pun. Propertius has set up this party with Phyllis and Teia to seek Venus or sexual satisfaction, but he craps out.] [The party, in spite of Propertius' best preparations, was ill-omened from the start. The lamps would not stay lit and the table kept collapsing. This is a wonderful moment of comic bathos.] [The reason for the poet's poor showing in the games of love is made clear. His mind was on Cynthia in Lanuvium.]

[Suddenly] [t]here is a noise of the front door bursting open, there are dim voices in the hall. Then Cynthia smashes her way out into the garden ("her hair a mess but lovely in her fury"). [The poet's lips, normally violet with unmixed wine, turn pale with fear as the cup drops from his hand; a wonderful example of Propertius' visual imagination.] The poet, temporarily safe from her anger, vividly describes the epic disruptions of her whirlwind entrance . . . [a]t this point, wakened by the uproar, people rush out into the street with torches and the whole neighborhood trembles. The two whores flee to a nearby tavern with Cynthia in hot pursuit. She tears at their hair, rips off their clothes, then races back to the house of her cheating man, clutching her victorious trophies [and] . . . proceeds to slap the poet silly. . . . [Propertius' ready concession that he deserves this abuse can be read two ways. First, continuing the inversion of sexual roles, Propertius is in the position of the woman whose infidelities are punished, often violently, while Cynthia occupies the position of the Roman man who philanders with impunity. Second, bites and even slaps are often portrayed in elegy as a form of foreplay. Considering that the estranged lovers wind up in bed, Propertius may be hinting at his own pleasure.] Worn out by these exertions, she catches her breath and then turns her attention to poor Lygdamus whom she spots cowering behind the adulterous couch. He begs his master to intercede on his behalf, to no avail.

[F]inished with Lygdamus, she pauses before resuming her efforts to punish the guilty poet who takes advantage of this moment to beg for a truce. He kneels before her, his hands raised in supplication, but she will barely allow him to touch her feet, let alone her knees. Exhausted at last, or moved perhaps by what she takes to be his abject sincerity, Cynthia, as merciful a victor as one could hope to encounter, decides to forgive him—on conditions. She demands that he desist from the practice of cruising for new acquaintances at Pompey's portico [According to Ovid a prime spot for picking up young women.] or at gladiatorial shows [Crowded spaces offered opportunities for amorous liaisons.], to stop ogling ladies in the upper section of the Theatre [Augustus allowed women to sit only in the upper rows of the theatre.], or to catch their eye as they peer out at him from their litters. And, of course, she requires him to cast Lygdamus into chains and send him off forthwith to the auction block. These are the terms she lays down, and he submits instantly. Then, like the priestess of the Religion of Love that she is, she fumigates the temple, sprinkling pure water over every spot the vile whores had polluted with their filth and infections [Cynthia's ritual purification of Propertius' house recalls the rites at Lanuvium with which the poem began.]. She then commands that all the lanterns be refilled with new oil, and three times she anoints the poet's head with cleansing sulphur.

When all the sheets on the couch had been changed, I reaffirmed my agreement to her condition (with an erection), and we solemnized the treaty by screwing our way over every inch of the newly cleansed love-bed (literally, "we lay down our weapons all over the entire bed"). ["We laid aside arms," but, since *arma* is a common euphemism for penis, it also means "we released our lust."]

It is here, in what is arguably Propertius' masterpiece, that we catch our last glimpse of Cynthia. The speeding Amazon charioteer (and cheating beloved) who opens this poem fits neatly with the female Odysseus, ferocious instrument of justice, who all but closes it. This creature, recognizably the Cynthia we have met with throughout the poet's earlier volumes [is] here allowed to reveal herself in all her passion and glory. . . . [Becoming], consummately, uniquely herself. (Johnson 2009: 85-89) (Miller 2002: 35-40)

Ovid

Less so for Catullus but mostly so for Propertius, and playfully, obviously so for Ovid: "Like his predecessors' descriptions of their mistresses/books . . . Ovid's representation of elegiac women's beauty, sartorial preferences, and deportment exemplify the stylistic sophistication of his own elegiac verse, transformed through metaphor into the figure of the mistress." So argues Keith (below), offering the clearest articulation yet of one of the key themes we've been following in the commentary on these poems.

Ovid elaborates the settings and themes of Propertian and Tibullan elegy in his *Amores*, a second edition of which survives, perhaps published two decades after Ovid first began to compose poetry *c.* 25 BCE. In the extant collection, Ovid offers the fullest and most coherent narrative of a love affair in Roman elegy, concealing the identity of his mistress under the pseudonym Corinna—if indeed she existed at all. Already in the *Amores* he jokes of knowing someone who claims to be Corinna (*Am.* 2.17.29), and elsewhere he reports contemporary speculation denying her very existence (*Ars amatoria* 3.538); we may note in addition her absence from Apuleius' notice concerning the girlfriends celebrated in Latin amatory verse (*Apol.* 10). Rather the name Corinna advertises her literary provenance, for it alludes to a famous Greek poetess of that name and is a Latinized diminutive of the Greek word for "girl" (*korê*) as well as the metrical equivalent of the Latin synonym, *puella*, regularly used of the elegiac "girlfriend." Ovid describes her physical charms in conventional language (*Am.* 1.5) and characterizes her inconsistently, usually as a courtesan (e.g., through comparison to famous courtesans, *Am.* 1.5.9–12) with a "procuress" (*Am.* 1.8), but occasionally as a married woman (e.g., through references to a "husband," *maritus, Am.* 1.9.25; 2.2.51; 2.19.57; 3.4.27; 3.8.63; and to adultery, *Am.* 3.4). Scholarly consensus has therefore seen in Corinna a composite figure of the conventional elegiac mistress rather than a real historical woman.

The first book introduces the elegiac mistress Corinna along with the stock scenes (party, locked out lover's complaint, quarrel) and standard characters (*vir*, door-keeper, bawd, hairdresser, go-between) of an elegiac affair; the second complicates the affair with the introduction of rivals to both Corinna and the speaker, but also with the separation of speaker and mistress while on journeys and in ill health; and the third recounts the waning of the speaker's passion, graphically figured as impotence in 3.7, and his increasing distance from and disillusionment with his promiscuous mistress. Ovid's elegy embodies a carnal physicality alien to that of Tibullus and Propertius, starting with a sexual double-entendre in his description of the rhythm of the elegiac couplet in the very first poem (1.1.17–18) and continuing in poems detailing Corinna's naked charms (1.5); the speaker's susceptibility to a variety of women (2.4), including Corinna's hairdresser (2.8); his stamina in bed (2.10, 2.15); and his unexpected impotence (3.7). Like his predecessors' descriptions of their mistresses/books, however, Ovid's representation of elegiac women's beauty, sartorial preferences, and deportment exemplify the stylistic sophistication of his own elegiac verse, transformed through metaphor into the figure of the mistress. (Keith 2012: 297).

But there's also this.

More often than not, Ovid – whether that name refers to the lover inside the world of the poems or to the poet standing outside that world and making it – just seems to be having too much fun to count as obsessed and tormented. Still, even Ovid portrays himself at the opening of his elegiac collection as wounded by Love's arrow and bound by the god's cruel command to live only for love and write only elegy (*Amores* 1.1). (Wray 2012: 27)

Commentary

Amores 1.5
This is "making love" literally—almost. A near-cinematic sex scene, at any rate. First, a slow-paced panning around the location: the narrator lies alone in a room darkened against the heat of noon (the time of day, *mediam . . . horam*, is explicit in the Latin). A sudden change of focus: enter "Corinna", stunningly beautiful, flimsily dressed. Next, a fast-action sequence: he tears off her frock (though she puts up a token resistance), surveys the perfection of her naked body from shoulder to thigh, hungrily presses her to himself. Then . . . cut! Use your imagination *(cetera quis nescit?*, literally "Who does not know the rest?")! Finally, forward to a quick shot of the aftermath: sleep following their exertions. . . . Despite this visual technique, however, the poem's format is still first-person narrative, with all the action in the past tense (or historic present) except for the narrator's closing wish for more of the same (*proveniant medii sic mihi saepe dies!*, "May such noontimes often come my way!"). (Booth 2009: 65)

Another piece stands out for its greater sense of realism. He evokes the heat of midday and a room with the shutters half closed to create a twilight suitable for seduction. Corinna comes; the poet tears her clothes off, as she puts up some unconvincing resistance. She stands naked before him and he coolly assesses the parts of her body, from the shoulders downward. And then – 'Who does not know the rest?' Here the woman has again become what the earlier elegists had found that she was not, an object. But is this an elegantly amoral picture of chilly lust, or is the 'I' of the poem laughing at his pose of practiced amorist? It is hard to say. Ovid is not deep, but he is quite often a little more elusive than one expects. (Jenkyns 2016)

In 1.5, the praeceptor's instructions bear fruit as the affair is consummated in the famous siesta poem in which Corinna is finally named. Compare this delay to the opening line of Propertius's *Monobiblos, Cynthia prima fuit*. Ovid through this and other techniques consistently foregrounds the artificiality of his chosen genre. Nonetheless, this poem appeals because of its seeming realism and its expression of frank joy in an uncomplicated erotic encounter. Such poems are rarities among the elegists, who mostly bemoan their disappointments or rail against rivals. The simplicity of the scenario, however, should not deceive the reader. The encounter is highly staged, filled with knowing winks and rhetorical nods.

1-2. *Aestus erat, mediamque dies exegerat horam*: Ovid sets the scene. Making love during the day was considered a decadent pursuit by traditional Roman moralists such as Cato the elder, who expelled a senator for embracing his wife in daylight. [*mid-time of the day*: when the gods were apt to be abroad and the prudent stayed indoors. Corinna's coming is treated as a divine epiphany; compare Catullus on Lesbia: "My radiant goddess came to me there soft-footed " (68.70). (Melville 2008: 178)] *Membra leuanda:* the sense of "resting" or "lightening one's limbs" conceals a sexual *double entendre*, "raising one's member." Catullus' hendecasyllabic poem 32 on a proposed afternoon encounter with Ipsitilla, which is one of Ovid's models, makes the image more explicit.

3-6. The window is half open allowing a kind of twilight in the afternoon. *Quale fere siluae luman habere solent*: compare 1.4.9-10 and its recollection of the forest home of the centaurs. Poem 1.5 represents the fulfillment of the desires thwarted by the *uir* [husband] in 1.4.

7-8. The voice of the *praeceptor amoris* [the teacher of love] from 1.4 returns. *Verecundis* [shy] is not an adjective that would normally be associated with girls who would show up for such an encounter.

9-10. *Ecce, Corinna uenit*: the shift to the present sets Corinna immediately before us. [*In came Corinna: ecce, Corinna uenit*; the suddenness of her appearance (ecce='lo!') suggests something superhuman. This is the first mention of her name. (Melville 2008: 178)] *Recincta*="unbelted." Tunics were normally one-piece garments bound at the waist by a girdle. *Candida*: compare Catullus 68.70. *Diuidua colla tegente coma*: Roman women normally wore their hair tied up in a knot or bun. Corinna's letting her hair down in this manner invites intimacy in a way hard to square with the term *uerecunda*.

11-12. *Sameramis*=Semiramis, on whom see Propertius 3.11.21-22. *Lais*=a famous Corinthian courtesan. This reference may be seen as connoting the fact that Corinna was a *meretrix* [registered prostitute], but it may merely imply that her favors were widely bestowed. [*Semiramis*: a legendary queen of Assyria. (Melville 2008: 178)]

13-14. The rapid shift from the slow and almost reverent description of Corinna's entrance to the violence of *deripui tunicam* is typically Ovidian. *Rara*: refers to the loosely woven, transparent quality of the tunic. *Nec multum ... nocebat*: a difficult passage, presumably referring to the fact that Corinna's robe, given its transparent quality, did not much get in Ovid's way, but nonetheless (*sed tamen*) she fought (*pugnabat*) to cover herself with it.

15-16. Indications of amorous violence, as seen in the use of verbs like *deripio* and *pugeo*, are common in Ovid (*Amores* 1.7 makes the violence explicit). This couplet's implication that Corinna's refusal of Ovid's advances were (*pugnaret tamquam quae uincere nollet*) not serious, while perhaps mitigated by the context, reveal the clear imbalance of power that characterized Roman sexuality. It is not clear that

Corinna has the right of refusal once she entered the *amator's* house. Through Ovid's recognition of the reality of Roman sexual power relations, the pose of *seruitium amoris* [the slavery of love] is shown in this and other poems to be a fiction in the service of poetry and masculine sexual ideology. Only those who have power can play at not having it.

17-18.   Note the distanced tone.   Ovid initially approaches the naked Corinna with the detachment of an art critic.

21-22.   *Castigato*=compressed or not restrained, and hence not sagging. The hexameter indicates that Corinna bore none of the physical marks of childbirth.

23-24.   *Singula quid referam*: this formula cuts off the description at the moment when it would have crossed the boundary from the erotic to the pornographic.

25-26.   *Cetera quis nescit*: a knowing wink that says everything and nothing. *Lassi*: their passion spent. (Miller 2002: 253-55)

This is among the most charming and direct of Ovid's erotic poems: a visually precise miniature, divided, triptych-like, into three neat and expressive sections (lines 1–8; 9–16; 17–24). The eternal Mediterranean siesta is caught with swift, economic strokes. Political interests are wholly absent, and satirical ones nearly so; but Ovid cannot resist one allusive flick at Corinna. Having compared her to Semiramis, the mythical Queen of Nineveh, Ovid then abruptly adorns this tired cliché by bringing in Lais as a second parallel–Lais having been one of the most famous and highly paid whores of antiquity. This is a straightforward account of a successful act of love. Such a description is, surprisingly, unparalleled in previous Roman love-poetry, and appears to be Ovid's own creation.

3–6.   The windows are in fact wooden shutters, with transverse slats, of the sort that are still common throughout the Mediterranean, and have changed little since those depicted in Pompeian wall-paintings.   The light filters through the slats; one shutter has been left ajar to catch whatever afternoon breeze may be going.

7–8. This is the first point at which we get a hint that the scene involves something more than a solitary siesta. So far Ovid's camera-eye has simply panned inquisitively round a bedroom empty except for himself. Now he reflects that the setting would be ideal for the seduction of a shy girl.

9–10. Corinna's entry is abrupt, and she is very far–except in the most perfunctory sense–from being a 'modest girl'. It has been suggested, in line with the Corinna-as-fiction theory, that from here on is a dream, or fantasy: that Ovid is simply having an erotic siesta vision, solo.

A potentially more profitable line of approach might be to ask a few pertinent questions about the domestic arrangements which this pleasant seduction scene implies. Where is Ovid? Presumably in his own house, since he is scarcely likely to set up a siesta in his mistress's bedroom without her knowledge. Then where does Corinna appear from? Has she come through the streets alone? Socially improbable to a degree. With a maid, then? If so, where is the maid now? And what about the other occupants of the house? We may assume, if we like, that Ovid, as a habitual Casanova, had a discreet and well-trained hall-porter. But where, we wonder, is his wife? While it is true that, on his own account, Ovid began writing about Corinna in late adolescence (*Tr.* 4.10. 57–60), he also tells us that he was married while still a mere boy (ibid., 69–70), twice in succession. Unless he maintained a discreet *pied-a-terre* (e.g., a friend's house, like Catullus)–this cannot be ruled out, but is unlikely–or alternatively, a theory that will always have takers, made up the whole relationship and incident from a mind well-stocked with Hellenistic poetic cliché, we have to ask ourselves how it came about that Ovid and his *inamorata*, not only here but on various other occasions, had such mysteriously easy access to each other. In this context the theory that the secret of Corinna's identity lay in her being, not Ovid's mistress, but his *first wife*, clearly has a good deal to recommend it. (Green 1982: 272-273)

The leisurely description of Corinna's figure in *Amores* 1.5 is one of the fullest portraits of a mistress in Latin elegy (*Am.* 1.5.17–22). . . . Ovid here employs the diction of Latin literary criticism to characterize Corinna's body and, implicitly, his own amatory verse, thereby conflating the physique of his elegiac girlfriend with the poetics espoused in his elegiac collection. Corinna's bodily perfection thus corresponds to the stylistic refinement privileged throughout the *Amores*. The poet-lover even implies that her poetic existence is more concrete than her physical existence, for he not only relishes the confusion about the identity of the real Corinna (*Am.*2.17.29–30; *Ars* 3.538) but he even promotes it (*Tr.* 2.339–340; 4.10.65–68). Indeed, Ovid playfully draws attention to her status as a literary construction: she is the inspiration for his poetry but also its sole subject (*Am.* 1.3.19–20; 2.17.33–34; 3.12.16; cf. *Tr.* 4.10.59–60), since she postures as an elegiac poet but is also the resulting written text (*Am.* 2.19.9–13; 2.17.10). Ovid thus insists that we recognize and appreciate the specifically literary qualities of the elegiac mistress: Corinna's style derives quite precisely from the literary conventions of elegiac verse. (Keith 2012: 297-98)

Amores 2.7 and 2.8

Poems 2.7 and 2.8 are a famous pair depicting the *amator's* dalliance with Corinna's maid, Cypassis. Both are of the same length. In the first, the poet strongly denies the accusation and bemoans the fact that Corinna is always casting unjust charges against him. In the second, the poet not only reverses the situation he also threatens to blackmail Cypassis by revealing the whole affair to Corinna if she does not continue to submit to his advances. . . . In this companion piece to 2.7 [that is, 2.8], the *amator's* cynical threat to expose his sexual relationship with Cypassis to her mistress as a means of insuring her continued compliance paints with brutal realism the image of a true *seruitium amoris* [the slavery of love]. The poem begins with an ingratiating attempt at flattery. This was a tactic borrowed from the rhetorical schools known as the *captatio beneuolentiae* [the "hunt for goodwill"]. The tone, however, soon changes. (Miller 2002: 258-60)

2.7 is actually a speech of self-defense, using legal language, in which his experience as one of the minor judges in civil cases has made Ovid expert . . . As McKeown notes, 2.7 plausibly rejects Corinna's accusations, though the opening, 'Am I always to be subjected to new charges', followed by 'I am weary of arguing the case so often', raises suspicion that Corinna has more cause for jealousy than lines 3-10 admit. The next section obliquely protests his innocence—if only I were guilty!—and first applies an argument from his own social pretentions: 'would I choose a low class girlfriend, or would any free man indulge in a love-union [*Veneris conubia*] with a slave scarred by lashings'; next an argument from Cypassis' loyalty to her mistress: if I had propositioned her she would have informed on me to you (*indicio*). He ends his defense with an oath by Venus and Cupid that he has been charged with a crime he did not commit . . . In 2.8 . . . the truth is unexpectedly revealed, as Ovid switches from insulting Cypassis to flattery . . . from moral indignation to aggressive intimidation of his slave partner. Now he is addressing Cypassis, whom he has found a sophisticated partner suited to his taste. [H]e calls up Homeric precedents . . . who loved captive women . . . [h]e boasts of the oath we heard him utter and Venus' tolerance of perjury . . . treating his own lies as a service he has performed for Cypassis, for which she now owes him sexual favors . . . [warning that] if she does not oblige, he will turn informer himself and report to her mistress where, how often, and in how many different positions the two of them had coupled. . . . If we thought that 2.7 aimed to persuade, the companion poem clearly overthrows the pretense; its appeal is the sheer impudence of this retooling and dismantling of any pretext of *fides,* whether 'truthfulness' or 'fidelity'. (Fantham 2009: 31-32)

Amores 3.11A and 3.11B

Though 3.11 appears in our MSS as one undivided poem, the sharp change of tone and attitude after line 32 has led many editors to print it in separate parts.

Rather more misleading as regards Ovid's fundamental attitude to his chosen theme is the vigorous (and oddly naive) debate between those who take the poem seriously, and those who treat it as a flippant literary *jeu d'esprit*–a debate which in some quarters extends to the *Amores* as a whole. This simplistic division badly underestimates Ovid's complex irony, his wryly amused self-knowledge, his abundant gift for emotional oxymoron. In particular, the argument that his emotions cannot be taken seriously here because of all those literary borrowings and allusions is a complete non-sequitur: to appreciate its shortcomings we need do no more than apply it to *The Waste Land*, Pound's *Cantos* or David Jones's *The Anathemata*. Joking about serious emotions is an unromantic habit; but then Ovid was not, in the modern sense, a romantic poet.

3.11A

1–4. The opening words echo *Am.* 2.19.49 (where Ovid is complaining, ironically enough, about an over-complaisant husband) and also Prop. 2.8.13–14. The image of a slave losing his chains and achieving emancipation (reinforced by lines 10–12, which emphasize the distinction between servile and freeborn actions) evokes, vividly, the conventional (but here all too real) *servitium amoris* [the slavery of love].

5–6. For horns as a symbol of strength see Ovid *AA* 1.239; to the best of my knowledge the phrase never in antiquity carried the implication of cuckoldry which it did, say, in Elizabethan times.

9–14. This stock description of the *exclusus amator*, the lover-shut-out gains added force from the image of the lover's successor, stumbling away exhausted–before his ousted rival's eyes–after a hard night's work.

15–16. There is an ironic echo here of an earlier passage by Ovid himself (*Am.* 2.10.15), where the fate he wishes for his enemies is to toss in an empty bed, without company.

17–18. There is an ambiguity here hard to reproduce in English. Two of the roles Ovid claims to have fulfilled are those of *custos* (guardian, as in the case of porter or eunuch, as well as escort) and *vir* (husband as well as lover). This ambiguity extends to lines 25–6, where it is by no means clear whose house Ovid is hurrying back to (*'veni'*)–his mistress's or his own.

23–4. The joke here, of course, is that Ovid's advice to his mistress (*Am.* 1.4.17–20) has been taken, learnt, and turned neatly against him.

29–30. For the garlanding of a vessel that had reached port safely see, e.g., Virgil *Georg.* 1.303–4; Ovid (cf. *RA* 811–12) uses this image to describe escape from sexual involvement. Ovid, furthermore, contrasts the state of his vessel (*lenta*= 'indifferent', often with a sexual connotation) with the 'swelling' (*tumescentes*) waters outside: the symbolism could hardly be more obvious.

3.11B

1–2. The second line is heavy with literary allusion, recalling not only Catullus' *Odi et amo*, but also a well-known line of Virgil's (embodying a motto that Chaucer put on the Prioress's brooch): *Omnia vincit amor, nos et cedamus amort* (*Eel.* 10.69): 'Love conquers all: let us too yield to love.'

7. Another famous line, imitated by Martial (12.47, a near-direct quotation), who also picks up line 9 in an earlier epigram (8.53.3–4).

13–16. The touchstone here is Tibullus (1.5.7–8); cf. also *Am.* 3.3.11–12.

19–20. In deliberate contrast to 11A 29–30, where Ovid's 'vessel' is safe from the storm raging outside the harbor, these lines show it running before the wind out at sea. (Green 1982: 328-30)

A . . . renunciation topic in *Am.* 3.11 metes out similar treatment to Catullus, agonizing over Lesbia. Announcing his decision to break with an unnamed woman, the Ovidian lover tells himself, 'Go through with it, and stand firm', clearly echoing Catullus 8.11: 'with mind made up, stand firm'. But the context of facetious self-review in which Ovid's near-quotation is embedded arguably undermines its original Catullan earnestness. Here too an immediate sequel . . . presents sudden second thoughts. These take the form of a pretended conflict in the lover's mind between love and hate, but actually the final decision in favor of love is from the start never in doubt, and the passage's bravura display of scintillating wit is at odds with any real pain. (Booth 2009: 68)

Amores 3.8

In Rome there was always an articulate upper (or, later, upper-middle) class eager to proclaim that those further down the social ladder were getting positions and privileges to which their rank–talent being irrelevant–did not entitle them. Senators grumbled about equestrians, old middle-class families poured scorn on *novi homines*, local squires grew apoplectic over jumped-up foreigners. They were money-grubbers (i.e. financially shrewder than those who denigrated them), they were vulgar, they had no proper sense of precedence. In the last resort, such critics would invoke the *Saturnia regna*, the lost Golden Age–pre-agricultural, pre-capitalist, an idyllic top people's fantasy of rural peace and plenty, analogous to the 'ancestral constitution' so popular as a rallying-cry among Athenian ultra-conservatives in the late fifth century BC.

In 3.8 Ovid reveals most of these traits, modified or partially camouflaged to suit his own special circumstances. To begin with, the scale of values he evokes is aesthetic rather than class-based: poetic genius should be (but is not) valued above a high credit rating. The argument is very much *ad hominem*, or, in this case, *ad feminam*, and recalls that of *Am*. 1.10: Ovid's mistress has ditched him for a wealthier man. But he is not only richer, he is a *parvenu*, Ovid, we know, took a conscious pride in his long equestrian pedigree (cf. *Am*. 3.15.5–6, *Trist*. 4.10.7–8), and contrasted it, specifically, with the pretentions of those *equites* whose status had been earned, all too recently, through military service–i.e. who had fought on the right side in the Civil Wars, and earned rich rewards as a result. These men provided the Augustan regime's most solid support and regularly used their army career as a means of entering the equestrian order. Equally, many merchants and traders (often freedmen) who had bought up the lands of the proscribed had no trouble in proving their assets at the figure (400,000 sesterces) required for civilian admission to the ranks of the *equites.*

So Ovid's objections to his successful rival are not only moral-aesthetic and dictated by sexual jealousy, but also based on the crudest sort of class-snobbery. In addition, we have a restatement of the poet's contemptuous revulsion at the whole notion of fighting and militarism together with a bitter reproach for the girls who–whether through avarice or sexual inclination–found soldiers attractive as lovers. Whether it was a covert sense of personal inadequacy that drove him to compensate by describing sexual conquest as *militia* we cannot tell. The argument here leans heavily on the charge of feminine gold-digging. The girl who can bring herself to touch a soldier does so because she is *avara,* rapacious (line 22): the myth of Jupiter (Zeus) and Danaë is couched in terms which reinforce such a hypothesis. The value of Saturn's reign (35–8) was, in the first instance, that precious metals, and thus *a fortiori* coinage and capitalism, remained unknown: beyond this, Ovid does no more than pay traditional lip-service to a kind of dim Mesolithic paradise, the nomadic hunter's world, minus all the back-breaking business associated with farming.

This line of thought leads him into somewhat dangerous political speculation. Having poured scorn on the class which constituted the backbone of the Augustan regime, having reiterated his contempt for military virtues as such, Ovid goes on (45–56) to equate the whole process of imperial expansion with greedy financial opportunism (a judgement with which not a few modern historians would concur); to label the Senate, the judiciary and the equestrian order as mere vulgar plutocracies; and to include in this programme of grab-as-grab-can the Caesarian deification principle–overseas acquisitions matched by a take-over bid in heaven. Having delivered himself of his scathing indictment, the poet proceeds

(57–66) to wash his hands of public life altogether. This, at least, was no empty rhetorical gesture, but a bold reminder of Ovid's earlier withdrawal from the *cursus honorum*. He had had the offer to a high official career under the regime, and had deliberately rejected it. To abstain from politics itself constitutes a political gesture, and Ovid's contempt for the aims, ideals, propaganda and supporters of Augustanism is only too apparent in his work. How seriously, in the last resort, could anyone who believed in poetic divinity take the idea of a deified emperor?

Yet the instinctive repulsion is also, inevitably, laced with envy. Ovid might reject contemporary Roman politics, and withhold himself, in fastidious disdain, from the military-imperial-financial ideal of expansion, conquest and provincial administration; but again and again he reveals his covert envy of the prerogatives (social, sexual or political) enjoyed by highly placed civil or military employees of the regime. From this viewpoint the impotence, whether physical or symbolic, which we find in some poems of Bk 3 is no accident: it extends through every aspect of life in Rome, from politics to love-making. Indeed, as 3.8 makes very clear, the categories tended to overlap. Ovid's physical impotence had its antecedents in the collapse of the Republic. By leaving him for a *nouveau-riche* military *eques* his mistress was simply acknowledging–and endorsing–the values of the new world in which she lived: she went with the fashion, while Ovid obstinately stood out against it. The bitterness which this poem reveals is rooted in something more subtle than simple jealousy.

1–4. The complaint that girls value cash above poetry is a regular one of Ovid's (cf. e.g. *AA* 2.273–6); it can also be found in Propertius and Tibullus. While a certain contempt for cash values does seem to characterize the landed-aristocratic phase of many societies (cf. the early medieval attitude to money-making and usury), there is little evidence to support Ovid's wishful thinking when he writes: 'Time was when poetic talent/Came dearer than gold'. Homer, surely, could have enlightened him on this topic.

29–34. For the legend of Danaë, impregnated by Zeus in the form of a shower of gold.

51–2. The temple of Romulus on the Quirinal dated back as far as 435 BC (Livy 4.21): it was burnt down in 49 BC, and its rebuilding completed by Augustus some thirty-three years later. (This latter date, 16 BC, is probably alluded to by Ovid, and would thus provide some slight corroboration for the publication of *Amores* at a subsequent point. Martial (1.71.9) refers to a temple of Bacchus on the Palatine. There were several temples to Hercules within Rome's city-limits, one of them at the Colline Gate, another near the Circus Flaminius. The temple of (Julius) Caesar referred to was the *aedes divi Iuh* adjacent to the Forum, dedicated, again, by Augustus.

55–6. Minimum qualifications of capital were laid down for both senators (800,000 sesterces, later raised to a million) and *equites* (400,000 sesterces). These figures were habitually far exceeded, and even a man such as the Younger Pliny–who was very far from the top of the pile, either socially or financially–astonishes us by the scale of his wealth and munificence. (Green 1982: 321-24)

Drawing a Few Conclusions

So what can we conclude from all this? After all, in the end aren't these *just* poems?

[In Propertius'] poem 4.8, the first-person narrator recalls the night when Cynthia caught him in the company of other women. The narrative of that night is . . . littered with apparently authenticating details such as the setting on the Esquiline, local girls, a dwarf, dice, a slave cowering behind a couch, and orders not to stroll in Pompey's portico. Yet Cynthia's sudden return finds her playing the role of an Odysseus to her poet's aberrant Penelope. Echoes of *Odyssey* 22 dissolve the poetic edifice of a real Roman event. (Wyck 2002: 26-7)

And even more forcefully.

I have argued, however, that even the realist devices of Propertian elegy can disclose the unreality of elegiac mistresses. Cynthia too is a poetic fiction: a woman in a text, whose physique, temperament, name, and status are all subject to the idiom of that text. So, as part of a poetic language of love, Cynthia should not be related to the love life of her poet but to the 'grammar' of his poetry.

The Propertian elegiac narrative does not, then, celebrate a Hostia [the alleged "real" woman behind the poet's Cynthia], but creates a fictive female whose minimally defined status as mistress, physical characteristics, and name are all determined by the grammar of the erotic discourse in which she appears. The employment of terms like 'pseudonym' in modern critical discourse overlooks the positive act of creation involved in the depiction of elegy's mistresses. Therefore, when reading Augustan elegy, it seems most appropriate to talk not of pseudonyms and poeticized girlfriends but of poetic or elegiac women. (Wyck 2002: 31)

Then the poet, his *domina*, these events—none of this is real? Well, maybe it's art (what the poet does), drawing upon the real, or at least the real as we might imagine it, in which case the question of *real* doesn't enter into it. I would, however, still be willing to argue that Catullus' Lesbia hews closer to autobiographical, that's even as I acknowledge the truth of Wyck's point about the largely fictive nature of Cynthia and Corinna; the difference, perhaps, between what later became a poetic genre (the elegist's *domina,* the *slavery of love*) and Catullus' earlier, and startling, originality. Elegiac women, the poet's personae, the question of what, if any, of this is real, all are questions we'll see again.

For more on the literary and social context of erotic elegy see Appendix Two. (Was it really subversive? Oppositional? No, the Romans had a problem with love, not sex. Yes, but what sort of love? Women in love elegy and Roman society: a less sanguine view. Just who were these young elegists? They'd lost the world and the world had lost them. More apologetic about their way of life than the kind of poetry they wrote.)

For now, here's Jenkyns' nice summation (*anguish was over*).

Before Catullus, the little love poetry that existed in Latin paraphrased or imitated Greek epigram. He began something dramatically new, and he drew the next generations after him: for half a century and more Latin poetry was to be saturated in the theme of love. It dominated the verse of Catullus, Gallus, Tibullus, Propertius and much of Ovid. It is a large part of Horace's *Songs*. Virgil explored it in the *Bucolics*; Propertius was right to hail him as one of the love poets. And Virgil ended the *Georgics*, a didactic poem, with something fairly rare in literature at any time, a story of passion burning within marriage, and indeed beyond death. His *Aeneid* put Dido's tragedy at its heart and celebrated the faithful love of the Trojan warriors Nisus and Euryalus. And then abruptly the theme vanished from Latin verse, as suddenly as it had appeared. It is natural to ask why.

As with Greek love poetry, it was crucial that the beloved could say no. In theory a Roman woman was entirely in the power of the head of her family; but whatever the law said, in the early first century there emerged an aristocratic milieu within which women could in effect do as they liked. Catullus' Lesbia was such a person. We have good evidence that she was a sister of Cicero's enemy Clodius – the very Clodia whom he attacked in his speech *For Caelius*, or possibly one of her sisters. It really does seem to be true: a young provincial aristocrat came to Rome, fell in love with the wrong woman, was driven to put his passion into verse, and changed the literature of Europe. Gallus' beloved was different: a glamorous Greek courtesan, whose favors Mark Antony enjoyed, and who impressed even Cicero by the charm of her company. The women in the later elegists –

Tibullus, Propertius and Ovid – are different again: typically they are educated, of good family, but ambiguous in status; they may be in need of a protector but they can choose among the suitors for that role. They are likely to reflect the consequences of years of civil war, when prosperous families were ruined and women lost their menfolk. Many of these will have drifted to Rome and entered that demi-monde which the elegists evoke. As the civil wars receded into the past, that world will have diminished, and with it the material that it provided for verse.

So there were social reasons for the rise and fall of Latin love poetry, but there were literary reasons too. Like Lucretius, Catullus discovered a wide new realm of possibility that the Greeks had not colonized. There had been nothing like Roman love elegy in Hellenistic literature. Of course poets had written in personal terms about their loves before – Sappho alone shows that – but new was the representation of one obsessing passion, of a sense of hidden narrative, its different moods, the ups and downs in a developing story, found not in one poem alone but fragmentarily in many. The elegists found variations on the theme, some indeed borrowed from epigram or comedy: the rival lover, the pimp, the lament outside the beloved's closed door, quarrel and reconciliation, love as warfare, and as slavery. As we find these topics turning up in one poet and then another, we come to realize that they are not limitless. In the end the material was used up, and once Ovid had made fun of it, anguish was over. (Jenkyns 2016)

But I've neglected the more *literary* issues; here's Miller's equally useful accounting.

The story, as it was once told in undergraduate classrooms, goes something like this. The Romans were a dour lot, interested only in money, war, politics and low entertainments. After the Punic Wars and the conquest of Greece, wealth, purveyors of Greek culture and sophisticated courtesans flowed into the capital. To match the tastes of their newly sophisticated men, Roman women, with time and money on their hands, began to play the part of courtesans themselves. The record of this change and the corresponding corruption of Roman values can be found not only in the fulminations of Cicero and Sallust but also in the love elegists of the first century BC: Catullus, Gallus, Tibullus, Propertius, Ovid, as well as the lone woman, Sulpicia. In their texts, we read stories of sophisticated *puellae* (literally 'girls') and the poets who pursued them. And while certain allowances must be made for poetic exaggeration and convention, the record that these poems provide tells us stories of passion, pursuit, and poetic perfection worthy of *La Bohème*. Such is the story as it was once told and often still is.

Nonetheless, by the 1980s, a reaction to this narrative had set in. While critics like Lyne still chose to speak of Catullus' and the elegists' desire for 'whole love' (1980), a new wave of criticism embodied in the work of scholars like Wyke (1989) and Veyne (1988) argued that the *puellae* were not real women in literary guise, but textual constructs. True, scholars had argued before against taking the poems as biographical evidence. However, the argument was largely aesthetic and formalist: appreciate the way a poem worked, not whether the poet was sincere or the beloved real. By contrast, Wyke and Veyne argued for the importance of the *puella's* fundamental textuality. While Veyne argued that all the beloveds were ironic fictions (Catullus' Lesbia excepted), Wyke's more nuanced view allowed for the historical determination of the elegiac beloved by other images of women circulating within contemporary culture, while leaving the *puella* herself oddly underdetermined.

For us, however, it is not a question of which of these perspectives is correct. On the one hand, the *puellae* are beyond doubt textual. They are the pretexts around which are constructed elaborate poetic collections. These women, at least as we know them, do not exist outside this written world. They are the organizing elements around which the basic scenario of elegiac love is constructed – the genre does not exist without them. But the texts and languages out of which they are made are not mere abstract systems. They are deeply embedded tools that exist only in so far as they are intelligible, useful and/or enjoyable by the inhabitants of their world. While the first explanation of how Romans came to create this poetry may be overly simplistic, we know from Sallust and others that the Romans did in fact believe their mores had changed, and that these changes were associated with what could be seen as an increasing liberation of the behaviour of Roman women from the constraints of tradition. We also know that Augustus in his attempt at reform clearly believed that there had been a decline in the standards of moral behaviour, or at least that it was useful to portray himself as believing such. Moreover, he saw that the link between elegiac love poetry and moral decline as sufficiently credible that he could list the *Ars Amatoria* as one reason for Ovid's exile without appearing ridiculous. The *puellae* may be textual, but they have oddly real effects.

What we see, then, as we examine the issue is that the choice between fiction and reality, textuality and history, or language and referent in regard to the elegiac *puella* is false. These women only exist to the extent that they function within the textual system known as Latin erotic elegy, and that system only existed because it was intelligible to and usable by the inhabitants of Rome during this period. The question is not, who were the *puellae*, but how do they function and what do they stand for? That is to say, what sets of values do they substitute for in the textual economies constructed by the poetic collections in which they figure? (Miller 2013: 166-67)

Again, for more see Appendix Two.

3

....

ALEXANDRIANS

Callimachus – subtle, learned, complex, influential. In some respects the most interesting of the poets. Of special interest to me not only for his profound influence on the Latin poets, but for his call for a new, *slender* poetics.

From Miller's *Latin Erotic Elegy:*

> [Callimachus was] by far the most important influence on Latin elegy . . . Catullus, Propertius, and Ovid list him as among their chief influences, and Tibullus, who refrains from making overt theoretical statements, alludes to him on several occasions. A brief introduction cannot do justice to his importance. The best that can be hoped for is to give a general idea of this complex and elusive poet, who was a scholar and librarian at the Museum in Alexandria. His poetry is characterized by learning, wit, and studied indirection. Unfortunately, most of his work survives only in fragments.
>
> One of the longest extant examples of his verse is a translation by Catullus of a poem called the "Lock of Berenice." A short except gives a sense of its flavor. It tells how a tress cut from the hair of Queen Berenice of Egypt was miraculously transformed into a new constellation discovered by the royal astronomer to the court at Alexandria, Conon. Berenice sheared the lock as an offering for the safe return of her husband and brother, Ptolemy III, from a campaign in Syria on which he had left immediately after their marriage.

> That same Conon saw me shining clearly on the threshold
> of the sky, a flowing lock from the top of Berenice's head,
> which she stretching forth her slight arms had promised to

many of the goddesses, in that season when it has pleased
the king, blessed with a new marriage, carrying with him
the sweet traces of their nocturnal struggle, when he had
borne off the young girl's spoils, to lay waste to the
Assyrians. (Catullus 66.7-14)

The precious imagery, the coy psychology of the pampered
tress, the witty compliments to the royal couple, and the
complex sentence structure are typically Callimachean. We
are a long way from Homer, archaic Greek elegy, or a typical
Roman panegyric of a triumphant general. In this passage, we
see the thematic and stylistic *mollitia* that the Latin elegists so
admired in the Alexandrian poet. At the same time, the
conflation of the amorous with the soldierly in the evocation
of the king and queen's nocturnal struggle would become one
of the signature motifs of Roman erotic elegy, the *militia*
amoris or "soldiering of love."

For all the convergences between the styles of Callimachus
and those of his later elegiac followers, there are certain clear
differences as well. Callimachus' poem does not adopt the
autobiographical pose that distinguishes the Latin elegists nor,
despite its clear interest in the erotic, does it form part of a
larger narrative of an amorous affair. The "Lock of Berenice"
is from Callimachus' most famous collection of poems, the
Aetia or *Causes*. This four-volume anthology of learned
elegies recounts stories that purport to give the origins or
causes of a variety of cultural, religious, and natural
phenomena. The "Lock of Berenice," therefore, offers an
explanation, however facetious it may be, of the origin of the
new constellation discovered by Conon.

These poems are anything but dry and scholarly, however
recondite their subject matter or abstruse their approach.
They are clever constructions of a court poet who appears in
his poems as an opinionated narrator and polemical poetic
theorist. Thus the *Aetia* (*Causes*) opens with a prologue in
which the poet defends himself against the charge that he is
incapable of producing a single continuous narrative of epic
proportions. His witty response is that Apollo had told him

to make his sacrifices fat, but to keep his muse slender. This notion of the slender style, as opposed to the fat bombast of epic, became one of the most important ways Roman elegy defined itself in contrast to epic. Thus in 2.1, for example, Propertius speaks of his inability to write heroic verse in his narrow bed, a metaphor that cleverly identifies lovemaking with the production of verse in the Callimachean style. Likewise, at the end of Callimachus' "Hymn to Apollo," the poet concludes not with the god's praises but with a swipe at his critics:

> And Envy whispered in Apollo's ear:
> "I am charmed by the poet who swells like the sea."
> But Apollo put foot to Envy and said:
> "The River Euphrates has a powerful current
> but the water is muddy and filled with refuse.
> The cult of Bees brings water to Deo
> but their slender libations are unsullied and pure,
> the trickling dew from a holy spring's height."
> [105-114] (Lombardo and Raynor 1998: 10)

The contrast between the slender purity of the Callimachean style and the swollen flotsam of epic bombast could not be better expressed. More importantly, however, what is clear from both this passage and the prologue to the *Aetia* is that we have in Callimachus not an unobtrusive or self-effacing narrative voice, but the very clear assertion of a singular point of view. . . . This does not however mean that anyone would confuse the stance of the Callimachean narrator with the Latin poet's pretense to write confessional verse.

In the end, Hellenistic models for elegy, while important, are all partial at best. Where Antimachus's *Lyde* possessed an erotic subjective frame for a series of narrative elegies, and Callimachus had presented an interventionist and opinionated narrator for the mythological tales told in the *Aetia*, no precedent for Catullus 68's combination of "autobiographical" narrative and mythological exempla, nor for Catullus 76's agonized internal dialogue can be found in Hellenistic poetry. Likewise, the Latin elegiac poet's complete subjection (*seruitium amoris*) [the slavery of love] to a single mistress (*domina, era*) is unprecedented in ancient Greek poetry of any era. Indeed, as I have argued before, Catullus represents the beginning of that uniquely interiorized voice that is commonly termed lyric poetry in the modern sense of the term and of which Latin erotic elegy is a subgenre. What Hellenistic literature offered at the end of the first century BCE was not a model to be slavishly copied by the erotic elegists, but an alternative value system to the Roman republic's traditional emphasis on *domus, dignitas*, and *gloria*, the *mos maiorum*. The Callimachean dedication to poetic excellence and the rejection of the common path were rhetorical tools the elegists deployed in their rejection of the traditional life of duty. Catullus and the elegists would exploit this resource, but from the unique perspective offered by a Roman cultural and political system that was at this time in the process of restructuring. Indeed, one of the great ironies of the relationship between Hellenistic poetics and the development of Roman erotic elegy is that the rhetoric of Alexandrian absolutism, which aided the elegists in their resistance to traditional republican ideology, may also have unwittingly prepared them for the emergence of Rome's own monarchy, the Augustan principate. (Miller 2002: 12-15)

On Callimachus' Influence on Ovid

Ovid was the latest and the most prolific in the cohort of Augustan poets: his *Amores* did not appear until the 20s, his *Metamorphoses* and *Fasti* sometime before AD 8, and the exile poems, *Tristia, Ex Ponto*, and *Ibis* between AD 8 and 18. His surviving poetry is written in elegiacs or hexameters; he experiments with a variety of genres; and his engagement with Callimachus is much more extensive than any of his Roman predecessors. Callimachus pre-figures Ovid both metrically and thematically in the varied scope of his poetry, which included hymns, epigrams, the *Aetia*, occasional court pieces, invective (the *Iambi* and *Ibis*), and the long hexameter poem, the *Hecale*. There was a lot of Callimachus, and Ovid matches or extends him in literary output, although not in metrical variety. Callimachus' appeal for Ovid included but extended beyond the narrow range of features adopted by Catullus and the elegists—the personal voice, poetic initiation, erotic themes, and the idea of a poetic "tradition" reformulated for one's own time and place. Callimachus provided at least three narrative strategies that Ovid's Roman precursors did not. One is a temporal scope from the distant past to contemporary events (even the *Aeneid*, as one expects with epic, ended well before Augustus). The second is the interweaving of a series of seemingly unrelated stories in multiple voices into one poetic fabric. The third is the reorganization of knowledge (whether poetic, religious, mythological, or philosophical) into an "ancestry" for a new royal house. And, ironically, Callimachus provided the only model outside of epic for the writing of long narrative poems.

It is obvious already in Propertius that the elegiac *recusatio* had become more than a bit shopworn. R. Tarrant points out that, when Ovid came to write his own version of the "Callimachean primal scene" at *Amores* 1.1, he felt no need to claim that he was incapable of writing epic. No doubt this in part reflects Ovid's own assessment of his talents. Yet he is the first (as far as we can judge) in Roman poetry to be faithful to Callimachus in his relationship with epic. Callimachus may have elected to write in a "slender" style, but as a matter of aesthetic preference (not generic hostility) and not because of a professed inability to write long poems. Equally, Ovid may have judged that the love elegy had become somewhat limited as a vehicle for poetic immortality, and throughout his subsequent career he opens up elegiac themes and meter to experiment with different genres and topics. (Acosta-Hughes 2012: 257-259)

A Few Brief Notes on Callimachus' Prologue to the *Aetia*

Books 1 and 2 of the *Aetia* are introduced by a Prologue in which the poet both answers his critics (the 'Telchines', as he calls them) and sets the stage for what follows.

Interpretation of the Prologue is riddled with difficulties. Not only has the text itself suffered severe damage, making it impossible to be certain what Callimachus wrote throughout, but even where we can tell what he wrote we often have a hard time deciding what he was referring to. (Nisetich 2001: 61-2)

[7] *for little stretches*: first of several expressions in the Prologue of a preference for the small and delicate in poetry.

[11] Philitas, born *c.* 340 BC on the island of Cos, became tutor of Ptolemy II Philadelphos, who was also born on Cos. Strabo described him as 'a poet and a critic'. He wrote, in addition to poetry, a treatise entitled *Miscellaneous Glosses* (rare words). His preference for 'leanness' in poetry was transferred later to his person, with the result that he was thought to have been so slight he had to wear lead in his boots to avoid being blown away by the wind.

[13] *Demeter*: Callimachus does not actually call her by name, using the epithet 'Thesmophoros' instead, in an apparent allusion to the famous *Demeter* of Philitas, a poem of elegiac couplets that described the wanderings of the goddess in search of her daughter Persephone.

[16] *Mimnermus*: of Smyrna, lived in the seventh century BC. He wrote elegiac poetry, apparently of two kinds . . . [one] light and discontinuous, the second a continuous narrative dealing with serious subjects. [Of the second type, the] *Song of Smyrna* may have included the foundation of the city by the Amazon of the same name; if it did, she could be the 'big woman' to whom Callimachus alludes.

[19-20] *the crane . . . Pygmies*: Homer compares the oncoming Trojan army to a flock of cranes flying off to battle with the Pygmies (*Iliad* 3.3-7).

[21-2] *the Massagetai . . . the Mede*: the Massagetai lived east of the Caspian Sea. Cyrus the Great ('the Mede') died trying to subdue them. According to Herodotus the battle began with both sides discharging arrows 'at a distance'.

[22] *nightingales*: poems.

[24] *Jealousy*: the Greek word here (*Baskanië*) has several meanings, all of them applicable to the Telchines: 'sorcery or witchcraft', 'malignity', 'jealousy'.

[30-1] *my own | Lykian Apollo*: the adjective 'Lykian' perhaps reinforces the feeling of intimacy between Callimachus and Apollo: Apollo was thought to have transformed himself into a wolf (*lykos*) when he mated with the nymph Cyrene, who gave her name to Callimachus' birthplace.

[37] *the shrill cicada's cry*: the cicada had a long history of association with poetry, beginning with Homer who compared the voices of the old men at Troy to that of the cicadas (*Iliad* 3.146-53). According to Plato (*Phaedrus* 259), some members of the first generation of men to experience the gift of the Muses were so enchanted by it that they went on singing for ever, forgetting to eat or drink and dying without noticing it. From them arose 'the race of cicadas', who, like their ancestors, do not eat or drink but only sing. After they die, their souls return to the Muses and report to them on how they are honored among mortals.

[42-6] *to sing | with dew upon my lips*: Callimachus continues with his emulation of the cicada: it was thought to feed only on dew and to shed old age when discarding its husk.

[44-5] *shedding | the years*: the wish to be free of old age is granted, at least momentarily.

[46] *Enkelados*: one of the giants who warred against the gods. Zeus smote him with a thunderbolt and buried him under Sicily. (Nisetich 2001: 231-34)

Annette Harder's Notes on the *Aetia's* Prologue

Fr. 1, generally considered to be the prologue to the *Aetia*, contains a spirited defense against literary opponents. Although the passage does not read as a complete and systematic literary program it gives a good impression of the literary issues that were at stake for Callimachus and of the way in which he positions himself in the literary tradition through both explicit statements and subtle allusions.

The fragment's contents can be summarized, roughly, as follows. In 1-6 the speaker, who represents himself as an old poet and is generally regarded as an impersonation of Callimachus, begins with a description of his critics, whom he calls the Telchines. The speaker summarizes their view that he is blameworthy, because he has not written one long, continuous poem on kings and heroes. In 7-20 the speaker reports his reaction to his critics: he rejects long and noisy poems and emphasizes that poetical skill, not length, must be the criterion by which poetry is judged. In 21-8 he explains that, when he first started to write poetry, Apollo told him that he should keep his Muse slender and go along untrodden paths. In 29-38 the speaker says that he has followed Apollo's instructions and expresses the intention and hope to be a subtle and refined poet, singing like the cicada and untroubled by old age, and he shows himself confident that the Muses will continue to be his friends. In 39-40 there seems to be a reference to a swan, which may be connected with the preceding passage on old age. In its overall arrangement the fragment consists of two main sections: in 1-20 the focus is on the rejection of the Telchines and on the importance of short and subtle works, in 21-40 the style of such works appears through a series of metaphors both in the speech of Apollo and in the speaker's own words. (Harder 2012: 6-7)

Scholars have sometimes thought that the prologue of the *Aetia* is a rejection of epic, but . . . for Callimachus works in elegiacs and hexameters were both part of the genre "epic" and therefore the issue in the prologue must have been style rather than genre. . . . In fact, as shown above, the prologue of the *Aetia* refers the reader in a highly allusive manner to a variety of literary genres and passages of literary criticism and is best read as referring to poetic style and quality in general. . . . The message seems to be that a poet should aim for the quality of small-scale, subtle, and original (and therefore "sweet") poetry, with *techné* as a more important criterion than length, and the reader is invited to read this message against the background of a kaleidoscopic and allusive picture of earlier Greek poetry and earlier literary criticism. This fits in with the character of the *Aetia*, which, in spite of its being basically an elegiac catalogue poem, shows a great deal of generic variety and alludes to many of the predecessors hinted at in the prologue. (Harder 2012: 10-11)

[Lines 1-20] Callimachus' answer to the Telchines begins with another negative description. He now draws attention to their envious nature and, as it were, accounts for the behavior and demands in 1-6. He then seems to focus on length and style, and these two aspects are intricately interwoven. In the much-disputed lines 9-12 Callimachus argues that brevity is better and seems to indicate his own position in the elegiac tradition as one who favors the short poems of Mimnermus and Philitas rather than the long poems of others. In 13-16 he rejects length and associates brevity with sweetness, while the choice of imagery suggests the notion that the grand subjects of mythological and historical epic should be avoided. In 17-18 Callimachus claims that poetry should be judged by its quality, not by quantity, and in 19-20 he rejects "noisy" poetry in the grand style, by implication indicating his preference for the slender style. (Harder 2012: 29)

[Lines 21-8] Callimachus now supports his answer to the Telchines with the authority of Apollo, the god of poetry himself, who at an early age urged him to write his special kind of refined and original poetry. Apollo offers the final legitimation, and as it were the *aition*, of Callimachus' style, but without confining his orders to a specific genre. . . . This scene has had a great influence on later poets, who, however, modified it into a *recusatio* to write specific genres, whereas in Callimachus the emphasis is on style instead of genre. (Harder 2012: 55)

[Line 23-8] In these lines Apollo orders Callimachus to write an original and refined kind of poetry and to accept that this might be hard work. The speech itself illustrates a kind of poetry: Callimachus makes Apollo speak in a highly poetic manner which may be intended to recall his own style, with a great deal of metaphor and allusion. (Harder 2012: 60)

[Lines 23-4] [W]hen Apollo demands that the sacrificial animal be fed so that it literally becomes "as fat as possible" he creates an effective contrast with the Muse, who must be kept slender in a metaphorical sense. Besides, he may also be thought to speak out of a certain greedy self-interest and the reader is probably expected to enjoy this joke. (Harder 2012: 61) [I]n contrast with the fat sacrificial animal the Muse must be kept slender . . . on a literal as well as metaphorical level and this slender Muse must stand for the fine and delicate poetry Apollo recommends. (Harder 2012: 62)

[Lines 25-8] In these lines Apollo elaborates on the notion of the slender Muse and adds further instructions. These are also wrapped in metaphor and show that Apollo's requirements include originality and the willingness to strive for achievement. The first notion is conveyed by the metaphor of the untrodden paths, the second through the addition that these paths might be narrow. . . . a contrast between the common and the select. (Harder 2012: 63)

[Line 27] Driving a chariot is a well attested metaphor for poetic activity, particularly in Pindar and Bacchylides, where the chariot generally belongs to the Muses, who might figure as its drivers. . . . The popularity of the metaphor in these poets has found an explanation in its relation to the most prestigious *agon* in the Panhellenic games, i.e. the chariot-race, which seemed well suited to convey a picture of poetic *impetus*. Here in Callimachus the poet himself drives the chariot, and Latin poets take over this image. This modification of the motif suits the way in which Callimachus shows himself to be in charge of his own poetry, which his contributions to the dialogue with the Muses also illustrate. (Harder 2012: 65) This might suggest that part of the ease of the well-trodden path is that one does not have to search hard for material and that there is no need to be selective, whereas the narrow roads force the poet to choose and to select his material carefully. (Harder 2012: 66)

[Lines 29-40] Callimachus describes how he followed Apollo's advice and became a poet of the slender style, singing like a cicada. He then complains of old age and expresses the wish to be young again, but also comforts himself, implicitly with the reference to the cicada, who represents Tithonus living on as "a voice", and explicitly with the certainty that in any case the Muses will still favor him, because they did so when he was a child. After that he seems to add something to the effect that swans sing most beautifully when old. (Harder 2012: 68)

[Line 30] [T]he cicada stands for the clear, subtle sounds of Callimachean poetry, whereas the braying of the asses stands for its opposite, i.e. poetry characterized by bombastic noise. . . . From early times onward the cicada is associated with pleasant sounds, often called "song." . . . Apart from this the cicada bears other connotations . . . and these too are evoked by Callimachus . . . an association with old age and immortality in combination with the ongoing qualities of one's voice . . . an ability to live on dew . . . the cicada's dedication to song as opposed to the careless improvisations of the ass, [the linkage of] the metaphor of the cicada to the notion of effort. (Harder 2012: 70) Callimachus wishes to be a light, winged cicada in *all* respects, as it would imply the shedding of old age and the ability to live on dew as well as the ability to sing like it. (Harder 2012: 76)

Commentary on Callimachus' Erotic Epigrams

Callimachus' *Epigrammata* [a lost collection] formed the most famous and admired of Greek epigram collections. Athenaeus informs us that it belonged to the canon of works read by boys in school (15.669c), and Martial, who was undoubtedly a connoisseur, awards Callimachus the palm of victory among earlier Greek epigrammatists(4.23). Pliny praises Callimachus' epigrams (obliquely, through comparison with a Latin epigrammatist) for their charm and human feeling, their sweetness, expressiveness, and wit (*Epist.* 4.3.3-4). We may also mention numerous echoes in the Roman elegists, whose claim to Callimachus as a model for love elegy was surely based, very largely, on his erotic epigrams. (Gutzwiller 1998: 183)

Eight of these thirteen epigrams (nine if Ganymede, a mythical example, is included) give the names of youths who are the objects of an older man's (or god's) erotic interest. Such a youth is called in Greek an *eromenos* ("desired, beloved"), the older man in love with him an *erastes* ("lover").

For each *eromenos* named in Callimachus' erotic epigrams (2, 5-10, 12), the poet himself is the *erastes* involved (he shares that role, in the last example, with another); he is the *erastes* in *Epigrams* 1, 3, and 4 also, where the object(s) of his affection are unnamed. That leaves only two (11 and 13) in which someone other than the poet figures as the *erastes*.

All but two (4 and 11) are addressed to someone: five of those in which the name of the *eromenos* is given are addressed to him (2, 7-10), the other three (5-6, 12) to different persons. Whether, and to what extent, the erotic epigrams reflect Callimachus' own experiences is uncertain. (Nisetich 2001: 294)

31 Pf
[5] *my passion*: of the thirteen love epigrams, only two [31 Pf and 43 Pf) are not explicitly homoerotic. (Nisetich 2001: 295)

[Perhaps we are] meant to imagine the poet at a symposium where sex is freely available, explaining to his drinking companion Epikydes why he doesn't take what is on offer. This epigram was well known to ancient readers and translated in part by Horace (in *Satires* 1.2.105-8), who however rejects Callimachus' conclusion and argues instead in favor of cheap prostitutes. (Fain 2010: 141-42)

28 Pf

[1] *recycled poetry*: . . . Callimachus would have disliked the Cyclic poems for their clumsy imitation of Homer and their lack of originality. In the present context, their popularity among the unsophisticated might tell against them too.

[3] *a boy*: Callimachus' word here is *eromenos*.

[5] *Lysanïes*: a man of this name is said by *Suidas* to have taught together with Callimachus, grammar to Eratosthenes. An erotic connection between this Lysanïes and Callimachus seems unlikely as such attachments were usually formed between a younger and an older man. . . . Callimachus' asseveration contains a vulgarism (*naichi*, 'sure'), and the whole statement is framed as if the poet were declaring in the poem what might be seen written on walls, vases, monuments, or even trees: the common erotic graffito declaring that "So-and-so-is-handsome (*kalos*)" or "beautiful (*kale*)." The modern equivalent, though it differs in naming both parties, is "So-and-so-loves-so-and-so." (Nisetich 2001: 295)

[T]he poet professes his dislike for anything that is ordinary, whether in poetry or in love [see the *Aetia*]. . . . The irony of the epigram comes from the definitive rejection at the beginning of the poem of whatever is ordinary, followed by an erotic compliment directed at the boy, Lysanïes. We expect Callimachus to end the poem by saying that Lysanïes may look great, but that the boy has clearly been around the block and is just the sort of lover Callimachus rejects. Or perhaps that Lysanïes looks great but not in any ordinary sort of way. What the poet says, of course, is that Lysanïes looks great but someone else got there first. So much for good intentions! In Greek, the name Lysanïes means "reliever of pain or sorrow" and was certainly intended to be ironic. (Fain 2010: 142-43)

46 Pf

[1] *Polyphemos*: the Cyclops encountered later by Odysseus (*Odyssey* 9). Theocritus 11 depicts him as a lover, singing of his hopeless passion for the sea nymph Galatea.

[3] *Philip*: a Coan doctor by the name of Philip is known to have been practicing medicine in Alexandria in 240 BC.

[3-4] *swelling . . . drug*: medical terminology.

[6] *the craze for boys*: there is no distinction made between homosexual passion, mentioned here as the poet's own, and heterosexual passion, felt by the Cyclops.

[10] *both charms*: poetry and hunger. The poet's poverty here (and in Epigram 7) is more likely to be conventional than autobiographical. (Nisetich 2001: 296)

41 Pf

Quintus Lutatius Catulus adapted this epigram into Latin (Aulus Gellius 19.9.14). (Nisetich 2001: 296)

The beginning of this epigram is based on Asclepiades VII, though the desperation in that poem has been replaced here by playful sophistication. Aristotle in the first book of his *Nicomachean Ethics* describes the soul as divided into rational and irrational parts, often at odds with one another. The notion that one part of the soul could go looking for the other, as one looks for a runaway slave, gives an amusing conceit to this familiar theme. Callimachus the poet writes with superb control of his technique about Callimachus the lover, who is so out of control that he has quite literally lost his mind (or at least half of it). This poem was apparently well-known to the Romans since it was translated by Quintus Lutatius Catulus, a general and consul unrelated to the poet Catullus and probably writing near 100 BCE, when many believe that Meleager's *Garland* arrived in Rome. The reading of Callimachus' epigram is uncertain . . . [t]he poem appears to be saying that we should look for the missing half of the poet's soul at the house of Theutimos, presumably intended to be the name of an adolescent with whom the poet had lately fallen in love. (Fain 2010: 143)

29 Pf

[1-2] The imperatives are second person singular, addressed, perhaps, to a servant at the symposium.

[1] *Dioklos*: another handsome boy (*eromenos*), with whom the poet is in love.

[2] *and leave the water out*: normally, the ancients diluted their wine with water. Here, toasting a beloved, the wine is taken neat. (Nisetich 2001: 296)

52 Pf
[1] *Hate him . . . love him*: addressed to Zeus, though we do not know it until line 3.
[2] *Theokritos*: perhaps a pseudonym, borrowed from the poet Theocritus, for a real or a fictitious lover of Callimachus'.
[3] *Ganymede*: son of Tros. Zeus fell in love with him and carried him off to Olympus where he became cup-bearer to the gods.
[4] *a lover once*: of Ganymede. (Nisetich 2001: 296-97)

[O]ne of the most charming of the love epigrams of Callimachus. [Here the] poet pleads with Zeus to show favor to Theocritus if Theocritus returns the poet's love. Zeus was notorious in antiquity for his love affairs, and one of his most famous liaisons was with the boy Ganymede, a Trojan prince who was brought by Zeus to Olympus and became his lover and cupbearer. The poet mentions this affair in support of his own suffering but tactfully abstains from elaboration. (Fain 2010: 144)

32 Pf
[1] *Menippos*: another *eromenos*, whether real or imaginary. The *eromenos* more interested in money than in love is attacked in *Ia* 3.
[2] *don't tell me my own dream!*: a proverbial expression, equivalent to "Don't tell me what I already know." (Nisetich 2001: 297)

Attractive young boys were often criticized in antiquity for selling themselves to the highest bidder, and Menippos seems to be among their number. What makes this poem touching is the poet's frank admission that he cannot satisfy his lover's expectations, and his hurt and disappointment when Menippos insists on pointing out the obvious. (Fain 2010: 144)

Pf 42

[1] *Archinos*: another *eromenos*, loved by the poet, evidently, from the distance.

I sang at your door: the poet seems to have gone, unaccompanied, from a drinking party to the house of Archinos.

[3] *wine at full strength*: a hint that he was toasting Archinos earlier in the evening.

[4] *the one . . . the other*: love . . . wine.

[5] *so-and-so son of so-and-so*: one gave one's full identification (name and father's name) when seeking to enter a house or join a party. Callimachus implies that he was content to stay outside, remaining, in spite of his condition, well-behaved. (Nisetich 2001: 297)

This poem was discovered in mutilated form as an inscription (probably from the first century CE) on the wall of a house on the Esquiline Hill, an expensive residential district rising above the Coliseum in Rome. It shows . . . Callimachus at his very best. . . . [T]he poet arrives inebriated at the door of his beloved but apologetic rather than vainglorious and does not ask to be let in. This apology seems to presage some horrible deed, such as breaking down the door or setting fire to the house. We then learn that "the poet has merely indulged in a harmless sentimental gesture" . . . The complexity of feeling rivals the best of the love poetry of the Latin poet Catullus. (Fain 2010: 144)

Pf 44

[1-2] *by Pan,* | *by Dionysos*: Pan might cause the sudden disturbance of feeling ("panic") the poet fears; Dionysos, god of wine, hints at the setting (a drinking party) and, possibly, at his tipsiness (and vulnerability) right now.

[3] *don't get too close!*: the *eromenos* here is perhaps more obliging than he ought to be.

[5] *Menexenos*: evidently, the *eromenos* on this occasion. (Nisetich 2001: 297)

The ashes and fire of love. . . . What gives the poem its poignancy is the poet's admission that he is powerless to alter his feeling. The "fire beneath these ashes" suggests a prior love affair from which he seems never to have recovered. Instead of steeling his own resolve . . . Callimachus acknowledges his own helplessness and places the responsibility entirely upon the shoulders of his lover. (Fain 2010: 145)

45 Pf
[1] *Menekrates*: another *eromenos*.
[4] *Hermes*: the god responsible for a lucky find. (Nisetich 2001: 298)

25 Pf
[1 *Kallignotos . . . Ionis*: otherwise unknown; if "Ionis" alludes to Io, both names would appear to be imaginary.
[3-4 *the vows | of lovers*: Zeus, caught in the act of being unfaithful to Hera with Io, swore that he had not made love to her. According to a fragment of Hesiod (124 MW), he then made all similar oaths taken by lovers free of sanction. (Nisetich 2001: 298)

30 Pf
[1] *Kleonikos of Thessaly*: evidently someone Callimachus met at a symposium.
[3] *the god I worship*: Eros
[5] *Euxitheos*: another *eromenos*.
You saw him too: a surprising development, perhaps ironical: Callimachus, in love with Euxitheos too, is taking it better than Kleonikos is. (Nisetich 2001: 298)

43 Pf
[3] *at the third toast*: the first libation at a symposium was made to Olympian Zeus, the second to the Heroes, and the third to Zeus the Saviour. Perhaps the guest despairs of being "saved."
[4] *garlands*: customary at symposia.
[5] *done to a turn*: in the fire of love. (Nisetich 2001: 298)

30 Pf and 43 Pf

These two poems have a similar theme. The poet in the first expresses surprise and shock that Kleonikos is reduced to skin and hair, and he then infers from his own experience that these are symptoms of overwhelming passion. The poet in the second poem sees the sighing and heavy drinking of a guest at a dinner party and concludes that that man, too, is in love, though trying to keep it secret. Both of these poems are written in a style similar to that one used by Asclepiades, with short sentences, sudden interrogatives, and a sharply focused ending. (Fain 2010: 145)

Commentary on Others of Note

Aetia 2.49-54 [i.e., fragment 43.12-17]

Amid all these personalities, it is the shifting persona of the poet himself that exerts the most fascination. We do not often find him without some mask on—the artist's mask, not the bandit's; meant to reveal, not to hide. Even when he seems to be taking it off, giving us a glimpse of his face, we find it was only to put on another. One such tantalizing moment occurs in a passage near the opening of *Aitia 2*, where, of all things, he happens to be revealing one of his aetiological sources. The passion of the man comes out, engaging, civilized, happy. The best thing about the party he went to, he says, was the conversation. [...suggests that here we have the *aition* of the aetiological story, which consists of careful listening at the right occasions. Harder 2012:310] (Nisetich 2001: xlix-l)

This sequence begins with Callimachus describing a banquet he attended, the physical pleasures of which quickly pass, while what was discussed remains in memory. It appears he is telling the Muses what he learned at the banquet; this is almost certainly an allusion to Plato's *Symposium*, during which ephemeral pleasures are put aside in favor of conversation. It would serve well as an introduction to fr. 178, where we find Callimachus, at a symposium, eschewing deep drinking in favor of conversation with his seat mate. (Stephens 2015)

Pf 2
Almost nothing is known about Heraclitus of Halicarnassus, the subject of this affecting poem. Diogenes Laertius calls him a poet of "elegy"—that is, of poems in elegiac meter, which includes epigrams. *Nightingales* was presumably the title of a collection of his poems, all of which have sadly disappeared except for a single epigram preserved in Meleager's *Garland* (*AP* 7.465) (Fain 2010: 137)

The first impressions we get of this epigram are its pathos and its conversational quality; its subject is death, but it is far from an ordinary sepulchral epigram, despite the fact that it touches on all the expected topics. A closer analysis reveals its artistry, not only in its use of unusual vocabulary and constructions and in its poetic forms, but also in its repeated theme of survival: conversation defeats sleep; poetry (i.e., the nightingales) escapes death.

Yet none of these impressions duplicate the ancient reader's reaction on reading the epigram's first few words, which lure him into a clever trap. Written without accentuation, these words would inevitably be read, not as "someone said," but as the more common sepulchral expression "tell me who." As the epigram goes on, this reading soon becomes unworkable and must be revised, but it leaves the reader with the lingering suspicion that a written poem's meaning does not survive as intact as the epigram claims. (Tueller 2014: xiv-xv)

Chariots and Callimachus' Great-Grandfather

It was Anniceris, Callimachus' great-grandfather, who, in an attempt to impress Plato, once drove his chariot several times round the Academy—the same Anniceris who later ransomed Plato from Dionysus of Syracuse. Unlike his poet progeny, he took the well-trodden path.

Anniceris of Cyrene was proud of his horsemanship and skill in driving chariots. On one occasion he even wished to give a display of his ability to Plato. So he prepared his chariot and drove it many times round the Academy, following the path so accurately that he never deviated from his own tracks but always followed them precisely. Everyone else was amazed, as was to be expected; but Plato was critical of his excessive meticulousness and said: "It is impossible for a man who devotes such care to petty things of no value to be serious about important matters. When his mind is entirely occupied with such things he is bound to neglect all that truly deserves admiration." (Here the translator notes: "Plato's riposte is ungenerous, since Anniceris allegedly ransomed him after he had been sold into slavery; see Diogenes Laertius 3.20. He was the great-grandfather of the poet Callimachus.") [2.27] (Aelian 1997: 99-101)

On Cicadas and the Muses (Plato's *Phaedrus* 259A-E)

Socrates: We have plenty of time, apparently; and besides, the locusts seem to be looking down upon us as they sing and talk with each other in the heat. Now if they should see us not conversing at mid-day, but, like most people, dozing, lulled to sleep by their song because of our mental indolence, they would quite justly laugh at us, thinking that some slaves had come to their resort and were slumbering about the fountain at noon like sheep. But if they see us conversing and sailing past them unmoved by the charm of their Siren voices, perhaps they will be pleased and give us the gift which the gods bestowed on them to give to men.

Phaedrus: What is this gift? I don't seem to have heard of it.

Socrates: It is quite improper for a lover of the Muses never to have heard of such things. The story goes that these locusts were once men, before the birth of the Muses, and when the Muses were born and song appeared, some of the men were so overcome with delight that they sang and sang, forgetting food and drink, until at last unconsciously they died. From them the locust tribe afterwards arose, and they have this gift from the Muses, that from the time of their birth they need no sustenance, but sing continually, without food or drink, until they die, when they go to the Muses and report who honors each of them on earth. They tell Terpsichore of those who have honored her in dances, and make them dearer to her; they gain the favor of Erato for the poets of love, and that of the other Muses for their votaries, according to their various ways of honoring them; and to Calliope, the eldest of the Muses, and to Urania who is next to her, they make report of those who pass their lives in philosophy and who worship these Muses who are most concerned with heaven and with thought divine and human and whose music is the sweetest. So for many reasons we ought to talk and not sleep in the noontime.

Phaedrus: Yes, we ought to talk.

Socrates: We should, then, as we were proposing just now, discuss the theory of good (or bad) speaking and writing.

Phaedrus: Clearly.

Socrates: If a speech is to be good, must not the mind of the speaker know the truth about the matters of which he is to speak? {259 A-E] (Plato 1914: 511-13)

4

....

EROTIC EPIGRAMS FROM BOOK 5
OF *THE GREEK ANTHOLOGY*

The history of *The Greek Anthology*, briefly stated, is as follows:

> *The Greek Anthology* contains some 4,500 Greek poems in the sparkling, diverse genre of epigram, written by more than a hundred poets and collected over many centuries. To the original collection, called *The Garland* (*Stephanus*) by its contributing editor, Meleager of Gadara (first century BCE), was added another *Garland* by Philip of Thessalonica (mid-first century CE) and then a *Cycle* by Agathias of Myrina (567/568 CE). In about 900 CE these collections (now lost) and perhaps others (also lost, by Rufinus, Diogenianus, Strato, and Palladas) were partly incorporated and arranged into fifteen books according to subject by Constantine Cephalas; most of his collection is preserved in a manuscript called the *Palatine Anthology* [discovered in 1606 in the Palatine Library in Heidelberg; it was written around 980]. A second manuscript, the *Planudean Anthology* made by Maximus Planudes in 1301, contains epigrams omitted by Cephalas. (Tueller 2014: 1)

And that of Book 5:

> Book 5 contains epigrams on the topics of desire, feminine beauty, love, and sex. The desire it manifests is fairly strictly heterosexual (though there are exceptions); this restriction is due not to ancient anthologists but rather to Cephalas, who (with some inaccuracy) separated homoerotic poems into what has now become Book 12 of the *Greek Anthology*.

Erotic epigram has no direct inscriptional precedent; it was created from a collision of epigrammatic models and elegiac themes. Among its earliest practitioners, and arguably its creator, was Asclepiades [see: 158, 162, 164, 189, 203, 209], many of whose erotic epigrams incorporate elements from dedicatory [see: 203] or sepulchral epigram; without these elements, his readers would not have recognized the poems as epigrams at all.

Many of the epigrams in Book 5 are bittersweet. They complain of any circumstance that impedes their love—the dawn that interrupts a liaison or a beloved who is unreliable or unfaithful [see: 164, 184, 186]. Equally, they complain of the state of being in love itself and curse the god Love for subjecting them to his forces. Others focus on the body of the beloved, waxing lyrical on her features [see: 70] or, more crassly, invoking the ravages of age or judging her body in a beauty contest. Many of the women seen in these poems are courtesans or prostitutes of a lower grade (complaints of their venality are common, e.g.), but this cannot be assumed of all of them; even the lemmatist occasionally misleads. Not every poem features sex, but a great many do; description of the act ranges from metaphorical admiration of the woman's skill [see: 203] to something nearer pornography [see: 127], or rape.

One recurring motif is the *paraclausithyron* [see: 189, 213]. In this adaptation of a folk custom, a lover, drunk and garlanded from a symposiastic party, makes his way to the door of his beloved and attempts to persuade the woman, or her servants, to let him in. In the epigrams, he is invariably unsuccessful, and expresses his disappointment in a variety of ways. (Tueller 2014: 198-99)

Tueller's General Introduction

The word *epigram* (Greek *epigramma*) was first used to mean an inscription. Though the great majority of Greek inscriptions are in prose, poetic inscriptions were especially striking, and it is to these that the word epigram came to apply more particularly. Epigrams were inscribed from the earliest days of the Greek alphabet, primarily for two reasons: to memorialize the dead and to address dedicated objects to a god. These, then, form the two earliest epigrammatic subgenres: sepulchral and dedicatory epigrams. Their meter, fitting the solemnity of their occasion, was generally dactylic hexameters, though many were also in the closely related elegiac couplets.

This much takes us to the close of the archaic period. It deserves notice that even at this early date, the epigram is an outlier in Greek literature. Despite its stately formal characteristics, its subjects are not mythic: they are ordinary people, making a bid for glory. It is also extremely brief. Although this brevity was common to all inscriptions for a time, the length of prose inscriptions gradually increased, while epigram remained quite short—at this time, nearly always two to four lines. Even more unusual is its literate character. Greek literature was at this time experienced almost exclusively orally. While the technology of writing was known, written texts functioned more or less as "prompt books" for performers; the audience would expect to hear, not read, these texts. Against this background, epigram stands out: a reader would come across an epigram without rehearsal, and would read the epigram aloud, being at once performer and audience—the epigram was consumed by reading. (And yet it also has undeniably oral features: meter, in particular, serves no purpose without vocal expression.) Literateness and brevity combined to cause interpretive difficulties: without an experienced performer or an explanatory context, the reader was forced to rely on the epigram's physical circumstances. The epigram was inscribed on an object, to which it would refer, and within a physical context—e.g., a temple or burial ground, or even by the side of a road—in which it was embedded.

Both the difficulty of reading and the delight that accompanies successful reading can be found in this epigram, from about 475 BC, which features a dialogue between the inscribed object and a passing reader:

"Engineered voice of stone, say who set up this ornament, honoring the altar of Apollo."

"Panamyes the son of Casbollis, if you in[sist?] that I speak out, dedicated this as a tithe to the god."

[*Carmina epigraphica Graeca* 429]

Here, a stone has acquired a voice by an artificial process—but its activation requires a certain amount of coaxing.

The most famous epigram of antiquity is inscribed at the beginning of the classical period. It memorializes the Spartan dead who fell at Thermopylae:

Stranger, report to the Lacedaemonians that we are lying here, obedient to their words.

["Simonides," *Anthologia Palatina* 7.249, though better known from its appearance in Herodotus, *Histories* 7.228.]

We see here a new impetus. This epigram is not satisfied with its fixity, and demands that its message be transmitted through space. While we can trace no direct causal relationship to this epigram, it was at about this time, the fifth century BC, that epigrams began to circulate in book form. The first such collection may well have been of epigrams by Simonides, to whom the above epigram is often attributed. These early collections gradually grew, as people found more inscribed epigrams that they deemed worth remembering. Inscribed epigrams were not "signed" by their authors, but their collectors nevertheless often attributed them to Simonides, Anacreon, or others—a judgment that in general implies nothing more than an ancient opinion that they sounded like the sort of thing that Simonides, Anacreon, et al. would have written. Hence, ascriptions of epigrams in the *Greek Anthology* to any figure from before the late fourth century BC must be regarded as speculative at best.

At the dawn of the Hellenistic period, epigram came into its own as a literary genre. We then begin to see epigrams that seem composed with no intention that they ever be physically inscribed. They retain the conventions of inscription, attempting to convince their readers that they could have come from a tomb or an object dedicated to a god, but their destination is paper, not stone. Epigram suited the stylistic leanings of the time: it was brief and unflinchingly literate, and it had not yet secured a place as a respected literary genre. Some of the greatest poets of the Hellenistic period made epigram a significant part—or even the entirety—of their work.

On the page, epigram was divorced from the physical surroundings that had given it an interpretive context. Literary epigrammatists soon discovered that they could turn this ambiguity into an advantage, creating what Peter Bing has termed the *Ergänzungsspiel,* or "supplementation game," in which the reader must find—or invent—clues in order to reveal the epigram's meaning. Alternatively, an epigrammatist could resolve ambiguity as the epigram went along, but in a different direction than the initial parts of the epigram had led the reader to expect. In a brief genre like epigram, this sometimes resulted in the wittiness that characterizes the common English use of the word *epigrammatic* to this day. In the hands of a master, an epigram could achieve both wit and depth.

The new freedom of the page also fueled the development of new subgenres of epigram. Without the need for inscription on an object, epigrams sometimes became, not verses fit for inscription on an object, but rather verses about an object: descriptions, ecphrases, and other more rhetorically developed reflections. Additionally, since most epigrams at this time were written in elegiac couplets (a feature that was to persist from then on), an epigram on a page could not easily be distinguished from an elegy, except in subject matter: elegy was usually on the topic of love or drinking—subjects fit for their sympotic setting. What is more, when literary epigrams were read aloud, it is likely that the occasion was also the symposium. Given these features, it was inevitable that the two genres would cross-fertilize. Many poets wrote erotic (i.e., amatory) epigrams; while some of these featured some connection to an inscribed context, most did not; they were simply brief and often witty encapsulations of an erotic circumstance. (Tueller 2014: ix-xv)

Further Remarks on Literary and Social Context

A dual connection with real life characterises early epigram: circumstance and the inscribed object. The monument celebrating the dead, the statue that is dedicated or the object that is personalised really exists and can repeatedly be looked at or read. Written text in fact changes in a permanent way the inscribed object. This fact gives an inscription the power to communicate on various levels: the lettering, the type of the material object, the context of this object (often mentioned in the text of the epigram) are all part of the overall meaning of an inscription, just as music and dance were an integral part of the sense of a partheneion by Alcman. Yet the forces of nature and history have done away with some of these semiotic elements; in some cases, as with the partheneion, all we have left is the plain text transmitted by the literary tradition. The history of epigram is characterised by a progressive dissolution of its ties with its physical and communicative contexts. From the fifth century on, epigram started freeing itself first from its material support—to become a literary and then bookish genre—and then also from the obligation to treat real events and people; this is particularly clear in the case of funerary epigrams which soon started commemorating people who were long dead and people who never lived. (Aloni 2009)

In considering the types of messages that were likely delivered by epigram books, we should look to the reasons that epigram, both in isolation and in collected form, appealed so strongly to Hellenistic writers and readers. Epigrams focus on individuals, in their particularity, in their personal relationships with family, friends, and deities, in the crucial moments of their professional and personal lives. In the cosmopolitan world of the Hellenistic era, individual subjectivities were no longer shaped by allegiance to a particular class or an independent political unit. Cities were mixtures of Greeks and non-Greeks, and the Greeks within them were of diverse origins and status, forming allegiance to an autocratic monarch for reasons of personal advantage or necessity rather than because of common political goals. By their focus on the personal and the particular, epigrams could reflect these new bonds—shifting, local, and pragmatic, and much altered from the earlier, inescapable and unquestionable, webs of relationship that enmeshed individuals in the cultural myths of their own polis. Epigram was a traditional poetic form that could yet avoid without excuse the larger social, religious, and political themes dominating earlier Greek literature. As a minor form elevated to major status, a marginal type brought to the center, epigram, matching form to content, could represent individuals as they now were—marginal, drifting, fragmentary and fractured selves. So too, epigram books, inasmuch as they lacked the unified and balanced structures of earlier literature, as discontinuous and fragmented entities without organic requirements of length or form, were effective representations of the changeable and unpredictable patterns of affiliation that linked Hellenistic individuals one to another. (Gutzwiller 1998: 13)

Posidippus' Papyrus Bookroll

In the second century BC, in the Fayum region of Egypt, an embalmer chose to reuse as mummy cartonnage a discarded papyrus bookroll. Recovered after more than two millennia and published in 2001, this papyrus contains a collection of about 112 Hellenistic epigrams in approximately 606 verses, apparently all by Posidippus of Pella. Although both the beginning and the end of the roll are missing, it nevertheless preserves a significant section of an epigram book, copied in the late third century BC. Divided into categories by headings, the epigrams celebrate early Ptolemaic monarchs and their courtiers, praise equestrian victors, famous Greek sculptors, and intricately carved gemstones, describe the use of omens for everyday life and for war, record cures of diseases, and commemorate many ordinary individuals through the old inscriptional forms of dedication and epitaph. In terms of amount of new poetry and its importance for understanding a literary era, the Milan papyrus constitutes the most significant find in decades, comparable to the papyrological recoveries of Bacchylides, Menander, and Sappho. In addition, this epigram collection is our earliest example of a Greek poetry book surviving in any substantial portion in artefactual form. Since Posidippus belonged to the first generation of poets who organized their short poems in aesthetically arranged collections, the new text offers invaluable information about the development of poetry books, which arouse in the crucible of the third-century courts and later migrated to Rome. (Gutzwiller 2005: 1-2)

The central question now at issue for scholars . . . is whether the Milan papyrus preserves part of . . . [an] authorially sanctioned epigram book or constitutes a different type of compilation, made to suit the idiosyncratic interests of an editor or as representative of some intermediate stage before the poetic possibilities of aesthetic arrangement were fully understood or utilized. (Gutzwiller 2005: 3)

5

....

PHILODEMOS' EPICUREAN GARDEN

Well, yes, I have taken an inordinate interest in Philodemos even though he's neither a Latin elegist nor one of their precursors (he's more or less a contemporary). Nevertheless, they do share poetic genres (amatory or erotic epigrams and elegies), and a new, and highly personal poetic persona. Still, having said that, what's of most interest to me is how Philodemos the Epicurean philosopher finds expression in Philodemos the poet. It's like this: with the Latin elegists the intent is primarily literary, but with Philodemos there's a deeper thread to tease out. And then there's *ataraxia*, for which I've always had a certain fondness.

But note this important point on how we're to read these poems (*the disjunction between personae*):

> The affinities of this group are clear, even if a name for it is lacking. Each presents a narrator or main speaker, whom it is easy to see as a mask for Philodemos, wrestling, somewhat successfully sometimes not, with the excessive passions of love and the fear of death. . . . Since, however, the "Philodemos" of the epigrams is designed to overlap only partially with the authorial persona implicit in the prose treatises, we are not meant automatically to read the epigrams as straightforward autobiography. Indeed, this disjunction between personae seems rather to warn us off from regarding the epigrams as factual documents. Even though we, unlike the original audience, are ignorant of Philodemos' real age, erotic/marital entanglements, and success or failure in adhering to Epicurean standards of behavior, we can still detect the rift between the serious promoter of Epicurean doctrine in the prose and the

intentionally somewhat comic character of the poetry who needs frank instruction from another. Poems like this are also more amusing—not an inconsiderable point in Hellenistic epigram—when read this way. (Sider 1997: 34)

Commentary

11

A double-sided topos of love poetry: Which woman is more desirable, the one who makes herself easily available (an adulterous wife or prostitute) or the one who is or plays hard to get? (Sider 1997: 101)

12

A description of a beautiful woman, feature by feature. . . . most of the body parts itemized are, at least at first, given their neutral anatomical rather than erotic names. The phrases in parentheses, on the other hand, reveal a barely concealed passion just below the neutral surface description. By v.5 the narrator can no longer keep up the façade and begins to list the beloved's sexy walk and tongue kisses. The dynamic point of the poem is thus the great difficulty if not impossibility of a man's maintaining his sang-froid—perhaps more specifically his Epicurean *ataraxia*—in the contemplation of a beautiful woman. The poem ends with the "X but comely" topos, of which Philodemos was so fond, where X here is the girl's low social status. (Sider 1997: 104) [He means she's a rural rustic, an Oscan from the Naples area. "A local, uncultured, Campanian girl," speaking a local dialect Latin and Greek speakers found amusing. (Sider 1997: 108)]

13

Once again, the persona adopted by Philodemos is that of someone who knows Epicurean teaching on the subject and who would like to follow its precepts, but who finds himself slipping from his ethical model. . . . While the rational part of the soul "speaks beforehand" (in warning) of desire for Heliodora, the soul's irrational part must also be speaking beforehand of this same desire—and so stirs it up. (Sider 1997: 111-12)

15

The topos illustrated here is a variation of the "Poet Caught by Love," in which we typically see the man willing to risk all. In this poem, however, the poet seems a prisoner less of Eros than of the woman who not only is herself subject to insatiable desires but who also, most likely because she is married, induces fear in the man as he thinks of the various punishments meted out to adulterers. This is particularly applicable to Rome . . . but this poem also presents a humorous counterexample to the Epicurean view that the sexual pleasures of adultery are more than cancelled out by the thought of punishment. (Sider 1997: 116-17)

25

The topos of the *segnis amator*: A would-be lover fails to satisfy . . . . Since the topos is an exercise in public self-humiliation, there can be no better way to accomplish this than by allowing the woman to revile the man. (Sider 1997: 147-48)

26

Another epigram narrated by a woman complaining about her disappointing lover. Normally it is the man who complains, often in *paraklausithyra,* of being rainsoaked. (Sider 1997: 150)

4

Philodemos' learned audience is alerted to the possibility that marriage is the subject of this poem . . . by the precise number thirty-seven, at which age Aristotle argues a man should marry (and marry "an eighteen-year old woman") . . . Philodemos' point is that Xanthippe is the koronis [a curved, elaborate marker denoting the end of a column of text on a papyrus roll] that marks the end of the manic stage of his life, and as a living koronis she fits into the book of Philodemos' life, as described at the poem's beginning. If she is to do this, she cannot be simply the last of his loves from his earlier life; a koronis that has disappeared cannot perform its proper function. Philodemos is certainly not claiming that henceforth (at age thirty-seven!) he will lead a celibate life. Xanthippe should rather be part of his new life in a way that demonstrates that his old ways are over. She can do this, first, by being his *patrona virgo*, like Lesbia,

Cynthia, et. al. . . . Xanthippe can also help Philodemos by acting as his partner/wife in their common pursuit of Epicurean virtues. (Sider 1997: 73-77)

5
A compliment to the longer and more complex 4. (Sider 1997: 78)

6
Throughout this short poem Philodemos plays with and thwarts audience expectations: (i) What starts as a desirable party is rejected; (ii) only midway through the poem does it reveal itself as a priamel; (iii) whose cap seems to be the narrator but is in fact the girl he wishes to marry. Finally, a poem seemingly addressed to friends turns out to take the form of a prayer to some unnamed deities. These alterations of poetic form and content brilliantly reflect the striking conversion of the narrator's life. (Sider 1997: 81)

7
A bedroom scene . . . The maid Philainis is told to fill (a presumably already lit) lamp and leave, locking the door behind her, before the lovemaking begins. The woman Xanthos is now addressed, but, although the inanimate lamp is called by its traditional appellation of witness, there remains one more animate witness to be gotten rid of: the reader. Xantho will need no further instructions. . . . Open expression of erotic feeling such as is found here of a husband for his wife is extremely rare in Greek literature; erotic poetry deals largely with pursuit and rejection. . . . The situation in Latin literature is far more complex, where mistresses are often spoken of as wives or at least with language more appropriate to wives than lovers. (Sider 1997: 86-90)

27
In a poem sent on the nineteenth of an unknown month (but quite likely not Gamelion – January-February – though Epicurus was born on the twentieth of that month), Philodemos invites Piso to attend on the next day the celebration in honor of

Epicurus (and some early Epicureans) known as the Twentieth. (Sider 1997: 152)

Since Philodemos invites Piso to his home and furthermore calls it a modest one (an Epicurean topos; Vergil does the same thing in his early poem to the Epicurean Siron), he clearly was not living in the Villa dei Papiri at that time (if ever). The poem is also clearly not only an invitation to the Twentieth, but also an oblique request for patronage. Philodemos cleverly uses the Homeric word for "comrade" (*hetaros*) as a synonym for *philos*, "friend," which had an almost technical status with the Garden for the relationship between fellow Epicureans; *philos* also equates with the Latin *amicus*, which in turn was the technical term for the patron-client relationship that Philodemos seeks from Piso. Thus Philodemos deftly asks Piso to be a "friend" in the ordinary, the Epicurean, and the Roman senses of the word. *Hetaros* is also the word used by Odysseus for *his* comrades. (Sider 2005: 83)

28
Like 29, a poem listing modest ingredients of a meal which would be appropriate for Epicureans, some of which occur in both poems. And once again friends are named, each of whom in good *eranos* fashion is expected to show up with his share of the meal. (Sider 1997: 161)

It would be rash to expect all Philodemus' epigrams to be heavily engaged with philosophy; he had, after all, outlets for his thoughts about Epicureanism in his lectures to his pupils, some of which, taken down in shorthand and copied by amanuenses, survive in Herculaneum papyri. But AP 11.35 [29] can be interpreted within a relaxed Epicurean (and symposiastic) context probably linked with his teaching. (Cairns 2016: 91) [We know] that Philodemus on occasion gave lectures to small select groups of students. [We know of one such class] "consisting of Plotius Tucca, L. Varius Rufus, Virgil and Quintilius Varus. . . . With such small numbers of students involved, and given the importance to Epicureans of communal dining, it takes little imagination to hypothesise that Philodemus, as part of a course of lectures, entertained his mini-classes to an Epicurean meal or meals at which the life-style preached by him in his classroom was practised and exemplified by him in the dining-room. If so, Artemidorus, Aristarchus, Athenagoras and Apollophanes were perhaps another small class of students honoured with an epigram as well as a meal." (Cairns 2016: 93)

29
The death a day earlier of two friends reminds Philodemos of the meals they will no longer share. . . . A boating accident would account not only for the death of Philodemos' friends together but also for his aversion to viewing the sea. But if this is the case Philodemos is failing to observe the proper emotional detachment from death expected of an Epicurean. . . . Sosylos, to whom Philodemos addresses his grief, seems to reply in the last distich, reminding him that their deaths have to be accepted: Well then, they prayed yesterday, today they are dead—from which the message to obviously be extrapolated is that they should enjoy today's (simple) pleasures . . . for tomorrow we too may be dead. (Sider 1997: 164-65)

The Garden

From Diskin Clay's article, "The Athenian Garden."

The conversation of the last book of Cicero's *De Finibus* is set in the Academy. Cicero recalls a day (in 79 BC) when he, his cousin Lucius, Pupius Piso and Titus Pomponius Atticus left the gymnasium called the Ptolemaeum and the lectures of the last member of the Academy, Antiochus of Ascalon, in the agora of Athens. They left the city and made for the quiet of the Academy a mile and a half from the Dipylon Gate. There the company was moved by the memory of Plato and his successors. On their way to the Academy they had passed Epicurus' Garden, which brought to the mind of the Epicurean, Atticus, the time he and the Epicurean Phaedrus had spent there. The young Cicero gives no hint of Sulla's destruction of these gardens of two very different schools of philosophers in 86. Epicurus was then still remembered not only in portrait paintings but his image on cups and rings. (Clay 2009: 27)

An interesting image: wealthy, cultivated young Romans spending a few months in Athens attending lectures at the various philosophical schools (e.g., Plato's Academy, founded first, located outside Athens' walls to the northwest beyond the Dipylon Gate; then Aristotle's Lyceum, also outside the city walls, but to the east; followed by the Academy's neighbor, Epicurus' Garden; and finally Zeno's school, located in the Painted Stoa near the Agora). And here's what Cicero has to say about this in the first few paragraphs of his Book V, *De Finibus Bonorum et Malorum* [*About the Ends of Goods and Evils*]):

I. My dear Brutus,—Once I had been attending a lecture of Antiochus, as I was in the habit of doing, with Marcus Piso, in the building called the School of Ptolemy; and with us were my brother Quintus, Titus Pomponius, and Lucius Cicero, whom I loved as a brother but who was really my first cousin. We arranged to take our afternoon stroll in the Academy, chiefly because the place would be quiet and deserted at that hour of the day. Accordingly at the time appointed we met at our rendezvous, Piso's lodgings, and starting out beguiled with conversation on various subjects the three-quarters of a mile from the Dipylon Gate. When we reached the walks of the Academy, which are so deservedly famous, we had them entirely to ourselves, as we had hoped. Thereupon Piso remarked: "Whether it is a natural instinct or a mere illusion, I can't say; but one's emotions are more strongly aroused by seeing the places that tradition records to have been the favorite resort of men of note in former days, than by hearing about their deeds or reading their writings. My own feelings at the present moment are a case in point. I am reminded of Plato, the first philosopher, so we are told, that made a practice of holding discussions in this place; and indeed the garden close at hand yonder not only recalls his memory but seems to bring the actual man before my eyes. This was the haunt of Speusippus, of Xenocrates, and of Xenocrates' pupil Polemo, who used to sit on the very seat we see over there. For my own part even the sight of our senate-house at home (I mean the Curia Hostilia, not the present new building, which looks to my eyes smaller since its enlargement) used to call up to me thoughts of Scipio, Cato, Laelius, and chief of all, my grandfather; such powers of suggestion do places possess. No wonder the scientific training of the memory is based upon locality."

"Perfectly true, Piso," rejoined Quintus. "I myself on the way here just now noticed yonder village of Colonus, and it brought to my imagination Sophocles who resided there, and who is as you know my great admiration and delight. Indeed my memory took me further back; for I had a vision of Oedipus, advancing towards this very spot and asking in those most tender verses, 'What place is this?'—a mere fancy no doubt, yet still it affected me strongly."

"For my part," said Pomponius, "you are fond of attacking me as a devotee of Epicurus, and I do spend much of my time with Phaedrus, who as you know is my dearest friend, in Epicurus's Gardens which we passed just now; but I obey the old saw: I 'think of those that are alive.' Still I could not forget Epicurus, even if I wanted; the members of our body not only have pictures of him, but even have his likeness on their drinking-cups and rings." [De Finibus 5.1-3] (Cicero 1931: 390-93)

Clay continues:

Years after his philosophical stay in Athens Cicero wrote (in 51 BC) to Gaius Memmius (the addressee of Lucretius' De rerum natura) on behalf of Patro, then the head of the Epicurean school in Athens who had followed Phaedrus. Cicero's purpose was to dissuade Memmius from pulling down the ruins of Epicurus' house in Melite within the city walls. He sent a copy of this letter to Atticus to reinforce his plea. Epicurus' house and small garden near the Hill of the

Nymphs were in ruins by the time Cicero wrote to Memmius and Atticus, but the school and Patro's feelings of reverence and duty to Epicurus and his fellow Epicureans in Athens is evident from Cicero's letter to Memmius. As for the fate of Epicurus' Garden on the road from the Dipylon Gate to the Academy and down to the Piraeus, we hear from Heliodorus' *Aethiopica* of a woman who planned to meet the husband of her mistress at a place 'where the monument of the Epicureans is'. When Pausanias visited the nearby Academy in the middle of the second century AD, he noticed a 'monument of Plato'. At the time of Pausanias' visit this monument to Plato was a desolate funerary monument. It has now vanished. As for Heliodorus' 'monument of the Epicureans' it is likely that in the fourth century and after the Herulian invasion of 267 AD no Epicurean still occupied Epicurus' Garden, yet it was still remembered in a context of pleasure. Epicurus' suburban Garden is now, however, a part of the industrial zone that has also enveloped the Academy. (Clay 2009: 27-28)

What we have here is not a philosophy or school, at least not in the traditional sense, but rather a shared, or communal and philosophical way of life.

The community of 'fellow philosophers' that gathered about Epicurus in his Garden during the last thirty-five years of his life is remarkable for including Epicurus' three brothers and perhaps his parents. More women are associated with Epicurus' Garden than are recorded for any other 'school'. They can be named in alphabetical order: Batis, Boidion, Demetria, Hedeia, Leontion, Nikidion and Themista. The name Hedeia (Pleasure) suggests that she and likely others were prostitutes. Epicurus provides for the children of his community in his will and for his philosophical slave Mus (Mouse), whom he frees on his death. Children and a slave were also important members of his community. Later Epicureans looked on the most prominent members of the Athenian Garden as 'those who led the way' (*kathēgemones*).

In the period of Zeno of Sidon a distinction was made between those who were being prepared for a life of philosophy (the *kataskeuazomenoi*) and their older directors, but no diplomas were granted to those who reached the end of the path of philosophy. (Clay 2009: 26-27)

And this, also from Clay's article: an invitation from Epicurus.

In Philodemus' treatise *On Epicurus* we have a remarkable record of an invitation to an Epicurean feast. It comes from a letter of Epicurus himself and reads:

. . . as concerns those who experience turmoil and difficulty in their conceptions of natures that are best and most blessed. [But Epicurus says] that he invites these very people to join in a feast, just as he invites others – all those who are members of his household and he asks them to exclude none of the 'outsiders' who are well disposed to him and his friends. In doing this [he says], they will not be engaged in gathering the masses, something which is a form of meaningless 'demagogy' and unworthy of the natural philosopher; rather, in practicing what is congenial to their nature, they will remember all those who are well disposed to us so that on their blessed day they can join in making sacred offerings that are fitting. Of the friends . . . (Clay 2009: 24)

And Philodemos?

It is high time to give Philodemus his formal introduction. We would know very little about him were it not for the 79 AD eruption of Vesuvius. It buried just outside Herculaneum a library which, when from the 1750s onwards it was recovered and made partly legible, proved to consist largely of Philodemus' works. It is therefore widely assumed to have originated as his own collection, especially as it includes works by Epicurus and other Epicureans, and variant drafts of some of Philodemus' own treatises. By a further well-founded conjecture, the magnificent villa which housed the library is widely held to have belonged to L. Calpurnius Piso Caesoninus, who, in addition to being the father-in-law of Julius Caesar, was Philodemus' Roman patron. The presence of Philodemus' library there further suggests that the villa had been the location of his school. Philodemus was born in Gadara in the late second century. At some point in his life he was in Alexandria, and it may have been there that he formed a lifelong friendship with the Academic Antiochus, as also with some of Antiochus' pupils. He studied Epicureanism in the Athenian Garden during Zeno of Sidon's headship, c. 100–c. 75. And before finally settling at Herculaneum he seems to have taught at Himera in Sicily, until he was exiled for causing religious offence. This sequence of moves, whatever its precise order may have been, by the late 70s BC had led him to Southern Italy. There he is thought to have remained until his death, probably in the 30s. Philodemus' new standing in Italy enabled him to create his own Epicurean circle at Herculaneum, and to exert his influence on aspiring young literary figures like Horace and Virgil. A contemporary Greek Epicurean, Siro, taught at or just outside the nearby Greek city of Naples, but Herculaneum was in a primarily Roman area, and although Philodemus wrote – and presumably taught – in Greek he is likely to have geared his teaching more to a Roman patrician clientele. His *On the good king according to Homer* (*PHerc.* 1507) is a good example: addressed to Piso, it sets out to extract the lessons about good and moderate government that can be gleaned from Homer despite the many abuses of power that he also portrays. One might have thought that the accident of Vesuvius' eruption had preserved for us the remnants of an unexceptional local philosophical school, perhaps one of a great many scattered around Italy, and that this very ordinariness was what made the find so illuminating about philosophical practice in the period. But this does not in fact seem to be so. When Cicero's Epicurean spokesman Torquatus (*De Finibus* 2.19) cites the authorities on whom he himself relies, he picks out Siro and Philodemus, with

Cicero's own express approval. We do not know of any other Greek Epicureans of comparable standing working in Italy at this date. Moreover Philodemus is, both intellectually and stylistically, a more significant writer than his reputation has generally conceded. Most of his works have to be recovered from badly damaged papyri, and the strained texts that confront readers are often the result of unsatisfactory editorial conjecture. Those passages which have been more or less fully preserved are in general lucid, not inelegant, and philosophically competent; and the best modern editions of his works – of which we may hope for more in the future – reach that same standard. (Sedley 2009: 32-33)

6

....

EXILE

The key, of course, is Ovid, as is noted by Ingleheart in her introduction to *Two Thousand Years of Solitude: Exile After Ovid*: "The poet Ovid stands at the head of the Western tradition of the exiled author: banished by the emperor Augustus in AD 8 from Rome to the far-off shores of the Black Sea [to Tomis; present-day Constanta in Romania], Ovid records his unhappy experience of political, cultural, and linguistic displacement from his homeland in the poems entitled *Tristia* ('Sad Things') and *Epistulae ex Ponto* ('Letters from the Black Sea')." The *archetypical exile*, the *iconic writer-as-exile*, the *Ur-exile*, for over two millennia Ovid has provided other writers the opportunity to articulate their own "experiences of dislocation and alienation via engagement with his exilic work and circumstances." (Ingleheart 2011: 1-2)

But there's been some late breaking news: "Better late than never: Rome revokes the exile of the poet Ovid, 2,000 years after his death." (Nick Squires in *The Telegraph*, December 15, 2017)

> Two thousand years after he was banished to the outer edges of the empire, the city of Rome has formally revoked the exile of the poet Ovid.
>
> A prolific writer famous for his *Metamorphoses* and *The Art of Love*, Ovid was exiled by the Emperor Augustus to a remote town on the coast of the Black Sea, in what is today Romania, in 8 AD.
>
> He remained there until his death, never seeing Italy again. He found life there uncouth and uncomfortable, sending endless pleas to the emperor asking to be allowed to return to Rome.

The reasons for his banishment are one of the great mysteries of ancient literature – the poet himself attributed it to *carmen et error*, or "a poem and a mistake".

No one has ever quite worked out exactly what he meant, but scholars have speculated that his indiscretion was linked to the adultery of the emperor's grand-daughter, who was banished at the same time.

A motion to officially revoke the exile order was approved by Rome city council, the distant successor to the imperial authority of Augustus, on Thursday.

It was put forward to mark the 2,000th anniversary of the poet's death, in 17AD, by politicians from the Five Star Movement, the anti-establishment party that has shaken up Italy's political landscape in the last five years.

They said they wanted to "repair the serious wrong suffered by Ovid by revoking the order with which the emperor sent him into exile in Tomis (modern-day Constanta)."

Yes, but what *did* happen?

Ovid's Exile

Ingleheart:

Ovid's account of his exilic downfall is an arresting study in a sudden, overwhelming misfortune, recalling Greek tragedies in which the protagonist is abruptly subject to a complete reversal of fortune. AD 8 is pivotal in Ovid's life and career: in that year having reached the age of 50, Ovid was Rome's greatest living poet, the feted author of numerous successful works, including the *Amores*, which continued the Roman tradition of first-person elegiac love poetry, the more experimental *Heroides* (or 'Letters of the Heroines'), which transfer the elegiac-erotic mode into fictional letters authored by mythical women to their absent lovers, and the *Ars amatoria* (or 'Art of Love'), which recast subjective love elegy as a step-by-step didactic guide to conducting love affairs with the opposite sex. But in the same year, a swift and unforeseen disaster befell the darling of Roman literary society, as Ovid was suddenly relegated [note: unlike exile, when relegated one still retained both citizenship and property; such relegation often being to a specific place and for a specified length of time] . . . from the capital of the Empire to Tomis . . . [then] at the very periphery of the civilized Roman world [where he died nine years later]. Ovid himself identifies two causes of his banishment: the notorious *'carmen et error'* ('a poem and a mistake', *Tristia* 2.207). The 'carmen' can be securely identified as the *Ars amatoria*, published nearly a decade before Ovid's banishment, which was accused of teaching adultery. It thereby constituted—at the very least—a provocation to Augustus' programme of moral reform, for, *circa* 18 BC, Augustus had passed laws which encouraged marriage and made adultery a criminal offence. It is easy therefore to imagine the offence that must have been caused by the witty, amoral *Ars* and its author. The 'error', conversely, constitutes what John C. Thibault labeled 'the mystery of Ovid's exile': Ovid never exactly reveals what this offence was, but it seems to have been committed just before the sentence of relegation, and to have involved Ovid seeing something which he failed to report. It is hardly surprising that readers have been attracted to this great mystery of literary history—indeed, Ovid sets the 'error' up as a topic for speculation and voyeuristic interest—and the combination of exile for both a literary offence *and* an unidentified personal error has appealed to the personal circumstances and/or curiosity of many of his readers. (Ingleheart 2011: 2-4)

A further "aggravating factor may have been Augustus' personal experience: he relegated both his daughter and granddaughter, Julia I and II, for committing adultery, in 2 BC and AD 8 respectively. Although the coincidence between these dates and those of the publication of the *Ars* and of Ovid's downfall should probably not lead us to the conclusion (unsupported by any evidence) that Ovid was directly involved in the offences of either of Augustus' family members, it seems reasonable to suppose that the offence caused by the *Ars* would have been compounded by the simultaneous flouting of Augustus' legislation by members of his own family. (Ingleheart 2011: 4, footnote 11)

This was serious. A number of his daughter's lovers were exiled, and one notable, Jullus Antonius, (son of Marcus Antonius [Mark Anthony] and Fulvia), was forced to commit suicide.

A Poem and a Mistake

And about that *carmen et error*:

[As we have seen], Ovid attributes his exile to *duo crimina, carmen et error* [two crimes, a poem and a mistake]. The latter—something which Ovid saw—has defied precise identification: Ovid claims he must remain silent about the *error* for fear of offending Augustus, and Ovid never reveals its exact nature, despite tantalizing hints, which afford great significance to references to both sight and silence in *Tristia* 2. The *carmen* is easier to identify: it can only be Ovid's *Ars amatoria,* a didactic handbook which purported to instruct Roman men and women on how to seduce members of the opposite sex, published around a decade previously; much of *Tristia* 2 attempts to defend the *Ars,* securing the identification. Ovid states explicitly and unambiguously that the *Ars* was charged with teaching adultery:

> Although two charges ruined me, a poem and a mistake,
>   the guilt of one crime must be passed over in silence by me;
> for I am not worth so great a price, that I might renew
>   your wounds, Caesar;
>   it is far too much that you should have grieved once.
> The other part [sc. of the case] remains, by which, having
>   composed a disgraceful poem,
>   I am accused of being a teacher of obscene adultery.
>   (Ingleheart 2010:41) [*Tristia* 2: 208-12]

To understand why such an accusation contributed to Ovid's exilic downfall, it is necessary to consider Augustus' innovations of 18 BC.

In 18 BC Augustus passed two 'logically linked' laws aimed at effecting serious changes in the marital and sexual *mores* of Rome's citizens. The provisions of the law *de maritandis ordinibus* were various: most importantly for the background to Ovid's exile, the law apparently prescribed ages between which citizens were expected to be married. Marriage was thereby strongly encouraged, a fact of obvious relevance to the law *de adulteriis coercendis*. Under this law, for the first time in Rome's history, adultery became a criminal offense with fixed penalties. We are only able to reconstruct the provisions of the original law from the later jurists, but it is clear that these penalties were harsh . . . a convicted adulteress stood to forfeit half her dowry and a third of her property, and faced relegation *ad insulam* [exile to an island]; men found guilty lost half of their property, and were relegated to a different island. The law aimed primarily at ensuring the fidelity of upper-class *matronae*.

Not only adulterers came under the scope of the new law; those considered accessories were also liable. For example, wronged husbands were legally obliged to first divorce and then take action against their adulterous wives: failure to do so was regarded as pandering (*lenocinium*), and was punished *pro adulterio* ('as if it were adultery'), as with providing adulterers with a venue for assignations.

'Teaching adultery' (the alleged crime of the *Ars amatoria*) was almost certainly not specified as an offense under the *lex Iulia*. However, since the law punished not only adulterers but also those who encouraged adultery, the *Ars*' teaching may have been considered equivalent to *lenocinium*. . . . The similarity of Ovid's punishment (relegation to a specified place) to the penalty for adultery and (by extension) *lenocinium* suggests that Ovid may have been arraigned for the latter offense.

The *Ars amatoria* was published (at least in part) in c. 2 BC, yet Ovid was not relegated until AD 8. How might we explain this substantial interval between crime and punishment? The best answer seems to be that the *error,* which apparently occurred more recently than the *carmen,* was the immediate precipitating factor in Ovid's relegation. (Ingleheart 2010: 2-4)

And specifically about that *error* (*lumina funesti conscia facta mali*: "made my eyes aware of a dreadful evil" [*Tristia* 3.6.28]):

Why did I see something? Why did I make my eyes guilty?
    Why was a crime uncovered by me, all unawares?
Unintentionally, Actaeon saw Diana divested of her clothes;
    no less was he prey for his own dogs.
It is clear that among the gods even misfortune must be atoned for,
    and an accident does not have forgiveness when a divinity is injured.
To be sure, on that day, on which a terrible error carried me away,
    a house small but without a stain perished;
[*Tristia* 2: 103-110] (Ingleheart 2010: 37)

[Here] Ovid introduces, for the first time in *Tristia* 2, the mysterious *error* that formed one of the two charges that led to his relegation. This passage contains the most information Ovid ever reveals on the subject . . . [i]t also establishes three important points: (i) that the *error* was something Ovid saw, (ii) that Ovid was an involuntary—and thus innocent— observer, and (iii) that Ovid's crime lay not in his unintentional act of seeing, but rather that what Ovid saw was itself a crime committed by others. . . . The other key piece of evidence for the *error*—that Ovid's crime lay in failing to report what he saw—is implied at 3.6.11-16, addressed to an anonymous friend [where Ovid suggests] he could have been safe . . . if he had told the secret that destroyed him: i.e., he could have avoided the 'living-death' of exile. (Ingleheart 2010: 121-22)

Note the self-mythologizing when Ovid suggests that the myth of Actaeon is analogous to his own situation. First, the myth: "In Callimachus' account, whilst out hunting, the young Actaeon unintentionally saw the goddess Artemis bathing naked. In punishment, Artemis transformed him into a stag; he was subsequently torn to pieces by his own hounds." And the parallel Ovid points to: "Thus both Ovid's and Actaeon's stories involve a man who through ill-fortune, inadvertently sees something which causes his punishment by an angered deity. In both cases, the offense could be labeled *error*, the punishment involved the fall of an entire house, and pardon might have been expected [though it never came]." The myth thereby serves a double purpose: "it affords him a tragic, elevated self-portrayal," evoking "for his own fate the pity and terror usually felt by the audiences of Greek tragedy for tragic characters" and "criticizes Augustus obliquely, by assimilating him with another angry and implacable deity." (Ingleheart 2010: 124-25)

Green's speculative recapitulation of the *mistake* and subsequent cruel exile:

> This is not the place to discuss in any detail the still-mysterious circumstances of Ovid's relegation by Augustus in the early winter of AD 8. For the reader of the exilic poems it is simply the fact of the poet's exile, rather than its possible antecedents, that is of primary importance. Briefly, Ovid himself offers two reasons for it: an immoral poem, the *Art of Love*, and a mysterious 'mistake' or 'indiscretion' (error), the details of which he declares himself forbidden to reveal, but which he clearly regards as the chief occasion of Augustus's wrath, with the poem as a subsidiary offence and probable diversionary cover.
>
> This *error* lay not in any specific act on his part, but in his having witnessed something, presumably of a criminal nature, done by others, and, it seems safe to assume, in having failed to report it to the authorities. The hints of *lèse-majesté* that he

scatters, the relentless hostility to him of Tiberius and Livia after Augustus's death, his clear partiality for the Princeps' grandsons and Germanicus, all combine to suggest that he was involved, however marginally, in some kind of pro-Julian plot directed against the Claudian succession (we know of at least two). If this is true, the *Art of Love* will have been dragged in (almost ten years after its publication!) to camouflage the real, politically sensitive, charge. A sexual scandal could — can — always be relied upon to distract public attention from more serious political or economic problems.

There was also a certain sadistic appositeness about Ovid's relegation which suggests the degree of angry resentment that his public attitudinizing had aroused. Enemies had brought his more *risqué* passages to the Princeps' attention, slandered him behind his back, and tried to lay hands on his property through the courts, presumably claiming the reward due to an informer. All this, given the climate of Julio-Claudian Rome, was predictable enough. But with the poet's removal to Tomis his sufferings acquired an ironic aptness that he himself must have recognized better than most. Now the poet who had mocked the moral and imperial aspirations of the Augustan regime, who had taken militarism as a metaphor for sexual conquest, who had found Roman triumphs, Roman law, and the new emphasis on family values equally boring and provincial, was being made to suffer a punishment that in the most appallingly literal way fitted the crime, while at the same time — since the victim of a *relegatio* retained his citizenship and property — offering a spurious show of imperial clemency.

The choice of Tomis as Ovid's place of enforced residence was a master-stroke. It cut him off, not only from Rome, but virtually from all current civilized Graeco-Roman culture. Wherever the intellectual *beau monde* might be found in AD 8, it was not on the shores of the Black Sea. Such residence rubbed the poet's nose in the rough and philistine facts of frontier life, the working of the *imperium* which he had so light-heartedly mocked. Life had caught up with literary fantasy and turned it inside-out: no metamorphosis now could rescue Ovid from the here-and-now of mere brute existence. His erotic exploitation of the soldier's life that he himself had so carefully avoided was duly turned back against him, in this dangerous outpost where he was exposed to raids from fierce unpacified local tribesmen, and might, in an emergency, be called on to help in the town's defense himself. Though we should take with a fairly large grain of salt his claims that he was forgetting his Latin, that his poetic skills were atrophying, that linguistically he was going native, it does remain true that, except through correspondence, he was now deprived of an alertly critical and sophisticated audience for his work-in-progress, such as he had enjoyed (and found essential for the creative process) in Rome. 'Writing a poem you can read to no one', he lamented in a famous aside, 'is like dancing in the dark.'

The charge against Ovid (whatever it may have been) was brought to the notice of Augustus and some of his more highly placed intimates, including Ovid's friend and patron Cotta Maximus in October or early November of AD 8. Ovid himself describes Cotta's reactions, and the fraught meeting they had on Elba when the news broke. The poet was summoned back to Rome for a personal interview with Augustus, during which he was given a severe dressing-down. Dealing with him in this way avoided a public trial — something, given the sensitive nature of the charge, the Princeps seems to have been very anxious to avoid: secrecy marks the proceedings throughout.

The sentence pronounced was, as we have seen, relegation *sine die* to the Black Sea port of Tomis, a Greek colonial foundation, in the barely settled province of Moesia. Little time was lost in forcing Ovid to settle his affairs and be on his way. This meant a December sea-voyage, so that (as we might expect at that time of year) he was exposed to several unpleasant storms during his journey, as well as being robbed by servants who clearly knew a vulnerable victim when they saw one. His severance from Rome was symbolically emphasized by the banning of the *Art of Love* from Rome's three public libraries. Sailing from the Adriatic through the

Gulf of Corinth he recalled making the same voyage on the Grand Tour; but then, in more carefree times, his destination had been Athens. From the Isthmus he took another boat to Samothrace, and from there (travelling as slowly as he might) to Tempyra in Thrace. He now (spring AD 9) completed the journey to Tomis overland. Despite his initial optimism — Book I of the *Tristia*, describing the events of this journey, clearly anticipated a speedy reprieve: perhaps he had Cicero in mind, exiled in the March of 58 BC and back home by August 57 — this remote provincial port was to be Ovid's home for the rest of his natural life. During the harsh winter of AD 17/18, in his sixtieth year, Publius Ovidius Naso finally gave up the unequal struggle for survival. He was buried — as he had foreseen, and feared — by the shores of the Black Sea. (Green 2005: xxiv-xxvi)

Concluding Remarks

Ovid's Paradigm of Exile

Green again:

The two volumes of poetry, the *Tristia* ('Sadnesses', 'Lamentations') and *Epistulae ex Ponto* (Black Sea Letters) that Ovid published during his years of exile have not, on the whole, had a good press from posterity. It is easy enough to see why. The brilliant literary prestidigitator who found imperial moralizing a dreary bore was now compelled, in his obsessional determination to escape from the barbarous backwater to which Augustus's fiat had doomed him, to grovel before the instrument of his downfall, and suck up to powerful patrons who represented the antithesis of everything in which he believed. Augustus's death left him at the mercy of two still more implacable enemies in Livia and Tiberius. The fashionable *flâneur* whose nearest approach to reality had been a fantasy-manual of seduction, whose most sustained creation was centered on outré metamorphoses and the ironic mockery of traditional myth, now found that Life, in its crudest form, had invaded his library and at one stroke deconstructed his lovingly fashioned literary persona. He became querulous, repetitive, self-pitying and self-obsessed, humorless. The egotism that had been a lightweight joy in Rome's *enfant terrible* of the boudoir became an embarrassing aberration when exercised, without elegance or proportion, at the expense of his wife. Tomis no longer let him be funny. The *praeceptor amoris* [the teacher of love] with his mask of myth, wit and literary allusion was now an all-too-human husband in a real-life situation. The poet was forced to adapt old genres and techniques to new uses for which they had never been intended.

This, in the event, he did with remarkable resourcefulness. Granted the fact that his poetry became the vehicle for an *idée fixe*, it is astonishing how much *variatio* he contrived to work into it. Nor, even more surprisingly, was his subservience always quite what it seemed. Despite everything, he fought back. The sardonic oblique shafts aimed — even from exile, even while ostensibly buttering up his tormentor — at Augustus's divine pretensions and moral revivalism astonish by their sly ferocity. Groveling, Ovid still contrived to insult.

More important, and a truth less often realized, the *Tristia* and the *Epistulae ex Ponto* offer an extraordinary paradigm of the fantasies and obsessions that bedevil every reluctant exile: loving evocations of the lost homeland, the personification of letters that are sent to walk the dear familiar streets denied to their writer, the constant parade — and exaggeration — of present horrors, spring *here* contrasted with spring *there*, the wistful recall of lost pleasures once taken for granted, the slow growth of paranoia and hypochondria, the neurotic nagging at indifferent friends, the grinding exacerbation of slow and empty time, the fear of and longing for death.

It is of extraordinary interest (and something seldom done, since readers of the exilic poems most often dip selectively rather than going through the two collections in sequence) to trace the graph of Ovid's emotional preoccupations during his decade of exile, as revealed to us by the testimony of his published poetic discourse. This remains true however we choose to characterize such testimony: somewhere between the two extremes of literary fiction and autobiography the truth must lie (Ovid's exile was, after all, not only a fact, but his sole theme from the moment he left Rome), and the current fashion for evaluating the poems exclusively in literary and rhetorical terms is no less partial, and no less misleading, than the earlier practice of seeing the corpus as *disiecta membra* of a factual record, an exile's diary and correspondence in verse. Of course we should be alert to the selectivity, *suppressio veri*, rhetorical artifice, conventional topoi, and carefully misleading implications that abound in these poems, just as we would in studying any forensic speech for the defense — which, indeed, is the main function that the *Tristia* and the *Black Sea Letters* are, cumulatively, designed to perform: they make a calculated appeal, not only to Augustus, but to literary readers at large. Ovid is presenting his case, as persuasively as he knows how, at the bar of public opinion. Yet he is also a consummate poet, who can no more help investing his brief with verbal elegance and images of haunting beauty than he could stop himself versifying as a boy; and if he mythicizes himself, it is in terms that spring directly from his own unhappy dilemma. The result is a paradigm of exile that has, in its timeless perceptions, served as a model and inspiration down the centuries, for writers as diverse as Seneca and Pushkin. (Green 2005: xxxvi-xxxvii)

The Transformation of the Suffering of Exile Into Art

Isn't that what this is all about: the poet's self-mythologizing transforming "the suffering of exile into art?" (Ingleheart 2011: 19) But this would be Ovid, no? Seeking "to express his personal circumstances by pointing up their parallels with those of various mythological characters;" a transformative act that makes him central to "[the] myth of exile, a myth to which later exiles can themselves turn." (Ingleheart 2011: 19) Turning, self-mythologizing, these are what offset the pain of exile and mute the personal. Ovid transcends "his personal circumstances . . . appropriat[ing] the roles of a dizzying array of archetypal suffering figures: for example, the human unjustly punished for a single lapse; the unremitting target of the vindictive revenge of a piqued, all-powerful deity; the artist and/or parent destroyed by their own creation; the lover bemoaning their separation from their beloved; the agonized, isolated individual unable to articulate and share the burden of his suffering; the wanderer doomed to eternal separation from his homeland." (Ingleheart 2011: 19) "[S]haping the discourse of exile, acting as an important cultural paradigm for later authors who have found themselves subject to exile or similar experiences of alienation or displacement." (Ingleheart 2011: 9-10) The "exile *par excellence*," whose exilic experiences are "uniquely susceptible . . . to being adapted to a wide range of aesthetic, intellectual, and political agendas" encompassing, "but by no means limited to: poetic transgression; censorship and creativity; linguistic isolation and cultural estrangement; artistic decline, the tragic effects of personal error; political rebellion; and (conversely) conciliatory or even fawning behavior towards a ruler." (Ingleheart 2011: 8-9)

Displacement, alienation, cultural estrangement (an *existential* homelessness?), it's these more interiorized modes of exile that interest me; forms of exile (often) of our own choosing, if not their circumstances. How is it that *these* forms of exilic suffering get transformed into art? Well, don't look to me for an answer, I just raise the question, though I must say *self-mythologizing* (these days) seems an unlikely candidate, but then again maybe this *is* how it's done—now—all the time—under any circumstances—like even right now.

The Slippage from Person to Personae

And here enters that slippage from person (or poet) to personae: "Ovid's first-person exilic poetry seems to give his readers direct, unmediated access to his experience and thoughts in a manner virtually unprecedented in ancient literature ["Only Catullus and Horace among ancient writers seem to offer such direct, unmediated access to their lives." (Ingleheart: 2011: footnote 29 p. 6)] (and rare in modern works too)—surely a major reason why readers identified with the figure of Ovid that emerges in these poems." (Ingleheart 2011: 6-7) Nevertheless, despite "the subjective voice of the exile poems, scholars now generally accept that the 'Ovid' of the exile poetry is a persona, which can be seen to draw upon earlier Ovidian personae, such as the elegiac lover of the *Amores*, the 'authors' of the *Heroides*, and the various suffering mythological characters in the *Metamorphoses*." All of which suggests "the constructed nature of the apparently autobiographical exilic letters." (Ingleheart 2011: 7, footnote 30) Yes, the person, the self-mythologizing exilic poet and his personae, but of this life, who he really was or what this meant to him . . . we really have no idea.

> I shall be read on the lips of the people,
> in fame through all the ages,
> if bards' prophecies have any truth,
> I will live.
> Ovid. *Metamorphoses* 15.878-9

Yes, but is that enough?

But Suppose They Invented Everything

> In Ovid's first two poems [in the *Amores*] there is not a beloved in sight, only the warring Cupid. The third poem introduces a desired girl, but as an entirely featureless figure. The fourth adds the detail of her unavailability, but nothing

more. The fifth gives her at last a name and a body, but no face (contrast the very first line of Propertius' first book: "Cynthia first captured wretched me with her eyes"). Nowhere in the *Amores* is Corinna appreciated for anything but her sex appeal, and, despite occasional focusing on her hair and complexion, she remains an empty outline. In the last poem in Book 2 she has been displaced by another, and in Book 3 she is eclipsed altogether: the sexy legs, long hair, peaches and cream complexion, dainty feet, tall, slim figure, and sparkling eyes that we glimpse there are not hers. Was Corinna even Ovid's girl at all?

The lover-narrator himself in the *Amores* remains cheerfully amoral. He is prepared to profess lifelong fidelity and to confess to incorrigible promiscuity; quick to berate a compliant rival for spoiling his sport and an obstructive one for being a prig. He is content to being lied to when confronted with his girl's unchasity and to lie shamelessly when taxed with his own: *Am.* 2.7 is an outburst of righteous indignation at being accused of bedding Corinna's slave-hairdresser, Cypassis, but is followed by immediate blackmail of Cypassis in private when she refuse to oblige him again (*Am.* 2.8.27-8):

And, Cypassis, I shall tell your mistress where I had you,
    and how often, and in how many and what kind of ways.

He dares to trivialize both his own violence in the course of a lover's row and his girl's distress after a hairdressing accident that left her (temporarily) bald (1.14.55, "Fix your face, and chin up: the damage is reparable"). For a generation more romantic as well as more prudish than our own, this was the work of an outrageous cad or else the pointless invention of an emotionally shallow mind. In either case, it was not the expected stuff of proper love poetry.

All Roman love elegy contains much thematic material that is standard (e.g., separation of lovers by a locked house door, control of the beloved by a madam (*lena*), illness of the beloved). Tibullus and Propertius were nonetheless end17ingly believed to have invested their stock situations and images (many inherited from Greek epigram and/or New Comedy) with at least emotional verisimilitude when transferring them to the social setting of first-century BC Rome; even a degree of authentic self-portrayal was not ruled out. The text of the *Amores*, however, itself strongly hints at the narrator's lack of interest in depicting unique and personal experience and emotion.

Hence the contention that Ovid applied his virtuoso talent to turning love elegy into comedy in the *Amores*, inventing for himself as lover an absurdly unbelievable *persona*, by means of which *he* could clown it where his amatory poetic predecessors had played it straight." (Booth 2009: 66-7)

Maria Wyke makes a similar point concerning Ovid: "Critics recognize that the narrative of the *Amores* is constructed within the framework of a general critical strategy they variously describe as a burlesque of elegiac conventions, a *reductio ad absurdum* of elegiac practices, a breaking of elegy's rules, a parody of Propertian poetry, a demystification of elegy's romanticism and its fiction of male erotic enslavement to one dominating mistress . . . [and a] decoding [of] the romantic and realistic practice of writing associated most notably with the Propertian corpus." Her point is that Ovid's first goal is an artistic one, "to construct a literary eroticism," noting that '[a]t this point the narrator is not yet in love," nor ready to "make the declaration of love for a specific woman that his audience might expect from a poet continuing the tradition established in Augustan elegies by Gallus, Tibullus, and Propertius." In fact, it's the role of the poet "that's given priority over that of lover . . . the Ovidian narrator express[ing] his metrical (rather than emotional) concerns." By "drawing attention to the creative process [Ovid] warns that realism is merely a property of the text. By describing the poet's mastery over his own material [he] exposes the conventions of elegiac romanticism and the fictionality of its mistress." (Wyke 2006: 197-98)

It's in this context that Booth raises an interesting question with regard to these elegists. Suppose, she says, these Augustan elegists wrote poetry not "to express love, but . . . [rather] confected love to write poetry—in other words, that not just Ovid in his *Amores*, but all of them invented everything? That hypothesis rests on the premise that Roman elegy is not mimetic but semiotic. That is, although its characters and situations may resemble those of the real world, its texts do not represent anything in that world: rather, their meaning is what the reader, as much as the author, constructs from their relation to one another and from the relation of the elegiac system as a whole to other poetic systems." (Booth 2009: 70-1) If so, then "the poet in the *Amores* will not be Ovid-the-author any more than the lover is Ovid-the-man, such resemblance as there is between the two being coincidental and insignificant. . . . This, then, is the collection in which Ovidius Naso (sometimes) plays himself as he makes and fakes love. Literary making and faking can amount to much the same thing. 'Play' in the *Amores* is both acting and fun. And what Ovid's text makes possible is more than what it says." (Booth 2009: 76)

Well, yes, perhaps Booth does take this a bit too far, but once we've freed ourselves from the notion that these elegies are autobiographical (at least in any straightforward sense), or refer to real (uniquely individual; identifiable) women, what we're left with are aesthetic considerations. In that context, talk of what's (really) real makes little sense. Or would we rather argue that there is a more refined truth, one that comes (only comes) by way of poetic insight? Callimachus might, contra Plato, but that's someone else's book. And I'm happy with this. That we've cleared enough ground to see what this *is* really about: aesthetics and poetics.

A FEW FINAL WORDS
FROM THE LAST OUTBACK
AT THE WORLD'S END

In the last outback, at the world's end.
Dylan. *Ain't Talkin'*

I'm in the last outback, at the world's end.
Ovid. *Epistulae ex Ponto*

Well, he does always seem to get there first, Bob Dylan, I mean, who was recently busted for appropriating a bit of Ovid's exile poetry for some of the lyrics on *Modern Times* (2006). Dylan has a history of this sort of thing—artistic appropriation—which is not something that overly concerns me (or his critics). For one thing, it's common artistic practice, and for another, he's got impeccable taste. From Richard Thomas's article (which he's recently updated: see the appended "Dylan's Metamorphosis" at the end of this chapter), *The Streets of Rome: the Classical Dylan*:

The Last Outback at the World's End: Into Exile with Ovid

One of the immediate classical resonances on *Modern Times* comes in the first song, "Thunder on the Mountain." Particularly in the wake of "Lonesome Day Blues" the sixth verse of "Thunder on the Mountain" pointed straight to Ovid, and his *Ars Amatoria*: "I've been sittin' down studyin' the art of love / I think it will fit me like a glove." But that was just the beginning. On October 10, 2006, Cliff Fell, a New Zealand poet and teacher of creative writing, wrote in the *Nelson Mail* (Nelson, New Zealand) of a striking discovery. He happened to be reading Peter Green's Penguin translation of Ovid's exile poetry, the *Tristia* and the *Epistulae ex Ponto* (Black Sea Letters), while listening to *Modern Times*:
And then this uncanny thing happened—it was like I was suddenly reading with my ears. I heard this line

> from the song "Workingman's Blues 2," "No-one can
> ever claim / That I took up arms against you." But
> there it was singing on the page, from Book 2.52 of
> *Tristia*: "My cause is better: no-one can claim that I
> ever took up arms against you." (Thomas 2007: 35)

So Thomas emailed Fell, which led to Scott Warmuth (a *Dylan aficionado*), who promptly added a few Ovidian intertexts of his own, and then back to Thomas again who, once he'd finally managed to get hold of Peter Green's translation, found a few more. They're all listed below, as presented by Stephen Harrison in his article *Ovid and the Modern Poetics of Exile* (Harrison 2011). But first, here's what Harrison has to say about all this:

> Dylan's thirty-second studio album *Modern Times* (2006)
> shows a strong interest in the exile poetry of Ovid, clearly
> using the translations in Peter Green's already mentioned
> *Ovid: The Poems of Exile* (1994). This late-career classical
> reception by one of the revered counter-cultural figures of the
> 1960s might seem surprising, but his pervious album *Love and
> Theft* (2001) included a prominent allusion to Virgil's *Aeneid*,
> and as we shall see the persona of the exiled Ovid presents a
> good fit for the ageing Dylan's approach to modern culture.
> Some of Dylan's imitations were picked up soon after the
> album's issue by classically minded Dylan fans (for example
> Fell 2006); Richard Thomas in particular has identified a full
> range of allusions (Thomas 2007). In this section I discuss in
> more detail than was possible in Thomas's original
> publication, add one or two to his list of passages, and argue
> that Dylan's development of Ovidian exilic material fits my
> tripartite schema of dislocation, politics, and lament.
>   The album begins with "Thunder on the Mountain".
> This track has no allusions to Ovid's exile poetry, but sets an
> Ovidian tone for the album by stating (verse 6): "I've been
> sittin' down studyin' the art of love | I think it will fit me like
> a glove." As Thomas points out, this is clearly an allusion to
> *Ars amatoria*; it might be worth adding that the next line, "I

want some real good woman to do just what I say," could refer to the precepts offered to women in the poem's third book, especially as that too was translated by Peter Green (*The Erotic Poems*, 1982). But it is in four other tracks that the exile poetry appears, which can be cataloged as follows in fifteen main allusions, with Dylan's lyrics followed by the lines in Green's translations to which they clearly relate: (Harrison 2011: 218-19)

And now the list, which I've modified for comprehension purposes.

Spirit on the Water (Track 2)
1. Verse 14: 'Can't believe these things would ever fade from your mind.'
Pont. 2.4.24: 'I cannot believe these things could fade from your mind.'
2. Verse 16: 'I want to be with you any way I can.'
Tr. 5.1.80: 'I want to be with you any way I can.'

Workingman's Blues no. 2 (Track 6)
3. Verse 2: 'My cruel weapons have been put on the shelf
Come sit down on my knee
You are dearer to me than myself
As you yourself can see.'
Tr. 2.179: 'Show mercy, I beg you, shelve your cruel weapons.'
Tr. 5.14.2; 'wife, dearer to me than myself, you yourself can see.'
4. Verse 4: 'Now the place is ringed with countless foes.'
Tr. 5.12.19-20: 'barred from relaxation | in a place ringed by countless foes.'
5. Verse 5: "Tell me now, am I wrong in thinking | That you have forgotten me?'
Tr. 5.13.18: 'May the gods grant . . . | that I'm wrong in thinking you've forgotten me!'
6. Verse 6: 'Them I will forget | But you I'll remember always.'
Pont. 4.6.42-3: 'Them I'll forget, | but *you* I'll remember always.'
7. Verse 7: 'No-one can ever claim | That I took up arms against you.'

Tr. 2.52: 'no-one can claim that I ever took up arms against you.'
8. Verse 8: 'I'm expecting you | To lead me off in a cheerful dance.'
Tr. 5.12.8: 'or Niobe, bereaved, lead me off some cheerful dance.'

The Levee's Gonna Break (Track 9)
9. Verse 10: 'Some people got barely enough skin to cover their bones.'
Tr. 4.6.42: 'there's barely enough skin to cover my bones.'

Ain't Talkin' (Track 10)
10. Verse 7: 'They will tear your mind away from contemplation They will jump on your misfortune when you're down.'
Tr. 5.7.66: 'tear my mind from the contemplation of my woes.'
Tr. 5.8.3-5: 'Why jump | on misfortunes that you may well suffer yourself? | I'm down.'
11. Verse 9: 'I'll make the most of one last extra hour.'
Tr. 1.3.68: 'let me make the most of one last extra hour.'
12. Verse 11: 'All my loyal and much-loved companions They approve of me and share my code I practice a faith that's long been abandoned Ain't no alters on this long and lonesome road.'
Tr. 1.3.65: 'loyal and much-loved companions, bonded in brotherhood.'
Pont. 3.2.38: 'who approve, and share, your code.'
Tr. 5.7.63-4: 'I practice | terms long abandoned.
13. Verse 13: "Who says I can't get heavenly aid?'
Tr. 1.2.12-13: 'Who says I can't get heavenly aid | when a god's angry with me?'
14. Verse 15: 'every nook and cranny has its tears.'
Tr. 1.3.24: 'every nook and corner had its tears.'
15. Verse 18: 'I'm in the last outback, at the world's end.' *
Pont. 2.7.66: 'In the last outback at the world's end.' *
(Harrison 2011: 219-20)
*Harrison muffs this (as, at one point, does Thomas). The actual lines are:
Dylan: "In the last outback, at the world's end." (Official Dylan website: https://www.bobdylan.com/songs/aint-talkin/)

Ovid: "I'm in the last outback, at the world's end." (Green 2005: 144)

Thomas's conclusion about the aptness of these intertexts is interesting. I mean, just how much does Dylan's singer identify with the exiled and aging Ovid? The answer: quite a bit. "Dylan, 65 years old, in the inner exile he has created for his own protection" invokes Ovid's exile poetry for a reason. "Indeed, the last words of the last song, "Ain't Talking," and therefore the last words of the third album of the trilogy . . . suggest a finality, a closing of the book, and they are straight from Ovid . . . as Dylan puts himself 'in the last outback, at the world's end.'" (Thomas 2007: 38). Yes, except poor Ovid had no choice, though it's not hard to imagine Dylan saying the same thing.

So just which of these am I guilty of: intentionally misleading exilic persona, an inner exile created for my own protection, cultural dislocation (it's clearly not physical dislocation), political exile, lament? Not political. I'm clear on that. I'm no political exile. It's more cultural, the result of the strange lives we live as we pass through time, the changes we note, what we find we miss or long for; so, yes, lament. But an inner exile only; one of temporal, cultural, or historical displacement; one experienced as we live, as the world changes more than we do. And that exilic persona? Well, there's always a bit of room between the me I am and the me I present to the world, or between what I mean and what I intend to mean. Or, better still, what I have some say in or control over and what I don't. Where my persona resides on that cline . . . I have no clear sense. But wherever that is, it truly is *my last outback at the world's end.*

I live,
exiled,
last outback
at the world's end,
the last place they'll look.

Dylan's Metamorphosis

Thomas has since updated (Thomas 2017) his original article in an attempt to stay abreast of the ever-mercurial Dylan (perhaps an impossible task for an academic). In this, *off the rails* would be my preferred cliché—and I don't mean Dylan—when he asserts: "that Dylan's borrowings – or thefts – are all transposed into new situations that have little to do with, but once noticed and activated evoke comparison with, those of the Ovidian models." So, we've moved on from explicitly quoting and referring, though never acknowledged as such, to situations that *merely evoke* comparison to Ovidian models? But doesn't that then raise the question of why, at one time, they held such appeal? A question he then asks for himself: "What is it about the Roman poet that made his voice, travelling across 2,000 years into Green's translation, so appealing to Dylan?"

> Why not Cicero, who was also exiled and wrote real letters back to friends, his wife, his brother, and various other figures? The difference is that while many of Ovid's poems pose as letters, they are not. The poems lament his condition, but they still show the wit, irony and character of the poet familiar to readers of Ovid's earlier and happier times. There is even a theory, in my view not ridiculous, that Ovid never went into exile [no, it's ridiculous]. Ovid's exile poems are poetic constructions, practicing the essence of an art that acknowledged, long before Rimbaud, that: "Je est un autre" – "I is an other", a quote Dylan repeats in connection with the personas he created from the very beginning. Ovid's exile poems are exercises in the genre of exile poetry, artistic creations of the voice of one suffering from solitude in a hostile setting at the ends of the earth. (Thomas 2017)

But there have been a lot of literary exiles, all of whom, presumably, partook of this "poetic construction," this "exercise in the genre of exile poetry," this essence: "I is an other" personae business. So, again, why Ovid? But maybe it no longer *is* Ovid? Is that what he's saying? That Dylan's broken ranks? As near as I can make out, yes, that it's, because it seems that Dylan is now pirating Homer, forcing Thomas, forever in the poet's train, to scramble to catch up.

> Like Dylan, Ovid was a trickster. And in his poems of exile Ovid aligns himself with the ultimate trickster, the hero of the *Odyssey*, though he claims to have suffered even more than Odysseus:

> > I was crushed by a god, with no help in my troubles
> > He had that warrior-goddess [Athena] at his side.
> > What's more the bulk of his troubles are fictitious,
> > Whereas mine remain anything but myth.
> > *Tristia* 1.5.59–80

> Dylan noticed this connection, and on his great album of 2012, *Tempest*, traded the Ovidian voice not merely for a Homeric voice, but specifically and exclusively the voice of Odysseus. (Thomas 2017)

So there's your connection between the older Dylan quoting Ovid and thinking of exile and a more recent version busily plundering Homer: Ovid and Odysseus were both *tricksters*. Well, you can read all you want to about Ovid starting right now and forever and never find anyone else who'd think to call him a *trickster* or compare him in any sane sense with Odysseus: a different sort of exile, not least in that one was real the other mythic; a different sort of journey—one always with home in mind, one to the world's end; and fundamentally different legacies within the literary genre of exile (is Odysseus even in that pantheon?). But here's Dylan referring to all this in his Nobel Lecture ("his alignment with Odysseus was completed when . . . he said: 'In a lot of ways, some of the same things have happened to you' . . . [that is, to] all of us in our own odysseys"), and since Thomas's article is about Dylan's metamorphosis there needs to be something not only from which he came, but something he *be*came, so I guess Ovidian to Homeric *is* called for. "And so Dylan closed his lecture where Homer began: 'I return once again to Homer', he said, 'Sing in me, o Muse, and through me tell the story'." His songwriting (his method of composition), so Thomas says (and this includes his constantly changing the lyrics to his songs: out with Ovid, in with Homer), "has always come from, and drawn meaning from, other places, not least the worlds of the Greeks and Romans. In the process, Dylan has become part of a stream that flows from the beginning of Western literature to the present." So he's changeable, but he's also deeply traditional, but where's the metamorphosis in that? (And those would be Ovidian metamorphoses, would they not?) I really must ask this: why do we even try to make sense of Dylan? I mean, has there ever been a better example of a poet repeatedly confounding our expectations with ever-mutable personae? And how is that like that trickster Odysseus? Isn't he just a man named Zimmerman hiding behind an elaborate façade (the many masks) of his own (and our) creation? Well, yeah, now here's a guy *living in exile*; one who's *never* coming home.

Coda

What started with a simple act of curiosity has led to a whole book of curiosities. I wish I'd had the time to track them all down, but then who ever does? Does that mean I set this aside, unsatisfied? Mostly, but then that's also a function of the many new threads I've uncovered, any one of which would be fascinating to follow—a vast array of tempting scholarship I've barely skimmed. So I've tried to stay with the theme I began, the poet and his *domina* ("elegy's romanticism and its fiction of male erotic enslavement to one dominating mistress"), but I have been tempted to wander by the epigrams of Philodemos and Callimachus (the *Epicurean* Philodemos; the *slender* Callimachus); the issue of how realistic, how autobiographical, these poems are and if that even matters (they aren't and it doesn't); the Ovidian theme of the writer-as-exile and how any suffering that might entail gets transformed into art; the fascinating slippage from person (or poet) to persona(e) (if we could get behind the mask(s) we'd find … *nothing* …?); and the historical and social context of this poetic activity. Not as tempting, and again mostly because I don't have the time, are the many more purely formal and literary considerations I've had to skirt to see this project through to conclusion.

Set aside the many disturbing aspects of Roman life that repeatedly parade through these poems (slavery, the lack of empathy, the deplorable treatment of women), the many clichés that make up so much of the love elegist's literary or thematic stock-in-trade, the rather foolish nature of these "love" relationships that look nothing like what we'd like to think of as love, and what we're left with are men whose actions as poets and Romans were often viewed as distinctly outré (which in Ovid's case proved to be fatefully consequential). And then there's the poet and his text, realistic, yet not, a "literary eroticism" bound by the conventions of a poetic genre lodged within a social world we find both eerily familiar and disturbingly alien. What's real here, I suppose, is just the text (Tom Stoppard's dog). That we have before us, the rest—the person/poet, their life, their world, all that it meant—is, if not just unknown, far less certain. We speak of what we can see, and even then we're just guessing.

Appendix One

The Circus Maximus and Roman Society

The Circus Maximus was the largest man-made structure in the Roman Empire, easily accommodating 150,000 people. Typically, there were twenty-four races on a game day (*ludi*), with sixty-six such days per year. Race entrants consisted of two- or four-horse chariots, each assigned to one of twelve starting gates by lot, the races being run counterclockwise around the *euripus* (central barrier) for seven laps (approximately five kilometers) in a typical time of 8-9 minutes. There were four large racing teams, or factions, that acted as contractors; large international operations with many employees (and fanatical fans), commonly known by their team colors: Red, White, Blue and Green. Although it's true that charioteers often achieved great fame and fortune, they were usually of low status—slaves, hired freedmen, foreigners—and rarely freeborn Roman citizens. Nevertheless, they were often famous celebrities hugely popular not only with the common people but the emperor and intelligentsia. And it's true, just as Ovid suggests, that unlike the seating at the theatre or amphitheater, seating at the Circus was not sexually segregated (seats were separated by painted lines or grooves in the stone benches), which allowed men and women to mix more freely than was typically possible elsewhere. Yes, there was betting.

Presented below, a small sample of the many fascinating contemporary accounts of both the Circus Maximus and chariot racing.

> Let sad Victory break the palms of Idumaea. Favor, beat your bare breast with merciless hand. Let Honor put on mourning. Grieving Glory, cast your crowned tresses on the

unkind flames. Ah villainy! Scorpus, cheated of your first
youth, you die. So soon you yoke black horses. The goal,
ever quickly gained by your hastening chariot - your life's goal
too, why was it so close? [10.50] (Martial 1993: 363-65)

I am Scorpus, the glory of the clamorous circus, your
applause, Rome, and brief darling. Envious Lachesis snatched
me away ere my thirtieth year, but, counting my victories,
believed me an old man. [10.53] (Martial 1993: 367)

Scorpus was a Green charioteer, "one of the most famous
drivers of the first century, known not just for his fabulous
prizes but for his outstanding successes as well as his early (and
thus tragic) death. Martial's epigrams hint at the deep
melancholy of the fans as Scorpus' death is given mythic
scope." (Futrell 2006: 191)

It is found in the *Acta* [likely the *Acta Diurna*, a gazette
published in Rome from the mid-first century BCE with news
of official events, ceremonies and so forth] that at the funeral
of Felix the charioteer of the Reds, one of his fans threw
himself upon the pyre—a pitiful story—and the opposing
fans tried to prevent this score to the record of a professional
by asserting that the man had fainted owing to the quantity of
scents. [7.53.186] (Pliny 1942: 631)

As above, so below: fanatical fans who deeply identified
with their teams; serious rivalries that often spilled over into
violent confrontations.

I have been spending all the last few days amongst my notes
and papers in most welcome peace. How could I—in the
city? The races were on, a type of spectacle which has never
had the slightest attraction for me, I can find nothing new or
different in them: once seen is enough so it surprises me all
the more that so many thousands of adult men should have
such a childish passion for watching galloping horses and
drivers standing in chariots, over and over again. If they were

attracted by the speed of the horses or the drivers' skill, one could account for it, but in fact it is the racing-colors they really support and care about and if the colors were to be exchanged in mid-course during a race, they would transfer their favor and enthusiasm and rapidly desert the famous drivers and horses whose names they shout as they recognize them from afar. Such is the popularity and importance of a worthless shirt - I don't mean with the crowd, which is more worthless than the shirt, but with certain serious individuals. When I think how this futile, tedious, monotonous business can keep them sitting endlessly in their seats, I take pleasure in the fact that their pleasure is not mine. And I have been very glad to fill my idle hours with literary work during these days which others have wasted in the idlest of occupations. [9.6] (Pliny the Younger 1969: 87-89)

[Here, Philostratus is quoting Apollonius of Tyana] Now the Alexandrians are devoted to horses, and assemble in the hippodrome to watch them. When they started slaughtering one another, Apollonius issued a rebuke to them on the matter. Entering the sanctuary, he said, "How long will you persist in dying not for your children's sake or for your sanctuaries, but in order to pollute the sanctuaries by entering them all covered with gore, and to perish within your own city wall? Troy, they say, was sacked by a single horse, cunningly built by the Achaeans of that time, but chariots and horses have been yoked to destroy you, and they prevent you from reining in your lives. You are being ruined, not by the sons of Atreus or Aeacus, but by one another, as not even the drunken Trojans were.

"Now in Olympia, there are prizes for wrestling, boxing, and the pancration, but no one has died because of the athletes, though over enthusiasm for a compatriot might perhaps be excused. But here mere horses make you unsheathe swords against one another and prepare to throw stones. Fire awaits such a city, where there is groaning and violence 'of the killers and the killed, and the ground runs red with blood.' Respect the Nile, the joint mixing bowl of

Egypt. But why do I mention the Nile to people who measure the rising of blood rather than of water?" [5.26] (Philostratus 2005: 47)

Let us now turn to the idle and slothful commons. Among them some who have no shoes are conspicuous as though they had cultured names, such as the Messores, Statarii, Semicupae and Serapini, and Cicymbricus, with Gluturinus and Trulla, and Lucanicus with Porclaca and Salsula, and countless others. These spend all their life with wine and dice, in low haunts, pleasures, and the games. Their temple, their dwelling, their assembly, and the height of all their hopes is the Circus Maximus. You may see many groups of them gathered in the fora, the cross-roads, the streets, and their other meeting-places, engaged in quarrelsome arguments with one another, some (as usual) defending this, others that. Among them those who have enjoyed a surfeit of life, influential through long experiences, often swear by their hoary hair and wrinkles that the state cannot exist if in the coming race the charioteer whom each favors is not first to rush forth from the barriers, and fails to round the turning-point closely with his ill-omened horses. And when there is such a dry rot of thoughtlessness, as soon as the longed-for day of the chariot-races begins to dawn, before the sun is yet shining clearly they all hasten in crowds to the spot at top speed, as if they would outstrip the very chariots that are to take part in the contest; and torn by their conflicting hopes about the result of the race, the greater number of them in their anxiety pass sleepless nights. [28.4.28-31] (Ammianus Marcellinus 1939: 157-59)

What, then; was the motive nothing at all which actuated you and induced you to leave your child? And how can that be? But it was a motive like that which impelled a certain man in Rome to cover his head when the horse which he backed was running,—and then, when it won unexpectedly, they had to apply sponges to him to revive him from his faint! [1.11.27-28] (Epictetus 1925: 85)

A more lighthearted view of the role of sport:

Her votaries announce the eighth hour to the Pharian heifer and the pike-carrying cohort returns to camp as another comes on duty. This hour cools the warm baths, the one preceding pants out immoderate heat, the sixth glows with Nero's excess. Stella, Nepos, Canius, Cerialis, Flaccus, are you coming? The sigma takes seven, we are six; add Lupus. The bailiff's wife has brought me mallows to relieve the stomach and the garden's various wealth. There is sessile lettuce and clipped leeks, belching mint is not to seek, nor the salacious herb. Slices of egg will top mackerel flavored with rue and there will be a sow's udder wet from tunny's brine. So much for the hors d'oeuvres. The little dinner will be served in one course; a kid, snatched from the jaws of a savage wolf, morsels requiring no carver's knife, workmen's beans and early greens. To these will accrue a chicken and a ham that has already survived three dinners. When my guests are satisfied, I shall offer ripe fruit and leesless wine from a Nomentan flagon twice three years old in Frontinus' consulship. To boot there will be merriment free of malice, frank speech that gives no anxiety the morning after, nothing you would wish you hadn't said. Let my guest talk of Scorpus and the Green; let my cups get no man put on trial. [10.48] (Martial 1993: 361-63)

But now adjourn your worries, put business matters aside, and treat yourself to a pleasant break, as you'll be free to relax for the entire day. There'll be no mention of interest due, and don't let your wife intensify your silent rage if she makes a habit of going out at dawn and coming back at night with her gauze dress damp and suspiciously wrinkled, her hair disheveled, and her face and ears flushed. Strip off anything that annoys you right in front of my doorstep. Leave behind your household and your slaves and whatever they've broken or lost. Most of all, leave behind the ingratitude of your friends. Meanwhile, the tiers of spectators are celebrating the Idaean ritual of the Megalesian flag and the praetor is sitting there as if in a triumph, the prey of the nags, and, if I may say so without offending the populace too huge to count, today the whole of Rome is inside the Circus. The shouting is ear shattering—and this tells me that the Green jackets have won. If they'd lost, you know, you'd see this Rome of ours dumbstruck and in mourning, as when the consuls were defeated in the dust of Cannae. The races are a fine sight for our young men, who are fit for the noise and bold betting, with a chic young woman at their side; my wrinkled skin would rather drink in the spring sunshine and escape the toga. You can head for the baths at once with a clear conscience, although there's still a full hour till midday. This is something you'd not be able to do for five days in a row, because even this kind of life is enormously tedious. Pleasures are enhanced by rare indulgence. [11.179-208] (Juvenal 2004: 415-17)

A dynamic account of one race.

Now the appointed day came, and the plain was filled with the noise of a crowd past numbering; and Scipio, with tears in his eyes, led the semblance of a funeral procession with due rites of burial. Every Spaniard and every soldier of the Roman army brought gifts to throw upon the blazing pyres. Scipio himself held goblets, filled either with milk or with sacred wine, and sprinkled fragrant flowers over the altars. Then he summoned the ghosts to rise up, and rehearsed with tears the glories of the dead, and did honor to their noble deeds. Thence he went back to the race-course and started the first contest—that which was to test the speed of horses. Even before the starting-gate was unbarred, the excited crowd surged to and fro with a noise like the sound of the sea, and, with a fury of partisanship, fixed their eyes on the doors behind which the racers were standing.

And now the signal was given, and the bolts flew back with a noise. Scarcely had the first hoof flashed into full view, when a wild storm of shouting rose up to heaven. Bending forward like the drivers, each man gazed at the chariot he favored, and at the same time shouted to the flying horses. The course was shaken by the enthusiasm of the spectators, and excitement robbed every man of his senses. They lean forward and direct the horses by their shouting. A cloud of yellow dust rose up from the sandy soil, concealing with its darkness the running of the horses and the exertions of the drivers. One man backs with fury the mettled steed, another the charioteer. Some are zealous for horses of their own country, others for the fame of some ancient stud. One man is filled with joyful hope for an animal that is racing for the first time, while another prefers the green old age of a well-tried veteran. At the start, *Lampon*, bred in Gallicia, left the rest behind; he rushed through the air with the flying car, galloping over the course with huge strides and leaving the winds behind him. The crowd roared with applause, thinking that with such a start their favorite had as good as won. But those who looked deeper and had more experience of the race-course, blamed the driver for putting forth all his strength at the beginning: from a distance they uttered vain protests, that he was tiring out his team with his efforts and keeping no reserve of power. "Where are you careering too eagerly, Cyrnus?" - Cyrnus was the charioteer - "Be prudent! Put down your whip and tighten your reins!" But alas, his ears were deaf: on he sped, unsparing of his horses, and forgetting how much ground had still to be covered.

Next came *Panchates*, a chariot-length and no more behind the leader. Bred in Asturia, he was conspicuous for the white forehead and four white feet of his sires. Though high-mettled, he was low of stature and lacked comeliness; but now his fiery spirit lent him wings, and he sped over the plain, impatient of the reins; he seemed to grow in stature and size as he ran. His driver, Hiberus, was radiant with scarlet of Cinyphian dye.

Third in order, neck and neck with *Pelorus*, ran *Caucasus*, a fractious animal that loved not the caressing hand that patted his neck, but rejoiced to bite and champ the iron in his mouth till blood came with the foam. *Pelorus*, on the other hand, was more tractable and obedient to the rein; never did he swerve aside and drive the car in crooked lines, but kept to the inside and grazed the turning-post with his near wheel. He was conspicuous for the size of his neck and the thick mane that rippled over it. Strange to say, he had no sire: his dam, Harpe, had conceived him from the Zephyr of spring and foaled him in the plains of the Vettones. This chariot was driven along the course by the noble Durius, while *Caucasus* relied upon ancient Atlas as his driver. *Caucasus* came from Aetolian Tyde, the city founded by the wandering hero, Diomede; and legend traced his descent to the Trojan horses which the son of Tydeus, successful in his bold attempt, stole from Aeneas by the river Simois. Atlas came last, but Durius was last and also moved no faster: one might have thought the pair were running peaceably side by side and keeping level.

And now, when near half the distance was completed, they quickened over the course; and spirited *Panchates*, struggling to catch up the team ahead, seemed to rise higher and at each moment to mount upon the chariot in front, and the hooves of his prancing forefeet struck and rattled on the car of the Gallician horse. When Hiberus, who came second, saw that the Gallician team of Cyrnus was tiring, that the chariot was no longer bounding ahead, and that the smoking horses were driven on by severe and repeated flogging, then, as when a sudden storm rushes down from a mountain-stop, he leaned forward quickly as far as the necks of his coursers and hung above their crests, and stirred up *Panchates,* who was chafing at being second in the race, and plied his whip, even while he called to the horse: "Steed of Asturia, shall any other get in front and win the prize when you are competing? Rise up and fly and glide over the plain with all your wonted speed, as if on wings! *Lampon* is panting hard; his strength is gone and he grows smaller; he has no breath left to carry the goal." At these words, *Panchates* rose higher, as if he were just starting in the race; and Cyrnus, though he strove to block his rival by swerving, or to keep up with him, was soon left behind. The sky and the race-course resounded, smitten by the shouts of the spectators. Victorious *Panchates* raised his triumphant crest still higher as he ran on; and he drew after him his three partners in the yoke.

The two last drivers were Atlas and Durius; and now they swerved aside and resorted to tricks. First, one tried to pass his rival on the left; and then the other came up on the right and strove to get in front; but both failed in their attempted strategy. At last Durius, young and confident, leaning forward and jerking at his reins, placed his chariot athwart his rival's course and struck the other car and upset it. Atlas, no match for the other's youth and strength, protested with justice: "Where are you rushing? or what crazy kind of racing is this? You're trying to kill me and my horses together." As he cried out thus, he fell head first from the broken chariot; and the horses too, a sorry sight, fell down and sprawled in disorder on the ground, while the conqueror shook his reins on the open course, and *Pelorus* flew up the middle of the track, leaving Atlas struggling to rise. It did not take him long to catch up the weary team of Cyrnus: he flew past with speedy car, though Cyrnus was learning too late the wisdom of controlling his pace. A shout of applause from his supporters drove the chariot on. And now Pelorus thrust his head over the back and shoulders of terrified Hiberus, till the charioteer felt the horse's hot breath and foam upon his neck. Durius pressed on along the plain, and increased the pace of his team by the whip. Nor was the effort vain: coming up on the right, he seemed to be, or even was, running neck and neck with his rival. Then, amazed by the prospect of such glory, he cried out: "Now, Pelorus, now is the time to show that the West-wind was your sire! Let steeds that spring from the loins of mere animals learn how far superior is the issue of an immortal parent. When victorious, you shall offer gifts to your sire, and raise an altar in his honor." And indeed, had he not, even while he spoke, been beguiled, by too great success and by his fearful joy, into dropping his whip, Durius would perhaps have consecrated to the West-wind the altars he had vowed. But now, as wretched as if the victor's wreath had fallen from his head, he turned his rage against himself, tearing the gold-embroidered garment from his breast, and weeping, and pouring out complaints to heaven. When the lash was gone, the team no longer obeyed the driver: in vain he flogged their backs with the reins for a whip.

Meanwhile, *Panchates*, sure now of victory, sped on to the goal, and claimed the first prize with head held high. A light breeze fanned the mane that rippled over his neck and shoulders; then with proud step he raised his nimble limbs, and a great shout greeted his victory. Each competitor received alike a battle-axe of solid silver with engraving; but the other prizes differed from one another and were of unequal value. To the winner was given a flying steed, a desirable present from the Massylian king; the second in merit then received two cups overlaid with gold of the Tagus, taken from the great heap of Carthaginian spoil; the third prize was the shaggy hide of a fierce lion and a Carthaginian helmet with bristling plumes; and lastly Scipio summoned Atlas and gave him a prize also in pity for his age and ill-fortune, though the old man had fallen down when his chariot was wrecked. To him was given a beautiful youth, to attend on him, together with a skin cap of Spanish fashion. [16.303-456] (Silius Italicus 1943: 409-19)

Below, from *Augustus,* John Williams' brilliant epistolary novel, and 1973's co-winner of the National Book Award for Fiction. Here, Ovid writes to Propertius, telling him of his remarkable day at the races with Augustus and Augustus' daughter, Julia. Sadly ironic, in light of what subsequently happened to Julia, her lovers, and Ovid.

III. Letter: Publius Ovidius Naso to Sextus Propertius, in Assisi (13 B.C.)

Dear Sextus, my friend and my master—how do you thrive in that melancholy exile you have imposed upon yourself? Your Ovid beseeches you to return to Rome, where you are sorely missed. Things here are not nearly so gloomy as you may have been led to believe; a new star is in the Roman sky, and once again those who have the wit to do so may live in gaiety and pleasure. Indeed, during the past few months, I have concluded that I would be in no other time and in no other place.

You are the master of my art, and older than I—yet can you be sure that you are wiser? Your melancholy may be of your own constitution, rather than Rome's making. Do return to us; there is pleasure yet, before the night comes down upon us.

But forgive me; you know that I am not suited for weighty talk, and once having begun cannot sustain it. I intended at the outset of this letter merely to tell you of a delightful day, hoping that I could persuade you by that to return to us.

Yesterday was the anniversary of the Emperor Octavius Caesar's birth, and thus a Roman holiday; yet it began for me unpropitiously enough. I was in my office disgracefully early—at the first hour, no less, just as the sun was beginning to struggle up from the east through the forest of buildings that is Rome, bringing the city to its feet—for though one may not plead a case on such a holiday as this, one may have to do so the next day; and I had a particularly difficult brief to prepare. It seems that Cornelius Apronius, who has retained me, is suing Fabius Creticus for nonpayment for some lands, while Creticus is countersuing, claiming that the title to the lands is faulty. Both are thieves; neither has a case; thus the skill of the brief and the persuasion of the pleading are most important—as, of course, is the chance of magistrate.

In any event, I had been working all morning; marvelous lines kept popping into my head, as they always do when I am laboring at something that bores me; my secretary was particularly slow and fumbling; and the noise that came from the Forum grated against my ears much more fiercely than it should have done. I was becoming increasingly irritable, and for the hundredth time swore that I should give up this foolish career that in the long run will only give me riches I do not need and the dull distinction of senatorial office.

Then, in the midst of my boredom, a remarkable thing happened. I heard a clatter outside my door, and laughter; and though I heard no knock, my door burst open, and there stood before me the most remarkable eunuch I have ever seen—coiffed and perfumed, dressed in elegant silks, with emeralds and rubies on his fingers, he stood before me as if he were better than a freedman, better even than a citizen.

"This is not the Saturnalia," I said angrily. "Who has given you leave to burst in upon me?"

"My mistress," he said in a shrill, effeminate voice; "my mistress bids you attend me."

"Your mistress," I said, "may rot, for all I care. . . . Who is she?"

He smiled as if I were a slug at his feet. "My mistress is Julia, daughter of Octavius Caesar, the August, Emperor of Rome and First Citizen. Do you wish to know more, lawyer?"

I suppose I gaped at him; I did not speak.

"You will attend me, I presume?" he said haughtily.

In an instant my irritation was gone. I laughed, and tossed the sheaf of papers I had been clutching toward my secretary. "Do the best you can with these," I said. Then I turned to the slave who waited for me. "I will attend you," I said, "wherever your mistress would have you lead me." And I followed him out the door.

As is my wont, dear Sextus, I shall digress for a moment. In a casual way, I had met the lady in question a few weeks before, at a huge party given by that Sempronius Gracchus whom we both know. The Emperor's daughter had returned only a month or so before from a long journey in the East, where she had accompanied her husband, Marcus Agrippa, on some business of his, and where Agrippa remains yet. I was anxious to meet her, of course; since her return, the fashionable people of Rome have been talking of nothing else. So when Gracchus, who seems to be on rather friendly terms with her, invited me, I of course quickly accepted.

There were literally hundreds of people at the party at Sempronius Gracchus's villa—really too large a gathering to be very amusing, I suppose, but it was pleasurable in its own way. Despite the numbers of people, I had the chance to meet Julia, and we bantered for a few moments. She is an utterly charming woman, exquisitely beautiful, and really quite intelligent and well-read. She was kind enough to indicate that she had read some of my poems. Knowing her father's reputation for rectitude (as do you, my poor Sextus), I tried to make a sort of rueful apology for the "naughtiness" of my verse. But she smiled at me in that devastating way she has, and said: "My dear Ovid, if you try to convince me that though your verse is naughty, your life is chaste, I shall not speak to you again."

And I said, "My dear lady, if that is the condition, I shall attempt to convince you otherwise."

And she laughed and moved away from me. Though it was a pleasant interlude, it did not occur to me that she would give me another thought, let alone remember my existence for two whole weeks. And yet she did; and yesterday I found myself in her company once more, following the circumstance which I have described.

Outside my door, attended by bearers, there were perhaps half a dozen litters, canopied with silk of purple and gold; they teemed with the movements of their occupants, and laughter shook the street. I stood, not knowing where to turn; my castrate chaperon had wandered away and was haranguing some of the lesser slaves. Then someone stepped from a litter, and I saw at once that it was she, the Julia who had so kindly interrupted my tedious morning. Then another stepped from the litter and joined her. It was Sempronius Gracchus. He smiled at me. I went toward them.

"You have saved me from a death by boredom," I said to Julia. "What now will you do with that life which belongs to you?"

"I shall use it frivolously," she said. "Today is my father's birthday, and he has given me permission to invite some of my friends to sit with him in his box at the Circus. We shall watch the games, and gamble away our money."

"The games," I said. "How charming." I intended my remark to be neutral, but Julia took it as irony. She laughed.

"One does not have that much concern for the games," she said. "One goes to see, and to be seen, and to discover less common amusements." She glanced at Sempronius. "You will learn, perhaps." She turned from me then, and called to the others, some of whom had stepped out of their litters to stretch their legs. "Who would share his seat with Ovid, the poet of love, who writes of those things to which you have dedicated your lives?"

Arms waved from litters, my name was shouted: "Here, Ovid, ride with us—my girl needs your advice!" "No, I need your advice!" And there was much laughter. I finally chose a litter in which there was room for me, the bearers hoisted their burdens, and we made our way slowly through the crowded streets toward the Circus Maximus.

We arrived at noon, just as the hordes of people were streaming out of the stands for a hasty lunch before the resumption of the games. I must say, it gave me an odd feeling to see those masses, recognizing the colors of our litters, part before our advance, as the earth parts before the advance of a plow. Yet they were gay, and waved to us and shouted in the most friendly manner.

We debarked from our litters; and with Julia, Sempronius Gracchus, and another whom I did not know leading our band, we made our way among those arcades that honeycomb the Circus toward the stairs. Occasionally from the doorway of one of these arcades, an astrologer would beckon and call to us, whereupon someone in our party would shout: "We know our future, old man!" and throw him a coin. Or a prostitute would show herself and beckon enticingly to one who seemed unattached, whereupon one of the ladies might call to her in mock terror, "Oh, no! Don't steal him from us. He might never return!"

We mounted the stairs; and as we approached the Imperial box there were shushings and calls for quiet, out of deference for the presence of Octavius Caesar. But he was not in the box when we arrived; and I must say that, despite the pleasure I was having in the company of this most delightful troop, I found myself a little disappointed.

For as you know, Sextus, unlike you—not being an intimate of Maecenas, as you are, nor needing that intimacy—I have never met Octavius Caesar. I have seen him from afar, of course, as has everyone in Rome: but I know of him only that which you have told me.

"The Emperor is not here?" I asked. Julia said, "There are certain kinds of bloodshed that my father does not enjoy." She pointed down at the open space of the course. "He usually comes late, after the animal hunt is over."

I looked to where she was pointing; the attendants were dragging away the slain animals and raking over the earth that was spotted with blood. I saw several tigers, a lion, and even an elephant being dragged across the ground. I had attended one of these hunts before, when I first came to Rome, and had found it extremely dull and common. I suggested as much to Julia.

She smiled, "My father says that either a fool is killed, or a dumb beast, and he cannot bring himself to care which. And besides, there are no wagers to be made on these contests between hunters and beasts. My father enjoys the wagering."

"It's late," I said. "He will be here, won't he?"

"He must," she said. "The games honor his birthday; and he would not be discourteous to anyone who so honors him."

I nodded, and recalled that the games were being presented to him by one of the new praetors, Jullus Antonius. I started to say something to Julia; but I remembered who Jullus Antonius was, and I checked my speech.

But Julia must have noticed my intention, for she smiled. "Yes," she said. "In particular, my father would not be discourteous to the son of an old enemy, whom he has forgiven, and whose son he has preferred to some who are his own kin."

Wisely (I think), I nodded, and did not speak more of the matter. But I wondered about this son of Marcus Antonius, whose name, even these many years after his death, still is honored by many of the citizens of Rome.

Yet there is little time to wonder about things of that sort in such gay company. The servants brought tidbits of food on golden plates, and poured wine into golden cups; and we ate, and drank, and chattered as we watched the crowd straggle back to their seats for the afternoon races.

By the sixth hour, the stands were filled, and it seemed to me overflowing with a good part of the population of Rome. Then suddenly, above the natural noise of the crowd, a great roar went up; many of the populace were standing, and were pointing toward the box where we reclined. I turned around, glancing over my shoulder. At the rear of the box, in the shadows, stood two figures, one rather tall, the other short. The tall one was dressed in the richly embroidered tunic and the purple-bordered toga of a consul; the shorter wore the plain white tunic and toga of the common citizen.

The taller of the two was Tiberius, stepson of the Emperor and consul of Rome; and the shorter was, of course, the Emperor Octavius Caesar himself.

They came into the box; we rose; the Emperor smiled and nodded to us, and indicated that we should seat ourselves. He sat beside his daughter, while Tiberius (a dour-faced young man, who seemed not to want to be where he was) found a seat somewhat removed from the rest of the party, and spoke to no one. For several moments the Emperor and Julia talked together, their heads close; the Emperor glanced at me, and said something to Julia, who smiled, nodded, and then beckoned me to join them.

I approached, and Julia presented me to her father.

"I am pleased to meet you," the Emperor said; his face was lined and weary, his light hair shot with white—but his eyes were bright and piercing and alert. "My friend Horace has spoken of your work."

"I hope kindly," I said, "but I cannot pretend to compete with him. My Muse is smaller and more trivial, I fear."

He nodded. "We all obey whatever Muse chooses us. . . . Do you have any favorites today?"

"What?" I said blankly.

"The races," he said. "Do you have any favorite drivers?"

"Sir," I said, "I must confess that I come to the races more nearly for the society than for the horses. I really know very little about them."

"Then you don't wager," he said. He seemed a little disappointed.

"On everything but the races," I said. He nodded and smiled a little, and turned to someone behind him.

"Which do you pick in the first?"

But whoever it was to whom he spoke did not have time to answer. At the far end of the race course, gates opened, trumpets sounded, and the procession entered. It was led by Jullus Antonius, the praetor who had financed the games; he was dressed in a scarlet tunic, over which he wore the purple-bordered toga, and carried in his right hand the golden eagle, which seemed almost ready to take flight from the ivory rod which supported it; and upon his head was the golden wreath of laurel. In his chariot drawn by his magnificent white horse, I must say he was an impressive figure, even at the distance from which I saw him.

Slowly the procession went round the track. Behind Jullus Antonius walked the priests of the rites, who attended the statues, thought by the ignorant to be the literal embodiments of the gods; then came the drivers who were to race, resplendent in their whites and reds, and greens and blues; and at last a crew of dancers and mimes and clowns, who cavorted and tumbled upon the track while the priests relinquished their effigies to the platform around which the racers would drive their chariots.

And then the procession made its way to the Emperor's box. Jullus Antonius halted, saluted the Emperor, and gave him the games in dedication of his birthday. I must say, I looked at Jullus with some curiosity. He is an extraordinarily handsome man— his muscular arms brown from the sun, his face dark and slightly heavy, with very white teeth and curling black hair. It is said that he closely resembles his father, though he is less inclined to fat.

The dedication over, Jullus Antonius came closer to the box and called up to the Emperor:

"I'll join you later, when I get them started."

The Emperor nodded; he seemed pleased. He turned to me. "Antonius knows the horses, and the riders. Listen to him. You'll learn a bit about racing."

I must confess, Sextus, that the ways of the great are beyond me. The Emperor Octavius Caesar, master of the world, seemed concerned only with the impending races; to the son of a father whom he had defeated in battle and whom he forced to commit suicide, he was warm and friendly and natural; and he spoke to me as if we both were the most common of citizens. I remember that I thought briefly of the possibility of a poem upon the subject; but just as quickly I rejected the idea. I am sure that Horace could have done one, but that is not my (or our) sort of thing.

Jullus Antonius disappeared into a gate at the far end of the course, and a few moments later reappeared in his enclosure above the starting gate. A roar went up from the crowd; Jullus Antonius waved, and looked down at the racers lined up beneath him. Then he threw down the white flag, the barriers dropped, and in a cloud of dust the chariots set off.

I stole a glance at the Emperor, and was surprised to see that he seemed hardly interested in the race, now that it had begun. He discerned my glance, and said to me: "One does not bet on the first race, if one is wise. The horses are made so nervous by the procession that they seldom run according to their natures."

I nodded, as if what he said made sense to me.

Before the chariots had completed four of their seven laps, Jullus Antonius joined us. He seemed to know most of the people in the box, for he nodded to them in a friendly manner, and spoke a few of their names. He sat between the Emperor and Julia, and soon the three of them were exchanging wagers and laughing among themselves.

And so the afternoon went. Servants came with more food and wine, and with damp towels so that we could wipe the dust of the track from our faces. The Emperor wagered on every race, sometimes betting with several persons at once; he lost carelessly, and won with great glee. Just before the beginning of the last race, Jullus Antonius rose to leave, saying that he had some last duties at the starting gate. He bade me good-by, and expressed the hope that we might meet again; he bade good-by to the Emperor; and then bowed with what I took to be an elaborate and private irony to Julia, who threw back her head and laughed.

The Emperor frowned, but said nothing. Shortly thereafter, when the crowd had streamed out of the Circus, we took our leave. A few of us gathered at Sempronius Gracchus's home for a while in the evening; and I learned what may have been the source of the little byplay between Jullus Antonius and the Emperor's daughter. It was Julia herself who told me.

Julia's husband, Marcus Agrippa, had once been married to the younger Marcella, daughter of the Emperor's sister, Octavia; early in Julia's widowhood, he had been persuaded by the Emperor to divorce Marcella and marry Julia. And only recently had Jullus Antonius married that Marcella who had been Agrippa's wife.

"It's rather confusing," I said lamely.

"Not really," said Julia. And then she laughed. "My father has it all written down, so that one might always know to whom one is married."

And that, my dear Sextus, was my afternoon and evening. I saw the new, and I saw the old; and Rome is again becoming a place where one can live. (Williams 1972: 207-16)

Appendix Two

Love Elegy: Social and Literary Contexts

Miller poses the following question: Yes, it's true that Ovid was exiled, but could Latin love elegy really be subversive? Apparently so, but perhaps not in the manner we might imagine.

> Not only do elegiac love affairs focus on love outside of marriage; they call into question the basic power relations that lay at the heart of traditional Roman life. The defining characteristic of the focus on an exclusive or dominant love affair as the genre's thematic center of gravity already casts it outside the mainstream of Roman cultural life. Love, in genres such as comedy and satire, was a regrettable extravagance to be tolerated in young men. They could have their flings with a courtesan or *meretrix*, provided they did not despoil the family fortune, but were then expected to settle down in a traditional arranged marriage and pursue a career in law, the military, or politics. Love was tolerated so long as it was temporary and did not endanger another man's fortune or legitimate sexual prerogatives. In Horace's lyric poetry, which was written during the twenties BCE, the heyday of the elegiac genre, love is a pleasant diversion to be indulged in with a variety of Greek flute girls and *meretrices*. In epic, which elegy always defines as its generic opposite, amorous intrigues such as Aeneas's with Dido are portrayed as endangering the very foundations of the state by distracting the hero from his divine mission. (Miller 2002: 3-4)

> The lovers . . . adopt[ing] the pose of the slave of love, *seruus amoris*, in which they pretend to subject themselves completely to the will of their beloveds . . . is an abdication of the normal rights of masculine domination that went without question in Roman society. For a man to submit to the will of a woman was to accept the label of effeminate softness or

mollitia. Moreover, the elegists go further still and cast themselves in the role of *praeceptores amoris*, teachers of love . . . present[ing] themselves not only as sexual nonconformists but also as the advocates of a lifestyle that, if taken literally, threatens the very bases of traditional power relations between the genders. (Miller 2002: 4)

[T]he elegists by questioning the nature of relations between the sexes and by envisioning their own subjugation to women—even if in an often ironic and humorous manner—present an interrogation of sexual norms unparalleled in Roman poetry. (Miller 2002: 4)

Elegy's potential to unsettle traditional mores, the *mos maiorum*, the return to which was a major part of the political program of the emperor Augustus, was not limited to its depiction of men subjected to women. The situations depicted by the genre also threatened what were considered the legitimate relations of power and property that governed the commerce between men and women. Elegiac romance, like that of the medieval courtly lovers who would follow in its wake, is always by definition extramarital. (Miller 2002: 4)

The elegists, therefore, are doubly subversive. Not only do they invert the power relations between men and women by adopting the position of the *seruus amoris* they also trouble the power relations between men by threatening the property rights of other men over their women. (Miller 2002: 6)

Really? Erotic elegy? Countercultural? Oppositional?

The period during which Ovid wrote erotic elegy saw significant developments in the relationship between Roman private life and the state. Augustus' moral legislation promoted marriage, punished adulterers, and made it illegal for a husband to overlook his wife's infidelity, but the propaganda went further than the legislation in its encouragement of associations between sanctioned sexual behaviour and other aspects of good citizenship, including loyalty to the princeps himself. Interaction between this propaganda and the poetic values developed during the late Republic and early imperial period had the effect of constructing a space in which the elegiac position construed itself as countercultural. Even though there may be no inherent reason why the elegiac mode should not be engaged in the service of the Augustan state (as both Propertius and Ovid were to explore in their later elegiac developments), the building blocks readily presented themselves whereby the poets could fashion the choice of elegy as an oppositional political as well as poetic stance. (Sharrock 2012: 80-81)

Sharrock also makes this important point: it wasn't *sex* the Romans had a problem with, it was *love*.

Ovid eventually got on the wrong side of the Augustan regime. It is important to stress, however, that it is not around a question of sexual obscenity that the political "problem" of Ovidian erotic elegy revolves. In this regard, Roman society maintains a fair degree of consistency over the centuries immediately before and after the publication of the *Ars Amatoria* in its lack of inhibition about the representation of sexuality, in art, literature, and indeed political invective. The "problem" for the elegists, and especially for Ovid, is twofold: first, the Romans, to generalise, don't have a problem with sex, but do have a problem with love, which makes a man lose his self-control and perhaps also his ancestral material wealth; and, second, the Augustan attempts to control what we loosely call morality are bound up not so much with personal sexual values but with the stability and control of middle and upper-class society. Adultery is an offence which you (as a man) commit, not against your own wife, but against the husband of your lover. In addition, and therefore, sexual behaviour became a site for the imposition and contestation of Augustus' authority. (Sharrock 2012: 82)

But what sort of love was this?

Theirs was a culture (the Roman Republic, first century BC) in which marriages were often arranged (girls as young as ten could be engaged, married at twelve), most often nothing more than legal arrangements meant to further political and economic advantage. Shifts in fortune, in power, in aim and purpose, meant divorce, which were easily obtained; remarriages common. In such a social world young women rarely had the opportunity to experience what *we* call love, or, if so, they lacked the freedom to do anything about it. The situation for young men, however, was—as always—different. So, yes, a loveless marriage, but that hardly meant love was not sought; but where? Mistresses, mostly, often courtesans, Greek courtesans in particular: cultured, well-read, often accomplished dancers and musicians, now drawn to Rome. But here, the irony, for as much "sought after by the fashionable set of young men," as these courtesans were, they also presented a challenge to "the more sensitive and passionate among the native Roman ladies," awakening in them both envy for "the glitter and excitements of a different way of life," and resentment born of "the tedious routine of their own households." It's in this dynamic context that "a curious social phenomenon" took root. "Ladies of the best families" began to live more independent lives, which is why it's often hard to say "whether the women we meet in the love-poetry of this period are Roman matrons or Greek freedwomen." (Luck 2002: 310) Or, as Green puts it: "But when the competition became more sophisticated and intelligent, from the late second century B.C.E. onwards, we can see a very different reaction developing. 'As the Hellenizing life of pleasure grew and prospered, some ladies started to want their cut' (Lyne 1980). They became witty and well read; they discovered that they, too, had sexual instincts and needs. . . . Anything the *demi-mondaines* could do [they] could do better. This included sex. . . . The tradition of the smart, adulterous wife was well established by the time Clodia entered the arena." (Green 2005: 9)

It's simple: as traditional ideals of marriage lost their meaning, men and women sought love outside marriage. For it wasn't like faith (*fides*), affection and respect (*pietas*), or chastity (*castitas*) had been forgotten, rather their location had shifted from that legal union between husband and wife we call marriage to the rather loose association between lover and mistress: *the ideal love-affair* (for example, Ovid swearing *by all the gods that he will never seek another mistress than Corinna.*). (Luck 2002: 311) It's in this context that we find our new Latin elegists, poets for whom the eternal union (*foedus aeternum*) between a man and a woman in a legal marriage not only no longer seemed possible, it no longer even seemed desirable. It needs to be pointed out, however, that even though these traditional values were in abeyance among the upper classes, such was not the case among middle and lower class families. Hence Augustus' concern for upper class morality, and why, as Luck notes, "the conjugal laws which he proclaimed at various times after 28 BC met with such violent opposition that he was obliged to postpone their enforcement until after AD 9, [which] by an act of curious brutality," was at about the same time as his banishment of "Ovid, the poet who had symbolized the frivolity" of this period. Ovid, banished "to the Black Sea, where he died obscurely in AD 17, without ever seeing Rome again." His exile effectively marking "the end of elegiac love-poetry in Rome." (Luck 2002: 311)

A much less sanguine view of the place of women in Roman society and Roman elegy.

During the last two centuries BCE, the legal and social regulations placed on women in Roman society became less restrictive, especially compared with ancient Greek women who were largely confined to the private spaces of their homes. Nonetheless, there is substantial evidence within the surviving texts of Roman literature that women continued to be relegated to a subservient role and that they were largely regarded as ungovernable creatures whose inherent irrationality and dangerous sexuality required them to be under the constant guardianship of males. The Roman elegists, however, appear to elevate women to a singularly exalted stature—a stature women did not enjoy in real life. (Greene 2012: 257)

But who were these young elegists?

[E]questrian and of provincial origins. The equestrian order was just below the senatorial. Its members had to possess a net worth of at least 400,000 sesterces, sufficient to live off their income and rents without other employment. This economic fact is of no little literary importance. These were men with the means and the leisure to pursue poetry and learning as a full-time occupation, with no need for external remuneration. Before Catullus, professional poets had been drawn from the lower classes and were often of Greek or servile origins. To make a living, they had to produce the kind of poetry for which Roman aristocrats were willing to pay. In practice, this meant made-to-order panegyrics of military and political triumphs or historical epics recounting the deeds of famous ancestors. The equestrian status of Catullus and his successors freed them from this necessity, at the same time as their provincial status made their entry into Roman politics unlikely. They were *noui homines*, men without consular ancestors. While it was possible for a talented *nouus homo*, such as Cicero or Marius, to claw his way to the top of the political heap and to achieve not only senatorial but consular status, it was rare. Thus all the elegists, like Catullus, were men of wealth, leisure, and learning, who were disengaged from the all-consuming political obsessions of the scions of the great aristocratic families. They were members of the first generation for which the duties of being a poet were compatible with those of being a free man. (Miller 2002: 17-18)

They'd lost the world, and the world had lost them.

Yes, Rome was changing: after nearly a half-century of civil wars the mechanics of Roman masculine identity were in disrepair. Even if these poets (Catullus' generation) had wanted to become normal Roman citizen-soldiers the opportunities for doing so were greatly reduced (you didn't want to find yourself on the wrong side in a civil war). It was under these circumstances that these young Roman poets created for themselves a new style or identity: the "erotic madman." The "obsessed, abject, un-Roman lover." What made this "crazy lover so suitable for this generation (and so repulsive to some of their immediate elders, the generation of Cicero) was the utter lack of [those] qualities that best define[d] the Roman-citizen soldier." Unwilling to "follow in the footsteps of the paterfamilias," unwilling, "as Propertius would blithely and famously admit," to "father a new crop of Roman citizen-soldiers," they likewise spurned military service, making speeches in the forum, increasing the wealth of their clan, running for public office, or supporting the candidacy of those who did. But what they did do was avidly pursue a life of total leisure. One they could squander on what mattered most to them "now and forever more: being in love with HER." This new person, "this poetic figure, this poetically rhetorical figure [became] the ideal writerly mold for what this generation [wanted] to say about who they [were] and who they [were] not." Yes, they were still Romans, but a new kind of "anti-Roman Roman, one "confused, ambiguous and ironic," [members of a] . . . losing, becoming-lost generation [whose] pathological idleness . . . utter self-absorption and glazed-eye dereliction," was in perfect accord with their awareness of the world they had lost and the world that had lost them. Well, if the public world had no place for them they'd just make their own "out of outrageous poetry and outrageous erotic adventure." (Johnson 2009: 5-6)

They were more apologetic about their way of life than about the kind of poetry they wrote.

> They knew that the life they led and the verse they wrote were not altogether respectable in the eyes of their contemporaries. Obviously they were not concerned with great religious and national issues. Sometimes they made a half-hearted attempt to defend their "naughtiness", *nequitia*. They always seem to remember that the love-elegy is a "playful" kind of poetry (*lusus*). This half-affectionate, half-deprecatory term could be applied to lyrics, epigrams, bucolics, satires, but certainly not to tragedies or epics.
>
> Both Horace and Vergil had composed "playful poems" in their youth, but they had gone on to more serious themes and modes in later years. Tibullus died too soon to follow their example; Propertius in his "Roman elegies" (Book IV), and Ovid in his *Fasti* tried to show that the elegiac metre, too, was suitable to more ambitious themes. But this was hardly more than an experiment, in the case of Propertius; and Ovid knew that he would be remembered by posterity as the "playful author of tender love-poems", *tenerorum lusor amorum*.
>
> The Latin elegists feel more apologetic about their way of life than about the kind of poetry they write. Like Callimachus who "shaped his verse on a narrow lathe", they claim to be conscious craftsmen. They are trying to raise the elegy to a higher rank, to distinguish it from the epigram and the light improvisation. (Luck 2002: 308)

Appendix Three

Selections from Ezra Pound's *Homage to Sextus Propertius*

This long set of poems (or "translations") has an interesting history. Both derided and defended at the time of their publication (1919; see below), and still the subject of debate, here are several that seem more closely tied to, or "inspired" by, their originals.

Yet you ask on what account I write so many love-lyrics
And whence this soft book comes into my mouth.
Neither Calliope nor Apollo sung these things into my ear,
    My genius is no more than a girl.

If she with ivory fingers drive a tune through the lyre,
    We look at the process.
How easy the moving fingers; if hair is mussed on her
    forehead,
If she goes in a gleam of Cos, in a slither of dyed stuff,
There is a volume in the matter; if her eyelids sink into sleep,
There are new jobs for the author;
And if she plays with me with her shirt off,
    We shall construct many Iliads.
And whatever she does or says
    We shall spin long yarns out of nothing.

Thus much the fates have allotted me, and if, Maecenas,
I were able to lead heroes into armour, I would not,
Neither would I warble of Titans, nor of Ossa
                              spiked onto Olympus,
Nor of causeways over Pelion,
Nor of Thebes in its ancient respectability,
          nor of Homer's reputation in Pergamus,
Nor of Xerxes' two-barreled kingdom, nor of Remus and his
    royal family,
Nor of dignified Carthaginian characters,

Nor of Welsh mines and the profit Marus had out of them.
I should remember Caesar's affairs ...
                              for a background,
Although Callimachus did without them,
                              and without Theseus,
Without an inferno, without Achilles attended of gods,
Without Ixion, and without the sons of Menoetius and the Argo
    and without Jove's grave and the Titans.

And my ventricles do not palpitate to Caesarial ore *rotundos,*
Nor to the tune of the Phrygian fathers.
Sailor, of winds; a plowman, concerning his oxen;
Soldier, the enumeration of wounds; the sheepfeeder, of
    ewes;
We, in our narrow bed, turning aside from battles:
Each man where he can, wearing out the day in his manner.
[Pound V.2/Propertius 2.1] (Pound 2005: 114-15)

Me happy, night, night full of brightness;
Oh couch made happy by my long delectations;
How many words talked out with abundant candles;
Struggles when the lights were taken away;
Now with bared breasts she wrestled against me,
                    Tunic spread in delay;
And she then opening my eyelids fallen in sleep,
Her lips upon them; and it was her mouth saying:
    Sluggard!

In how many varied embraces, our changing arms,
Her kisses, how many, lingering on my lips.
"Turn not Venus into a blinded motion,
        Eyes are the guides of love,
Paris took Helen naked coming from the bed of Menelaus,
Endymion's naked body, bright bait for Diana,"
            —such at least is the story.

While our fates twine together, sate we our eyes with love;
For long night comes upon you
                    and a day when no day returns.

Let the gods lay chains upon us
                so that no day shall unbind them.

Fool who would set a term to love's madness,
For the sun shall drive with black horses,
          earth shall bring wheat from barley,
The flood shall move toward the fountain
           Ere love know moderations,
           The fish shall swim in dry streams.
No, now while it may be, let not the fruit of life cease.

        Dry wreaths drop their petals,
               their stalks are woven in baskets,
        To-day we take the great breath of lovers,
                    to-morrow fate shuts us in.

Though you give all your kisses
                    you give but few.
Nor can I shift my pains to other,
        Hers will I be dead,
If she confer such nights upon me,
              long is my life, long in years,
If she give me many,
        God am I for the time.
[Pound VII/Propertius 2.15] (Pound 2005: 117-18)

Light, light of my eyes, at an exceeding late hour I was
    wandering,
And intoxicated,
              and no servant was leading me,
And a minute crowd of small boys came from opposite,
                   I do not know what boys,
And I am afraid of numerical estimate,
And some of them shook little torches,
                 and others held onto arrows,
And the rest laid their chains upon me,
          and they were naked, the lot of them,
And one of the lot was given to lust.

"That incensed female has consigned him to our pleasure."
So spoke. And the noose was over my neck.
And another said "Get him plumb in the middle!
          Shove along there, shove along!"
And another broke in upon this:
            "He thinks that we are not gods."
"And she has been waiting for the scoundrel,
          and in a new Sidonian night cap,
And with more than Arabian odours,
          God knows where he has been.
She could scarcely keep her eyes open
            enter that much for his bail.
              Get along now!"

We were coming near to the house,
        and they gave another yank to my cloak,
And it was morning, and I wanted to see if she was alone, and
    resting,
And Cynthia was alone in her bed.
              I was stupefied.
I had never seen her looking so beautiful,
      No, not when she was tunick'd in purple.

Such aspect was presented to me, me recently emerged from
    my visions,
You will observe that pure form has its value.
"You are a very early inspector of mistresses.
Do you think I have adopted your habits?"
      There were upon the bed no signs of a voluptuous
        encounter,
     No signs of a second incumbent.

She continued:
      "No incubus has crushed his body against me,
      Though spirits are celebrated for adultery.
      And I am going to the temple of Vesta..."
                 and so on.
Since that day I have had no pleasant nights.
[Pound X/Propertius 1.3] (Pound 2005: 120-22)

Varro sang Jason's expedition,
        Varro, of his great passion Leucadia,
There is song in the parchment; Catullus the highly
        indecorous,
Of Lesbia, known above Helen;
And in the dyed pages of Calvus,
        Calvus mourning Quintilia,
And but now Gallus had sung of Lycoris.
        Fair, fairest Lycoris—
The waters of Styx poured over the wound:
And now Propertius of Cynthia, taking his stand among these.
[Pound XII] (Pound 2005:126)

[Varro is the Latin poet Publius Terentius Varro. His love
poems to Leucadia are lost. Calvus, orator and poet, whose
love poems to his wife or mistress, Quintilia, are lost.
Cornelius Gallus was a friend to Virgil and first prefect of
Egypt who wrote four books of love poems, since lost, to the
actress Cytheris, called Lycoris in the poems.]

Homage to Sextus Propertius
    First appeared as "Poems from Propertius Series" in *Poetry*
(XIII, March 1919) and subsequently in six parts in *The New
Age* (June-August 1919). Published in book form in *Quia
Pauper Amavi* (1919). Its first separate printing was in 1934.
Pound referred to the poem as a "major persona," or mask,
praising and criticizing the first-century Roman poet
Propertius, employing irony, mockery, and humor, which
Pound defined as *logopœia*, "the dance of the intellect among
words," emphasizing the "ironical play" of language.
Logopœia, he added "does not translate; though the attitude of
mind it expresses may pass through a paraphrase" (*Literary
Essays*, 25). What he seeks in his translation is "the original
author's state of mind" (*Literary Essays*, 25).
    Homage to Sextus Propertius is alternately satiric and
political, drawing parallels between Pound's critique of Britain
in 1917 and Propertius's critique of the Roman Empire. In
uncovering and emphasizing the irony in Propertius, Pound
frees him from Victorian obfuscation and sentimentalizing.

But when four sections of the poem appeared in *Poetry* in March 1919, it aroused the anger of the classicist W. G. Hale, who attacked its numerous errors, declaring Pound ignorant of Latin. Pound replied that he had not done a translation of Propertius but attempted to restore vitality to the poet's work (see *Selected Letters*, 149, 229-30). The translation is "creative" and closer to an adaptation. Eliot, in the introduction to Ezra Pound, *Selected Poems* (1928), called it "a paraphrase, or still more truly ... a *persona*" (*Selected Poems*, 19).

Pound explained that he used the term "homage" as Debussy did in "Homage *à Rameau*," a piece of music recalling the manner of Rameau. In 1922, Hardy told Pound that the poem would be clearer retitled as "Propertius Soliloquizes." Later editions added "1917" after the title. Pound based his work on a series of poems from the extant four books of the Roman elegist Sextus Aurelius Propertius (born c. 50 B.C.E.). (Pound 2005: 364)

Appendix Four

Marlowe's *Amores* 1.5

Christopher Marlowe's (1564-1593) maligned translation of *Amores* 1.5 (c. 1582, printed posthumously c.1602).

> Liber Primus. Elegia 5.
> Corinnae concubitus
>
> In summers heate, and midtime of the day,
> To rest my limbes, uppon a bedde I lay,
> One window shut, the other open stood,
> Which gave such light, as twincles in a wood,
> Like twilight glimps at setting of the sunne,
> Or night being past, and yet not day begunne.
> Such light to shamefaste maidens must be showne,
> Where they may sport, and seeme to be unknowne.
> Then came *Corinna* in a long loose gowne,
> Her white necke hid with tresses hanging downe,
> Resembling faire *Semiramis* going to bed,
> Or *Layis* of a thousand lovers sped.
> I snatcht her gowne: being thin, the harme was small,
> Yet strivde she to be covered therewithall,
> And striving thus as one that would be cast,
> Betrayde her selfe, and yeelded at the last.
> Starke naked as she stood before mine eie,
> Not one wen in her bodie could I spie,
> What armes and shoulders did I touch and see,
> How apt her breasts were to be prest by me,
> How smoothe a bellie, under her waste sawe I,
> How large a legge, and what a lustie thigh?
> To leave the rest, all likt me passing well,
> I clinged her naked bodie, downe she fell,
> Judge you the rest, being tyrde she bad me kisse.
> *Jove* send me more such afternoones as this.

It is unclear when Marlowe undertook the translation of the *Amores* but most critics agree it dates from his time in Cambridge. The first edition included ten of Ovid's elegies (the Elizabethan term for epistolary poems of love or complaint), although later editions extended to translations of all three books. The first edition, which also included Sir John Davies's *Epigrams*, satirical poems which were always published with Marlowe's *Elegies*, was published without a date on the title page, but is thought to date from 1594-5. Such circumspection on the part of printers is usually a sign that there is something dangerous about the publication. Marlowe's decision to translate the *Amores* was certainly a scandalous one, given that Ovid's text was widely held to be pornographic, and Marlowe's *Elegies* were eventually banned by the censors in 1599. (Brown 2004: 110-111)

Appendix Five

Sulpicia: Not a Written Woman, a *Writing* Woman

It's not that I've saved Sulpicia for last, rather it's that I came to see her rightful place in this book too late for inclusion elsewhere. But she certainly belongs with these elegists both as a poet and as one concerned with the (Roman) ways of love. And note how the role reversal—the woman writes about a man—makes for interesting comparisons. Still, the most fascinating point, I think, is that here the *puella* writes: giving voice (our only voice) to a woman's thoughts and feelings. Invaluable.

> Though one can argue that Roman elegy is among so many other things playing with gender, the active players are almost exclusively male. Cynthia, Delia and Corinna are objects of male desire and male poetry. Although these elegiac *puellae* can be both *dominae* and *doctae*, they are 'but a tune to play' on the poet's pipe. They are metaphors and muses, but mainly mute. There is an exception to this rule: the voice of Sulpicia. (Skoie 2013: 83)

Translated by Mary Maxwell (Maxwell 1995: 84-85):

3.13
At last it's come, and to be said to hide this kind of love
    would shame me more than rumors that I'd laid it bare.
Won over by the pleading of my Muse, Cytherea
    delivered him to me. She placed him in my arms.
Venus has fulfilled what she promised: Let my joys be told
    by one who is said to have no joy of her own.
I would hate to keep what I've written under seal where none
    could read me sooner than my lover, for pleasure
Likes a little infamy; discretion is nothing but a tedious pose.
    Let it be known I have found a fitting partner.

3.14
The hated birthday approaches. A grim celebration
  in the backwaters, without Cerinthus, is planned.
What's sweeter than the city? Could a cottage satisfy a girl?
  Could farms along the freezing river of Arretium?
You're overanxious about me, Messalla, it's time you calmed
  down;
    for journeys, dear kin, are by no means always opportune.
Here soul and sense will remain though my self is abducted,
  as compulsion makes no note of my opinion.

3.15
Did you hear? Your girl has been relieved of her onerous trip,
  so now I'm allowed to stay in Rome for my birthday.
That day I was born will be celebrated by all of us,
  and by mere chance will be shared by once-skeptical you.

3.16
I'm grateful that, now you've so blithely left me behind,
  I am saved from taking a precipitous fall.
You prefer the simple toga and a basket-burdened
  whore to Sulpicia, daughter of Servius:
Others worry about me and the pain it would cause
  should I yield my high place to an inferior.

3.17
Are you, Cerinthus, still devoted to your girl
  now my feeble body's vexed with fever?
I would not pray to overcome this grim disease
  unless I could suppose you wished me well.
What use to me is conquered distress if your heart
  remains indifferent to my suffering?

3.18
No longer care for me, my light, with such fervor
  as you seem to have felt for the last few days,
If ever in my youth I'd done something so foolish,
  anything at all I could regret even more
than what I did last night when I left you alone,

desiring as I did to hide my own fire.

The eleven poems concerning Sulpicia are located in book three of the *Corpus Tibullianum* (3.8–18) and were until the nineteenth century read as by Tibullus. Of these, three are written in the third person about Sulpicia (3.8, 3.10 and 3.12) while eight are written from the first person perspective of Sulpicia herself (3.9, 3.11 and 3.13–18). While the first eight poems are between twenty and twenty-six verses, the latter six are much shorter – between six and ten verses each. This has given rise to different theories of authorship once Tibullan authorship of the entire corpus was ruled out.

The most widely held hypothesis is that these poems make up two different groups. The short first-person poems, 3.13–18, are attributed to a real Augustan Sulpicia, *Serui filia* ('daughter of Servius'), as she presents herself in poem 3.16. This Servius might be the son of Cicero's friend Servius Sulpicius, and Messalla, who is addressed in another poem (3.14), might be her maternal uncle and even guardian. This places Sulpicia in one of the major literary circles of Augustan Rome and gives us a possible date for the poems in the twenties BC. The longer poems, 3.8–12, are within this paradigm regarded as by someone else. These poems are often called the 'garland of Sulpicia' or 'Sulpicia cycle' and ascribed to an *amicus Sulpiciae* or *auctor de Sulpicia*. The idea is that these might be written by a poet who has taken Sulpicia's invitation in poem 3.13 – that someone might tell her joys (*mea gaudia narret*, 5) – seriously. This fits nicely with a reading of the third book of the *corpus Tibullianum* as a kind of *Hauspoetenbuch*, a collection of poems written by different members of Messalla's literary circle who all knew each other and met in what one might call his literary salon. This hypothesis is substantiated by the way several of the long poems elaborate on issues from the shorter ones as well as the idea of a poetic circle responding to Sulpicia. (Skoie 2013: 83-84)

Commentary

3.13

The first poem of Sulpicia's short collection is programmatic. It announces her theme and makes clear the distance she takes from the male elegists. The daughter of a noted jurist who died early and left his daughter in the charge of her mother's brother, Messalla Corvinus, Sulpicia was not only a woman of aristocratic background and upbringing, she was also privy to the most recent artistic and literary trends. As a young woman in the twenties BCE, she would have heard both Tibullus's poetry recited at her uncle's salons and that of the young Ovid. In such an environment, it is inconceivable that she would not have known the poetry of Catullus and Propertius or that when she sat down to write her own verse she would have done so in a naïve or artless manner. Rather as Santirocco, Lowe, and Tschiedel have shown, by far the most economical assumption is to presume that when Sulpicia deviates from the elegiac norm, she does so consciously and deliberately (14, 45–46). Thus, where it was once fashionable to dismiss her poetry as "feminine" – meaning untutored, unsophisticated, and ungrammatical – it is now possible to view it as a woman's poetry – meaning written from a fundamentally different position from that of Tibullus, Propertius, or Ovid.

This poem offers an important test case for all such readings. Even recent critics often assume that 3.13 has slipped out of its proper order in the collection. Since the poem speaks of a love that has been consummated, many critics find it difficult to square its subject with their preconceived image of Sulpicia as a proper young maiden of good family. They have therefore moved it to the end of the sequence where, they claim, it celebrates Sulpicia's marriage to Cerinthus. This interpretation, while transparently ideological, was made easier by a false etymology of Cerinthus's name put forward by Renaissance humanists. Deriving Cerinthus from the Greek *kera* or "horn," they identified him with the Cornutus whose marriage is alluded to in Tibullus 2.2. But *Kerinthos* is both the name of a city in Euboia mentioned in the "Catalog of Ships" (*Iliad* 2.538) and the Greek word for "beebread," a substance fed to young bees that the ancients thought of as a compound of honey and wax. As Roessel has shown, these qualities identify Cerinthus with both the honey-sweetness that the Greeks from Homer to Callimachus associated with poetry and the wax tablets on which deliberate poetic composition took place. Thus Cerinthus, like Cynthia and Delia, is both the subject of the poetry composed in his name and a synonym for the act of composition and the fame resulting therefrom. It is this fame that is the concern of the opening poem, not the celebration of a marriage. As such, 3.13 is well designed to be the opening poem of Sulpicia's sequence.

1–2. Love has finally come and it is of such a sort that it would be more a shame to keep still than to reveal it to everyone. The first clause is simple and straightforward, but Sulpicia immediately plunges us into the syntactical complexity for which her poetry is known. The subject of the indirect question that forms the second clause is *fama*. This is also the subject of the poem as a whole, what shall Sulpicia's reputation be? In conventional elegiac poetry, the love affair must be kept secret since it is either *de facto* or *de iure* adulterous. Likewise, a young aristocratic girl, out of *pudor* ("shame"), would conventionally keep an extramarital affair secret and avoid *mala fama*. But Sulpicia argues that this love is of such a quality (*qualem*) that the reputation (*fama*) of having kept it a secret (*texisse*) would be more (*sit magis*) a cause for shame (*pudori*) than would that of having exposed it (*nudasse*). The medium of that exposition, of course, is this very poetry, which in conventional elegiac terms insures her *fama*. As Santirocco has noted, the predominance of indirect discourse in the poem contributes to its syntactical difficulty while dramatizing the workings of *fama* in all its senses.

3–4. Venus has answered the prayers I have addressed to her through the Muses and placed him in our lap. This emphasis on the fulfillment of love is unusual in male-authored elegy.

The sexual image implicit in *sinum* in the same sentence with *exorata meis . . . Camenis* clearly associates Sulpicia's lovemaking with her poetry. The image of Venus coming to Sulpicia's aid recalls Sappho 1.

Cytherea = Venus. Cythera is an island south of the Peloponnesus where Aphrodite had an important shrine. *Camenis* = the name of traditional Italic goddesses who had become identified with the Greek Muses. Note the artful alliteration and learning of ending the hexameter with these two proper names. Their corresponding adjectives, *exorata* and *meis*, begin the line.

5–6. This couplet is addressed to Sulpicia's male counterparts in elegy who constantly bemoan their lack of fulfillment in love. Venus has kept her promises to Sulpicia and let anyone who has had less luck in love recount the story of her joys. Sulpicia here clearly adopts a different model of desire from that of her rivals.

7–8. Sulpicia rejects the elegiac tradition of sealed letters exchanged between lover and beloved in favor of the open publication that is also her declaration of poetic arrival. The postponement of the main verb, *uelim*, to the end of the couplet makes the couplet more difficult but effectively maintains the reader in suspense about the poet's intentions until the last possible moment.

9–10. Sulpicia proclaims her independence of social convention. *Cum . . . fuisse: cum esse* is a common euphemism for sexual relations. (Miller 2002: 159-61)

In this poem Sulpicia presents herself as the ardent lover and gives a framework for the reading of all the other poems, a sexual relationship with a man blessed by the goddess Venus. Though some commentators would like this to be no more than a kiss, *esse cum* is a common euphemism for sexual intercourse, cf. Varro *Ling.* 6.80. Furthermore *peccare* (to sin) has connotations of extramarital sex. This worthy man is usually read as Cerinthus, who is the beloved of most of the other poems. The name is most likely a pseudonym in analogy with Cynthia, Delia and Corinna with equally rich connotations. *Cerinthum* (from the Greek κήρινθος) means bee-bread and thus has a connection both with honey and wax, love and literature. Because of metrical equivalence and placement in the *Corpus Tibullianum*, many have read him as the Cornutus who is mentioned in Tibullus' poem 2.2.19. In that case one might even argue that the couple got married – an attractive option for many a commentator. (Skoie 2013: 85-87)

[In] 3.13, Sulpicia shows an unusual awareness of an aspect of poetry that does not seem to play any important part in the rest of the elegiac corpus, a concern with publishing. In his commentary, Oliver Lyne goes so far as to call poem 3.13 a 'publication poem'. In this poem Sulpicia is not only publishing her love, she is making a feature of the actual publication, or telling, of it. Yet the actual publication is far from straightforward. While the statements might be called 'bravado', the way they are told is not quite as brave. The poem is notoriously difficult to translate precisely because she does not tell the story in a straightforward manner, but in a convoluted way using passive, subjunctive and hypotaxis. Hence she does not say explicitly that she herself would rather tell it than hide it, but wraps this statement up in a passive construction (*sit mihi fama*, 2); likewise she does not say that she has been with a man worthy of her, rather she urges herself to 'be said' (*ferar*, 10) to have been with such a man. Thus there is a double process of telling and not telling. Likewise, she uses the metaphor of undressing (*nudasse*, 2) and what has been called a 'rhetoric of disclosure' while she at the same time verbally veils herself behind passive constructions. A similar move is made in poem 3.18 where Sulpicia regrets having hidden her passion, but at the same time hides this same passion in what one scholar has called a 'bewildering web of multiple hypotaxis' at the very end of the poem. (Skoie 2013: 87)

3.14

This poem is written on the occasion of Sulpicia's birthday. It forms a pair with the following poem and together they look back to Catullus's practice of pairing epigrams (see 70 and 72), with the second always looking at the same phenomenon from a later point in time. This will be one of Ovid's favorite devices as well.

The birthday poem was a common set piece in Messalla's circle. Tibullus wrote two (1.7 and 2.2). Those pieces are happy occasional verses that celebrate the joys of country life. Sulpicia here playfully inverts the topos making the birthday a source of unhappiness because she will have to spend it in the country away from Cerinthus. Moreover, the cause of her unhappiness is her uncle, the same Messalla whose birthday Tibullus celebrates in 1.7. The joke would have been appreciated by those in the know.

1–2. The statement is unusually straightforward. Its poignancy comes from its inversion of expected values. Cerinthus is named for the first time.

3–4. Like Delia, Sulpicia knows love is not a country pleasure. *Arretino . . . agro* = ablative of location, denoting a wine-growing region of Tuscany.

Frigidus amnis = the Arno, which comes from the north.

7–8. The loss of the senses in love was made famous by Sappho in poem 31 and in Catullus's translation (poem 51). (Miller 2002: 161-62)

3.15

This is the companion piece to 3.14. Sulpicia celebrates being allowed to remain in the city for her birthday.

1–2. *Triste* looks back to line 2 of the previous poem. *Ex animo* = the journey has ceased to be a source of anxiety.

3–4. "Let that birthday be celebrated by us all, which comes with you perhaps not now expecting it!" The syntax is difficult. (Miller 2002: 162)

3.16

This sarcastic little poem shows Sulpicia's capacity to turn elegiac convention to her own advantage. The *marita fides* that the elegists claimed to practice in relation to their own, often fickle, mistresses was, of course, more honored in the breach than the observance (see Ovid). Here, however, Sulpicia proclaims her lover's obligation to be faithful to her, not just her to him. She thus deploys elegiac convention while revealing the role reversal implied in it for what it was, a convenient weapon in the arsenal of masculine seduction. In the process, she makes a proud declaration of her own high social standing in relation to Cerinthus's *scortum*, "hussy," and of his consequent obligations to her. Power in Rome was distributed along a variety of intersecting axes; two of the most prominent were gender and social class. Sulpicia's gender may have been traditionally submissive but her social standing was near the top of the aristocratic hierarchy.

1–2. "It is a good thing that you now permit yourself to act without a care for me, otherwise I might have quickly made a most foolish mistake" (i.e., fallen in love with you). This is a very difficult couplet. Sulpicia expresses mock gratitude (*gratum est*) because (*quod*) Cerinthus at this point (*iam*) gives himself such wide latitude (*multum . . . tibi permittis*) that she is able to avoid making a grave mistake (*ne male inepta cadam*).

3–4. *Togae*: prostitutes were the only women who wore the toga, thereby signifying their transgression of the norms of gender behavior.

Quasillo: wool spinners were at the bottom of the social hierarchy. Their status should not be confused with the traditional piety associated with women who spin wool and make clothes for their own husbands. Spinners, *quasillariae*, were slaves or freed women given large quantities to spin each day for their *dominae*.

Serui filia Sulpicia: Sulpicia was the daughter of the patrician Seruius Sulpicius Rufus, himself the son of a famous jurist known to Cicero. He died young after marrying Valeria Messalla, the sister of Tibullus's patron. The latter became the young girl's guardian when her mother refused to remarry. Note the way the formal three-word appellation balances the three-word epithet, *pressumque quasillo scortum*, thereby

underlining the differences in status. This is the only
pentameter in Sulpicia that does not end in a disyllabic word.
This deviation from accepted metrical practice calls attention
to her name at the end of the line.
5–6. "There are those who are troubled on our behalf to
whom the greatest cause of pain is that I might yield to a
humble bed." Cerinthus may be *securus* but there are those
who do have *cura* for Sulpicia and they worry lest she be made
to yield her position to one of low status, the *scortum* whose
bed Cerinthus currently occupies. It cannot be Cerinthus
himself since we know from the anonymous poems on
Sulpicia and her beloved, which precede her own work in the
Tibullan corpus, that Cerinthus was of a sufficiently elevated
social status to practice the aristocratic sport of boar hunting
(3.9). Nonetheless, there may well be a dig here at Cerinthus
having a less exalted pedigree than Sulpicia, or an implication
that he has debased himself by consorting with a *scortum*.
(Miller 2002: 162-64)

In this highly ironic and difficult poem, Sulpicia, not only sets
herself apart from her lowborn rival (the toga-dressed and
woolbasket-carrying prostitute, 3–4), but also presents herself
as very different from the elegiac *puellae*. First, she gives
herself a proper Roman name which can be placed in
Augustan society: she is a member of the *gens Sulpicia*, part of
the aristocracy. Second, while Paul Veyne famously called the
elegiac *puellae* 'not such high society', Sulpicia here places
herself in 'high society deluxe'. She is a noble woman, and
class obviously matters in the powerplay with Cerinthus
which seems to take place here. Unlike Cerinthus, who is so
sure (*securus de me*), she is uncertain of his commitment.
However, here Sulpicia uses the opposite tactics to 3.17 where
she explicitly plays weak to prompt a response. Instead she
uses the weapons she has at hand, her social status and those
concerned about her (*solliciti*, 5) – presumably her peers.

The other elegists employ the metaphor of *seruitium
amoris* ('the slavery of love') when describing the power
structure involved in their love affairs. In this imagery the

beloved woman is placed on top as *domina* in a gender-bending game. In poem 3.16 Sulpicia is admittedly presented as a *domina* in the social sense. It is more doubtful whether she also represents an elegiac or gender-bending *domina*. After all, she seems to have little power over her beloved. One might therefore ask what happens to gender-reversal when a woman plays the part of the weak lover? Might not this simply reaffirm normal sexual roles in Augustan society? (Skoie 2013: 91-92)

3.17

As we have already seen in Tibullus 1.5, the illness of the beloved is a topos that allows both the lover to demonstrate his devotion and the *domina* her ingratitude. Once more, Sulpicia inverts expectations. Here she is ill and her lover far from waiting on her appears distracted, perhaps by the *scortum* of the previous poem.

1–2. The question is straightforward. *Cura* recalls *securus* from the opening line of 3.16. *Calor* = fever.
3–4. The desire for mutuality expressed in 3.13.10 and rearticulated in 3.16's demand for fidelity is here taken to its extreme: I do not wish to recover unless you wish so too.
5–6. This couplet restates and expands upon the thought expressed in the previous one. What use is health if you can be happy with me sick? (Miller 2002: 164)

This is not simply a poem by which to diagnose Sulpicia but a poem asking for proof of the beloved's feelings. In the *Ars* (2.3.15–36) Ovid recommends that the lover grab any opportunity to display his piety (*pietas*, 2.3.15); compare Sulpicia's *pia cura* ('true concern', 1). Both Tibullus (1.5.9–18) and Propertius (2.9.25–8) describe similar situations. Further, as Santirocco points out, 'the sustained medical imagery on which the lines turn is standard in Latin love poetry, the calculated ambiguity between real fever and the heat of passion, between real disease and the illness that is love'. Despite the fact that some of the terminology used is of a more technical nature, the reader is reminded of Catullus

76, where the disease is his love. The use of *lentus* in verse 6 also links to amatory discourse, e.g. Prop. 1.6.12 where the lover exclaims that the man who can be indifferent (*lentus*) in love should perish. (Skoie 2013: 89)

3.18

The theme of *cura* returns, but in the final poem it is Sulpicia who worries that she has needlessly given Cerinthus cause for anxiety when she fled an encounter in an effort to conceal the height of her passion. The topic of misplaced *pudor* first broached in 3.13 returns here, rounding off the sequence in a form of ring composition. The *feruida cura* of the first line recalls not only the previous poem's *pia cura* but also its *calor*. The burning fever has been transformed into the fire of passion. Each couplet appears to be syntactically complete until the reader reaches the next. The poem thus unfolds as a series of surprises.

1–2. The couplet is difficult. "May I not, my love, at any time (*iam*) be so burning a cause of anxiety [but also "passion"] as I seem to have been a few days before." *Cura* is often used as a synonym for the beloved. See Propertius 1.1.35.
3–4. We here realize that the poem is a conditional statement. May I not be a cause of burning passion to you if I have ever done anything so stupid!
    Tota . . . iuuenta = ablative of time, emphasizing Sulpicia's youth. She was probably around twenty years old. Her subsequent poetic silence, like that of many of her later renaissance counterparts, was probably the result of marriage.
5–6. At last, we find the cause of the speaker's embarrassment. (Miller 2002: 164-65)

Works Cited

Acosta-Hughes, Benjamin and Susan A. Stephens. *Callimachus in Context: from Plato to the Augustan Poets.* Cambridge University Press, 2012.

Aelian. *Historical Miscellany.* Translated by N.G. Wilson. Loeb Classical Library 486. Cambridge: Harvard University Press, 1997.

Aloni, Antonio. "Elegy: Forms, Functions and Communication," in *The Cambridge Companion to Greek Lyric.* Edited by Felix Budelmann. Cambridge: Cambridge University Press, 2009.

Ammianus Marcellinus. *History, Volume III: Books 27-31. Excerpta Valesiana.* Translated by J. C. Rolfe. Loeb Classical Library. 331. Cambridge: Harvard University Press, 1939.

Booth, Joan. "The *Amores*: Ovid Making Love," in *A Companion to Ovid.* Edited by Peter E. Knox. Oxford: Wiley-Blackwell, 2009.

Brown, Georgia E. "Marlowe's Poems and Classicism," in *The Cambridge Companion to Christopher Marlowe.* Edited by Patrick Cheney. Cambridge: Cambridge University Press, 2004.

Brown, Tina and Philip Roth. "Philip Roth Unbound: Interview Transcript." *The Daily Beast.* October 30, 2009.

Butrica, James. "Editing Propertius," in *Propertius.* Oxford: Oxford University Press, 2012. Edited by Ellen Greene and Tara S. Welch.

Butrica, J. L. "History and Transmission of the Text," in *A Companion to Catullus*. Oxford: Blackwell, 2007. Edited by Marilyn Skinner.

Cairns, Francis. *Hellenistic Epigram: Contexts of Exploration*. Cambridge: Cambridge University Press, 2016.

Cicero. *De Finibus Bonorum et Malorum*. Translated by H. Rackham. Loeb Classical Library 40. Cambridge: Harvard University Press. Second edition, 1931.

Clay, Diskin. "The Athenian Garden," in *The Cambridge Companion to Epicureanism*. Edited by James Warren. Cambridge: Cambridge University Press, 2009.

Dyson Hejduk, Julia T. "The Lesbia Poems," in *A Companion to Catullus*. Oxford: Blackwell, 2007. Edited by Marilyn Skinner.

Epictetus. *Discourses, Books 1-2*. Translated by W. A. Oldfather. Loeb Classical Library 131. Cambridge: Harvard University Press, 1925.

Fain, Gordon L. *Ancient Greek Epigrams. Major Poets in Verse Translation*. Berkeley: University of California Press, 2010.

Fantham, Elaine. "Rhetoric and Ovid's Poetry," in *A Companion to Ovid*, edited by Peter E. Knox. Oxford: Wiley-Blackwell, 2009.

Fitzgerald, William. *How to Read a Latin Poem: if you can't read Latin yet*. Oxford: Oxford University Press, 2013.

Futrell, Alison. *The Roman Games: a sourcebook*. Oxford: Blackwell, 2006.

Gibson, Roy. "Love Elegy," in *A Companion to Latin Literature*. Edited by Stephen Harrison. Oxford: Blackwell, 2004.

Gigante, Marcello. *Philodemus in Italy: The Books from Herculaneum*. Translated by D. Obbink. Ann Arbor: University of Michigan Press, 1995.

Green, Peter. *Ovid. The Erotic Poems*. Translated with an introduction and notes by Peter Green. London: Penguin Books, 1982.

Green, Peter. *The Poems of Catullus*. Berkeley: University of California Press, 2005.

Green, Peter. *Ovid. The Poems of Exile: Tristia and the Black Sea Letters*. Translated with an introduction, notes, and glossary by Peter Green. Los Angeles: University of California Press, 2005.

Greene, Ellen. "Gender and Elegy," in *A Companion to Roman Love Elegy*. Edited by Barbara K. Gold. Oxford: Blackwell, 2012.

Gutzwiller, Kathryn. *Poetic Garlands: Hellenistic Epigrams in Context*. Berkeley: University of California Press, 1998.

Gutzwiller, Kathryn. Editor. *The New Posidippus: a Hellenistic Poetry Book*. Oxford: Oxford University Press, 2005.

Harder, Annette. *Callimachus: Aetia. Volume 1: Introduction, Text, and Translation. Volume 2: Commentary*. Oxford: Oxford University Press, 2012.

Harrison, Stephen. "Ovid and the Modern Poetics of Exile," in *Two Thousand Years of Solitude: Exile After Ovid*. Edited by Jennifer Ingleheart. New York: Oxford University Press, 2011.

Heyworth, S. J. "The Elegiac Book: Patterns and Problems," in *A Companion to Roman Love Elegy*. Edited by Barbara K. Gold. Oxford: Blackwell, 2012.

Heyworth, S. J. and H. W. Morwood. *A Commentary on Propertius, Book 3*. Oxford: Oxford University Press, 2011.

Ingleheart, Jennifer. *A Commentary on Ovid, Tristia, Book 2*. Oxford: Oxford University Press, 2010.

Ingleheart, Jennifer. *Two Thousand Years of Solitude: Exile After Ovid*. Edited by Jennifer Ingleheart. New York: Oxford University Press, 2011.

Jenkyns, Richard. *Classical Literature: An Epic Journey from Homer to Virgil and Beyond*. New York: Basic Books, 2016.

Johnson, W. R. *A Latin Lover in Ancient Rome*. Columbus: The Ohio Sate University Press, 2009.

Juvenal, Persius. *Juvenal and Persius*. Edited and translated by Susanna Morton Braund. Loeb Classical Library 91. Cambridge: Harvard University Press, 2004.

Katz, Vincent. *The Complete Elegies of Sextus Propertius*. Princeton: Princeton University Press, 2004.

Keith, Allison. "The *Domina* in Roman Elegy," in *A Companion to Roman Love Elegy*. Edited by Barbara K. Gold. Oxford: Blackwell, 2012.

Lee, Guy. *Ovid's Amores*. Translated by Guy Lee. New York: The Viking Press, 1968.

Lee, Guy. *Propertius: The Poems.* Translated with notes by Guy Lee. Oxford: Oxford University Press, 1994.

Lombardo, S. and D. Raynor. *Callimachus: Hymns, Epigrams, Select Fragments.* Baltimore: Johns Hopkins University Press, 1988.

Luck, Georg. "Introduction to the Latin Love Elegy," in *Latin Love Elegy: An Anthology and Reader.* Edited by Paul Allen Miller. London: Routledge, 2002.

Martial. *Epigrams, Volume I: Spectacles, Books 1-5.* Edited and translated by D. R. Shackleton Bailey. Loeb Classical Library 94. Cambridge: Harvard University Press, 1993

Martial. *Epigrams, Volume II: Books 6-10.* Edited and translated by D. R. Shackleton Bailey. Loeb Classical Library 95. Cambridge: Harvard University Press, 1993.

Melville, A.D. *Ovid. The Love Poems.* Translated by A.D. Melville. Oxford: Oxford University Press, 2008.

Miller, Paul Allen. *Latin Love Elegy: An Anthology and Reader.* Edited with an introduction and commentary by Paul Allen Miller. London: Routledge, 2002.

Miller, Paul Allen. "The *Puella*: Accept No Substiutions!" in *The Cambridge Companion to Love Elegy.* Edited by Thea S. Thorsen. Cambridge: Cambridge University Press, 2013.

Morgan, Llewelyn. "Elegiac Meter: Opposites Attract," in *A Companion to Roman Love Elegy.* Edited by Barbara K. Gold. Oxford: Blackwell, 2012.

Morwood, James, Iain Ross, S.J. Heyworth and Soo-Lin Lui. "Explorations of Ovid, 'Amores' 3.2, 3.4, 3.5, and 3.14."

Greece & Rome. Second Series, Vol. 58, No. 1 (April 2011), pp. 14-32.

Mozley, J.H. *The Art of Love and other Poems.* Revised edition. Translated by J. H. Mozley. Revised by G.P. Goold. Loeb Classical Library 232. Cambridge: Harvard University Press, 1979.

Nisetich, Frank. *The Poems of Callimachus.* Translated by Frank Nisetich. Oxford: Oxford University Press, 2001.

Papanghelis, T. D. "Catullus and Callimachus on Large Women." *Mnemosyne* 44: 372-86.

Parker, Dorothy. *The Viking Portable Library Dorothy Parker.* New York: Viking, 1944.

Plato. *Euthyphro. Apology. Crito. Phaedo. Phaedrus.* Translated by Harold North Fowler. Loeb Classical Library 36. Cambridge: Harvard University Press, 1914.

Philostratus. *Apollonius of Tyana, Volume II: Life of Apollonius of Tyana, Books 5-8.* Edited and translated by Christopher P. Jones. Loeb Classical Library 17. Cambridge: Harvard University Press, 2005.

Pliny. *Natural History, Volume II: Books 3-7.* Translated by H. Rackham. Loeb Classical Library 352. Cambridge: Harvard University Press, 1942.

Pliny the Younger. *Letters, Volume II: Books 8-10. Panegyricus.* Translated by Betty Radice. Loeb Classical Library 59. Cambridge: Harvard University Press, 1969.

Pound, Ezra. *Early Writings: Poems and Prose.* Edited with an introduction and notes by Ira B. Nadel. London: Penguin Books, 2005.

Maxwell, Mary. *Lyric and Elegaic Poetry: An Anthology of New Translations.* Edited by Diane J. Raynor and William W. Batstone. New York: Routledge, 1995.

Richardson, L. Jr. *Propertius. Elegies I-IV.* Edited, with introduction and commentary. Norman: University of Oklahoma Press, 2006.

Sedley, David. "Epicureanism in the Roman Repubic," in *The Cambridge Companion to Epicureanism.* Edited by James Warren. Cambridge: Cambridge University Press, 2009.

Sharrock, Alison R. "Ovid," in *A Companion to Roman Love Elegy.* Edited by Barbara K. Gold. Oxford: Blackwell, 2012.

Sider, David. *The Epigrams of Philodemos.* New York: Oxford University Press, 1997.

Sider, David. *The Library of the Villa dei Papiri at Herculaneum.* Los Angeles: Getty Publications, 2005.

Silius Italicus. *Punica, Volume II: Books 9-17.* Translated by J. D. Duff. Loeb Classical Library 278. Cambridge: Harvard University Press, 1934.

Skinner, Marilyn B. "Authorial Arrangement of the Collection: Debate Past and Present," in *Companion to Catullus.* Oxford: Blackwell, 2007. Edited by Marilyn Skinner.

Skoie, Mathilde. "The Woman," in *The Cambridge Companion to Love Elegy*. Edited by Thea S. Thorsen. Cambridge: Cambridge University Press, 2013.

Stephens, Susan. *Callimachus: Aetia*. Carlisle: Dickinson College Commentaries, 2015. [http://dcc.dickinson.edu/callimachus-aetia/book-2/sicilian-cities]

Stoppard, Tom. *The Invention of Love*. New York: Grove Press 1997.

Thomas, Richard F. "The Streets of Rome: The Classical Dylan." *Oral Tradition*. Vol. 22, No. 1 (2007), pp. 30-56.

Thomas, Richard F. "The Metamorphosis of Bob Dylan." *The Times Literary Supplement*. December 6, 2017.

Tueller, Michael A. *Greek Anthology, Volume* I. Translated by W. R. Paton. Revised by Michael A. Tueller. Loeb Classical Library 67. Cambridge: Harvard University Press, 2014.

Welch, Tara S. "Whose Reading of What Propertius," in *Propertius*. Oxford: Oxford University Press, 2012. Edited by Ellen Greene and Tara S. Welch.

Williams, John. *Augustus*. New York: Viking Press, 1972. Wray, David. "Catullus the Roman Love Elegist?" in *A Companion to Roman Love Elegy*. Edited by Barbara K. Gold. Oxford: Blackwell, 2012.

Wyke, Maria. "Reading Female Flesh: *Amores* 3.1," in *Oxford Readings in Ovid*. Edited by Peter E. Knox. Oxford: Oxford University Press, 2006.

Wyke, Maria. *The Roman Mistress: Ancient and Modern Representations*. Oxford: Oxford University Press, 2002.

* 9 780099 622048 4 *